What others are saying about
The Post-Corporate World

"**First, David Korten warned us** what was and would become more wrong in *When Corporations Rule the World.* In *The Post-Corporate World* he gives us a road map to a more humane future. For every reader who senses that today's disasters of inequality, the environment, and consumerist obsessions just can't go on but finds no hope from experts, David Korten describes a new economic culture in which everyone matters."

—Gloria Steinem

"*The Post-Corporate World* **does for our view of corporatism** what Betty Friedan did for our view of women and Rachel Carson did for our view of the environment. It is passionately and gracefully written and takes our obsession for goods and growth and turns it on itself. It will twist your mind about the world and how you are living in it. Read this book."

—Peter Block, author of *Stewardship* and *The Empowered Manager*

"**If you secretly wonder why the hyped promise of capitalism** doesn't match the all too common and difficult struggle to make ends meet, you will be fascinated by this account of where our economy went wrong and how we can change. A stunning, illuminating, and extremely important book."

—Vicki Robin, coauthor of *Your Money or Your Life*

"**The turmoil in the financial markets in 1998** has shown us that the globalization process needs to take much more into account the social dimension and the real interests of people. David Korten's new book is a refreshing signpost for the future."

—Klaus Schwab, President, World Economic Forum, Geneva

"**An earthshaking book—a product of brilliant thinking** from one of history's most groundbreaking intellectuals and activists. Korten's clarity and uncompromising integrity come through on every page and empower the reader to take a new stand for a world that is sustainable, responsible, and steeped in the principles of relationship, community, and consciousness."

—Lynne Twist, Co-chair, State of the World Forum

"**If you want to understand what is really happening in the world,** read David Korten. *The Post-Corporate World* points to what must come next if human beings and other creatures are to have a livable future."
—John B. Cobb, Jr., Professor Emeritus of Religion, Claremont Graduate School, and coauthor of *For the Common Good*

"**A breakthrough contribution** to an essential rethinking of the human purpose and our institutions. One of the most important books of this century."
—Dr. Robert Muller, Chancellor, University for Peace, Costa Rica, and Former Assistant Secretary General of the United Nations

---

"**A practical, yet ennobling vision of the future of our economy,** a future that is worthy of the best of our hopes and dreams. You can have no more compassionate and humane guide to the future of a humane economy."
—Paul Ray, author of *The Integral Culture Survey* and *The Cultural Creatives*

"**Chilling and inspiring!** From Adam Smith to Planetary Consciousness, David Korten provides a comprehensive, intelligent analysis of the economic forces and assumptions that have shaped our past, and the necessary choices we need to alter the course of our future."
—Alisa Gravitz, Executive Director, Co-op America

"**Re-establishes connects that embed us in the real world and lift our spirits** with a new vision of human and natural communities."
—David Suzuki, author of *The Sacred Balance*

"**Korten's central message is loud and clear,** hard-hitting, eminently readable, provocative, and important!"
—Gar Alperovitz, President, The National Center for Economic and Security Alternatives

---

"**An important and inspiring contribution** to a world badly in need of a new story."
—Carl Frankel, author of *In Earth's Company*

"**Shows that business, jobs, production, and finance can serve life,** community, ecological vitality, and soul-satisfying ways of life, rather than economic growth at all costs. This may be among the most important books of the late 20th century."
—Sarah Van Gelder, Executive Editor, *Yes! A Journal of Positive Futures*

David C. Korten

The Post-Corporate World

Life After Capitalism

A Copublication of
Kumarian Press, Inc.
and Berrett-Koehler Publishers, Inc.

Berrett-Koehler Publishers

Kumarian Press

Copublished by Berrett-Koehler Publishers, Inc., and Kumarian Press, Inc.

Berrett-Koehler Publishers, Inc.
450 Sansome Street, Suite 1200
San Francisco, CA 94111-3320
Tel: (415) 288-0260
Fax: (415) 362-2512
www.bkpub.com

Kumarian Press, Inc.
14 Oakwood Avenue
West Hartford, CT 06119-2127
Tel: (860) 233-5895
Fax: (860) 233-6072
www.kpbooks.com

Ordering Information

Individual sales. This book can be ordered direct from either Kumarian Press or Berrett-Koehler Publishers at the addresses above.

Quantity sales. Special discounts are available on quantity purchases by corporations, associations, and others. For details, contact either Kumarian Press or Berrett-Koehler Publishers at the addresses above.

Orders for college textbook/course adoption use. Please contact Kumarian Press at (800) 289-2664.

Orders by U.S. trade bookstores and wholesalers. Please contact Publishers Group West, 1700 Fourth St., Berkeley, CA 94710. Tel: (510) 528–1444; Fax: (510) 528-3444.

Printed in the United States of America

Printed on acid-free and recycled paper that is composed of 50% recovered fiber, including 10% postconsumer waste.

Library of Congress Cataloging-in-Publication Data

Korten, David C.,
    The post-corporate world: life after capitalism / by David C. Korten.
      p. cm.
    Includes bibliographical references and index.
    ISBN 1-57675-051-5 (alk. paper)
    1. Corporations. 2. Capitalism. 3. Big business. 4. Industrial policy.
  I. Title.
  HD2731.K67   1998
  338.7'4—dc21   98-51489
                                    CIP

First Edition
01 00 99   10 9 8 7 6 5 4 3 2 1

Copyediting: Sandra Beris
Interior design and production: Joel Friedlander, Marin Bookworks
Indexing: Leonard Rosenbaum
Proofreading: Elissa Rabellino
Cover design: Richard Adelson

To two leading-edge thinkers from the field of biology,
Mae-Wan Ho and Elisabet Sahtouris,
whose pioneering work on living systems inspired this book

To Thomas Berry,
who drew me to the search for a new story

and

To my friends and colleagues of the Positive Futures Network,
who are helping the new storytellers recognize themselves,
find one another, and share what they are learning of the possibilities ahead.

Contents

Acknowledgments vii
Prologue: A Story for the Third Millennium 1

Part I: The Deadly Tale 19
   1. The Sirens' Song 21
   2. The Naked Emperor 37
   3. The Midas Curse 65

Part II: Life's Story 85
   4. The Incredible Journey 87
   5. Organism as Metaphor 103
   6. Embracing Life's Wisdom 119

Part III: Envisioning a Post-Corporate World 135
   7. Responsible Freedom 137
   8. Mindful Markets 151
   9. Economic Democracy 163
  10. The Rights of Living Persons 183

Part IV: Coming Home to Life 209
  11. Culture Shift 211
  12. The New Storytellers 225
  13. Life Choices 243
  14. Engaging the Future 261

Epilogue: Planetary Consciousness 277
Notes 283
Index 305
About the Author 317

Acknowledgments

ANY BOOK OF THIS SCOPE is necessarily a collaborative product of many minds. The primary inspiration for the underlying framework comes from the work of Mae-Wan Ho and Elisabet Sahtouris. These two leading contributors to the new biology have also shared insights and provided constructive feedback throughout the drafting process. My special thanks to these remarkable women.

Following a now long-standing practice, Fran Korten, my life partner and most valued critic, has shared with me in the development of many of these ideas and has critiqued and extensively edited every chapter several times during the course of the manuscript's preparation. I am especially grateful that she found the time for this task even as she was holding down highly challenging full-time professional assignments of her own. Whatever merit this book may have, substantial credit is hers.

In a world of predatory publishing houses, I've been blessed to work with two extraordinary independent publishers—Berrett-Koehler Publishers and Kumarian Press—which maintain a commitment to the nearly forgotten tradition of publishing books because they matter and which have worked closely together in an unusual publishing partnership to give me extraordinary support in the completion and presentation of this project. At Berrett-Koehler, Steve Piersanti worked with me on every aspect of the book's writing and presentation. I will never forget faxing him a new draft chapter for comment on a Saturday afternoon and getting back his faxed handwritten comments at 11:00 P.M. that same night. Among all the wonderful people at Berrett-Koehler, special mention also goes to Pat Anderson, who has planned the marketing program; Elizabeth Swenson, who supervised the production; Karla Swatek, who worked with me on publicity; and Valerie Barth, who helped me master the media publicity process with *When Corporations Rule the World*. Sandra Beris completed the copyediting task with thoughtful and meticulous care. At Kumarian Press, Krishna Sondhi was at my side all along the way as she has been with each of my previous Kumarian books—continuing a valued partnership that extends back to the early 1980s.

John Adams, Gar Alperovitz, Alan AtKisson, Patricia E. Barrett, Linda Beyus, Ira Chaleff, Tony Clarke, Stuart Cowan, Dorothy Craig, Charles Derber, Thomas H. Greco Jr., Forrest Hawes, Pamela Johnson, Gabriela Melano, Kenneth Murrell, Barbara Shipka, Alis Valencia, Sarah vanGelder, and Thad Williamson all provided detailed critical feedback on the manuscript at various stages of its preparation. Jeff Shaw provided research assistance in locating key references. Sarah vanGelder also inspired the title of the book with her workshop on "Envisioning a Post-Corporate World" at The Other Economic Summit (TOES) conference held in Denver, Colorado, in 1997 as a citizen counterpoint to the Denver meeting of the G-8.

Other colleagues on whose thinking and inspiration I've drawn include Sharif Abdullah, Bella Abzug, Fatma Alloo, Gavin Anderson, Peggy Antrobus, Jean-Bertrand Aristide, Winifred Armstrong, Marcus Arruda, Jill Bamburg, Tariq Banuri, Jeff Barber, Maude Barlow, Gerald Barney, Brent Blackwelder, Walden Bello, Gerard Bentryn, Thomas Berry, Agnès Bertrand, Peter Block, David Bonbright, Hartmut Bossel, Barbara Brandt, Robin Broad, Tim Brodhead, Jerry Brown, Ruth Caplan, Fritjof Capra, John Cavanagh, Nilo Cayuquo, Rick Clugston, Clifford Cobb, Annemarie Colbin, Chuck Collins, Richard Conlin, Michael Conroy, Herman Daly, Kevin Danaher, Susan Davis, Chris Desser, Joe Dominguez, Richard Douthwaite, William Drayton, Ronnie Dugger, Alan Durning, Don Edwards, Duane Elgin, Paul Ehrlich, Ralph Estes, Anwar Fazal, Kevin Fong, Carl Frankel, Tracy Gary, Robert Gilman, Tom Gladwin, Susan George, Teddy Goldsmith, Alisa Gravitz, William Greider, Elaine Gross, Richard Grossman, Ted Halstead, Wendy Harcourt, Willis Harman, Paul Hawken, Randy Hayes, Hazel Henderson, Judy Henderson, Noeleen Heyzer, Jim Hightower, Nicholas Hildyard, Collin Hines, Dee Hock, Mika Iba, Rick Jackson, Josh Karliner, Sadruddin Aga Khan, Tom Keehn, Marjorie Kelly, Danny Kennedy, Martin Khor, Andy Kimbrell, Michael

Kinsley, Alicia Korten, Smitu Kothari, Satish Kumar, Sarah Larrain, Kathy Lawrence, Michael Lerner (*Commonweal*), Michael Lerner (*Tikkun*), Tina Liamzon, Bernard Lietaer, Lance Lindblom, Chee Yoke Ling, Luis Lopez-llera Méndez, Joanna Macy, Jerry Mander, Atherton Martin, Donella Meadows, Marilyn Mehlmann, John Mohawk, Michael McCoy, Victor Menotti, Susan Mika, Robert Monks, Ward Morehouse, David Morris, Jane Anne Morris, Ralph Nader, Wally N'Dow, Helena Norberg-Hodge, Sharyle Patton, Ignacio Peón Escalante, Nicky Perlas, Gifford Pinchot, Libba Pinchot, Carl Pope, George Porter, Tony Quizon, Tracy Rysavy, Paul Ray, William Rees, Jeremy Rifkin, Carl Riskin, Mark Ritchie, Karl-Henrick Robèrt, James Robertson, Vicki Robin, Anita Roddick, Tom Rogers, Atila Roque, Jonathan Rowe, Sixto Roxas, Najma Sadeque, Nola Kate Seymoar, Klaus Schwab, Michael Shuman, Isagani Serrano, Bart Shaha, Vandana Shiva, Bishan Singh, Corazon Juliano-Soliman, Claude Smadja, John Stauber, Felix Sugirtharaj, Akio Takayanagi, Betsy Taylor, Victoria Tauli-Corpuz, Robert Theobald, Sarah Timpson, Doug Tompkins, Lynn Twist, Steve Usher, Edgardo Valenzuela, Jakob Von Uexkull, Lori Wallach, Paul Wangoola, Paiboon Watanasiritham, Jae Hyun Yoo, Svet Zabelin, and Simon Zadek.

The book was prepared as a project of the People-Centered Development Forum (PCDForum), an informal alliance of organizations and activists dedicated to the creation of just, inclusive, and sustainable societies through voluntary citizen action. Its preparation was funded largely by royalties from *When Corporations Rule the World,* speaking honoraria, small donations, and a core support grant to the PCDForum from NOVIB in the Netherlands. The PCDForum is a purely voluntary organization that pays no salaries. I have received no personal compensation from any source for the preparation of this book, and all royalties go to the PCD-Forum. Information on the PCDForum and its publications is available on our Web site, generously provided and maintained by the International Institute for Sustainable Development Canada at http://issd.ca/pcdf.

If you wish to keep in contact with the kind of work and thinking that is moving us toward a post-corporate world, I urge you to subscribe to *YES! A Journal of Positive Futures,* published by the Positive Futures Network (PFN), P.O. Box 10818, Bainbridge Island, Washington 98110. I am a cofounder and chair the board of directors. For information call (800) 937-4451 or (206) 842-0216; fax (206) 842-5208, or visit the *YES!* Web site at www.futurenet.org. The Positive Futures Network is dedicated to creating awareness of the forces behind the positive cultural and institutional changes described here and to helping those engaged in creating a positive future find one another and meld their efforts into an effective transformative social movement.

The views expressed in this book are mine alone and do not necessarily represent those of the PCDForum and its contributors or those of the Positive Futures Network.

David C. Korten
Bainbridge Island
December 1998

Prologue: A Story for the Third Millennium

> *Because of the interconnectedness of all minds, affirming a positive vision may be about the most sophisticated action any one of us can take.*
> —WILLIS HARMAN[1]

IN THE 1980s capitalism triumphed over communism. In the 1990s it triumphed over democracy and the market economy. For those of us who grew up believing that capitalism is the foundation of democracy and market freedom, it has been a rude awakening to realize that under capitalism, democracy is for sale to the highest bidder and the market is centrally planned by global megacorporations larger than most states.

My previous book, *When Corporations Rule the World,* shared insights from my personal awakening to the realities of a world ruled by financial speculators and big business. Since its publication in September 1995, the troubling trends it described have steadily worsened. Mergers and acquisitions have continued to concentrate corporate power. Our political system is even more beholden to corporate money. Negotiators press ahead to complete new international trade and investment agreements that further strengthen corporate rights at the expense of human rights. Growth in the gap between the very rich and the rest of humanity has accelerated. The global financial system is now so unstable that even the speculators who create and profit from the instability are sounding warnings. Institutional legitimacy has further declined. Unsustainable demands on the environment have increased. And the social fabric has further eroded.

The Post-Corporate World takes the growing threat of social and environmental collapse driven by the excesses of an economic system that is blind to human need as its point of departure. In contrast with *When Corporations Rule the World*, however, it focuses less on the dysfunctions of the new global capitalism and more on the nature and form of democratic, market-based alternatives. It is written to challenge the story that has become the daily mantra of public discourse, a story that goes something like this:

> Like it or not—with the death of socialism—the forces of economic globalization and the new global capitalism are immutable and irreversible. There is no alternative. We must deepen our commitment to consumerism, free trade, and economic growth even as we endure the current trials of capitalism's creative destruction. In the end we will be rewarded with universal peace and prosperity. In the meantime, those who would survive and prosper must learn to win in the global economy's relentless and unforgiving competition.

For those of us who believe there is more to life than making money and shopping in megamalls for products we didn't know we needed until we saw them advertised on television, this story is a demeaning and dehumanizing counsel of despair and resignation that stirs resistance deep in the core of our being. Yet given the power and seeming support enjoyed by the institutions involved, capitalism's message of inevitability—if not its promise of universal freedom and prosperity—seems all too credible. Too often, those of us who long for alternatives feel powerless and alone. In fact, however, we are not alone. There are hundreds of millions of us— possibly billions—a part of the evidence I see that our species is in the midst of a profound awakening to a new appreciation of what it means to be truly human.

Indeed, millions of people, unsung heroes of a new era, are already hard at work constructing the building blocks of a post-corporate–post-capitalist civilization. They are demonstrating alternatives far more attractive and viable than socialism or the failed economic models of the former Soviet Union. The most promising alternatives center on applying the familiar principles of democratic governance and market economics to create societies that function in service to life and treat money as a facilitator, not the purpose, of our economic lives.

These determined pioneers are creating new political parties and movements, strengthening their communities, deepening their spiritual practice, discovering the joyous liberation of voluntary simplicity, building networks of locally rooted businesses, certifying socially and environmentally responsible products, restoring forests and watersheds, promoting public transportation and defining urban growth boundaries, serving as peacemakers between hostile groups, advancing organic agriculture, practicing holistic health, directing their investments to socially responsible businesses, organizing recycling campaigns, and demanding that trade agreements protect the rights of people and the environment.

They are present in every country. They come from every race, class, religion, and ethnic group. They include landless and illiterate peasants but also corporate executives; they include union members, shareholders, ranchers, teachers, housewives, small-business owners, farmers, local government officials, inner-city kids, loggers, wealthy intellectuals, and reformed gang leaders. The majority are women. Fed up with the failures of elitist leadership and distant bureaucracies, they are demonstrating the powerful potential of truly democratic forms of leadership in which people take direct responsibility for the health and well-being of themselves, their families, their communities, and the planet.

They are demonstrating through action that the mantra's message of inevitability is as false as its promise of universal freedom and prosperity. They—we—are creating a new story of the human and planetary future.

Stories

When I was a graduate student, I came across a remarkable book called *The Imagel,* by Kenneth Boulding. Boulding's thesis was simple but profound. We each organize our knowledge into a personal image of the world, which serves as a kind of map in guiding our behavior. To understand behavior, understand the image. *To change behavior, change the image.* It is an idea that deeply influenced my subsequent thinking about the processes of institutional change.

Most of the information we receive leaves our image of reality unaffected, which means the information conveys no new meaning. Or the information may alter the image in some way that does not change its basic structure. There are, however, times when new information reconstitutes our image of the world—and consequently our behavior. Changing the image shared by a culture can change its collective behavior and thereby create a new cultural reality.

Our deepest images are often best expressed as the stories on which we rely to give context and meaning to our lives. My own experience is a testimony to the fundamental change a new story can bring to the direction of an individual life. In 1959, I was completing my senior year of college. My political values were conservative and I was preparing to return to the town of my birth to succeed my father, as he had succeeded his father, as the head of our family business selling musical instruments and kitchen appliances. Aside from a journey of a few days in Canada and a border crossing of a few hours into Mexico with my parents as a child, I had never ventured outside the United States. Nor did I see much point to foreign travel, since within my limited worldview most everything of value or interest was to be found right here, in the good old United States of America.

Then for reasons I do not even recall—perhaps related to my concern that communism posed a threat to the American way of life—I chanced to take a course on modern revolutions from history professor Robert North. I became immersed in a simple, widely shared story that changed my life in a most dramatic way. The story, which you might call the classic American development story of the cold war era, went like this:

> Our world is divided into a small group of highly developed Western industrial countries and a much larger group of countries whose people are deprived of the benefits of development due to a lack of capital and technical and managerial skills. Their resulting poverty makes them easy targets for the false promises of communist revolutionaries. For reasons of self-interest, as well as humanitarianism, we must reach out to bring the benefits of American society to the poor countries of the world by providing them with the capital and expertise needed to spur their economic growth.

One fateful night I called my family in Longview, Washington, and informed them that I would not be returning to take my place in the family business. I had decided to become a development worker and devote my life to ending the poverty of the world's underdeveloped countries. As I had been destined for a business career and had already applied for graduate study in business, it seemed fitting that my contribution would come through helping bring modern management education to the rest of the world.

In the end, I spent some thirty years on this path, in places as far from my hometown as Ethiopia, Nicaragua, the Philippines, and Indonesia, the countries in which I've lived most of my adult years. I now look back on that experience as my real education—a time during which I became aware of the stark difference between the myth and the reality of the development story that had drawn me to my life's vocation.

In each of these countries, plus the dozens more I've visited, I witnessed the development progress promised by the classical development story. Year by year there were more modern international airports with well-stocked duty-free shops, freeways crowded with late-model cars leading from the airports to elegant five-star hotels located near bustling air-conditioned shopping malls where one could buy the latest in imported designer labels and consumer electronics. There were more grand homes and ever larger numbers of modest but comfortable middle-class residences with air conditioning and other modern conveniences. Those structures are development's facade, monuments to the good fortune of the few whom development has favored.

Yet there was another ever present reality that the classical development story had not foreseen. Behind the facade, millions of people were living in dehumanizing destitution—many as a consequence of development's intrusion into their lives. Shocking numbers had been driven by development projects from homes and communities that had afforded them a modest but dignified living. Dams, forestry projects, and many other interventions financed by the World Bank and other foreign assistance agencies had disrupted their lives for purposes that benefited those already better off. Environments were being stripped bare of life for the short-term profits of the rich and the short-term survival of the displaced. The deep social fabric of once-rich cultures was being ripped asunder.

Although a few were enjoying new material comforts, the lives of many more were deteriorating. Nearly everywhere, it seemed, inequality was increasing. It was ever harder to escape the pollution, even in the gated compounds of the rich. Something was very wrong.

My unease turned to horror when I turned my gaze back to the land of my birth and realized that similar processes of social and environmental deterioration had become well established in the United States and other Western industrial countries. Development seemed to be turning us all into what we now call Third World countries. The supporting structures of the story that had guided my life began to disintegrate.

Subsequently, I worked for several years with a network of colleagues, largely from nonprofit organizations in the Third World, in an effort to understand the nature of the problem. A new story began to emerge. In this story, the solutions that had defined much of my life as a development worker turned out to be a source of terrible problems. I soon found myself a leading narrator of a new development story—a story that largely explains the social and environmental crisis spreading throughout both industrial and preindustrial societies.

When Corporations Rule the World told the new story as I had come to understand it:

> Our relentless pursuit of economic growth is accelerating the breakdown of the planet's life support systems, intensifying resource competition, widening the gap between rich and poor, and undermining the values and relationships of family and community. The growing concentration of power in global corporations and financial institutions is stripping governments—democratic and otherwise—of their ability to set economic, social, and environmental priorities in the larger common interest.
>
> Driven by a single-minded dedication to generating ever greater profits for the benefit of their investors, global corporations and financial institutions have turned their economic power into political power. They now dominate the decision processes of governments and are rewriting the rules of world commerce through international trade and investment agreements to allow themselves to expand their profits without regard to the social and environmental consequences borne by the larger society. Continuing with business as usual will almost certainly lead to economic, social, and environmental collapse.
>
> To a considerable extent the problem originates with the United States. Its representatives are the primary marketeers of the false promises of consumerism and the foremost advocates of the market deregulation,

free trade, and privatization policies that are advancing the global consolidation of corporate power and the corresponding corruption of democratic institutions.

Resolving the crisis depends on civil societies, mobilizing to reclaim the power that corporations and global financial markets have usurped. Our best hope for the future lies with locally owned and managed economies that rely predominantly on local resources to meet the livelihood needs of their members in ways that maintain a balance with the earth. Such a shift in institutional structures and priorities may open the way to eliminating deprivation and extreme inequality from the human experience, instituting true citizen democracy, and releasing presently unrealized potential for individual and collective growth and creativity.

The timing of the book's release coincided with a receptive moment, a turning point in public consciousness. Corporate excesses were becoming ever more obvious and a significant segment of the population was becoming fed up. A number of citizen groups were beginning to take on corporate power and the related issues of international corporate-rights treaties disguised as trade agreements. Though the corporate-controlled press took little note of these initiatives, a variety of books and articles began circulating, mainly from small and alternative presses, and conferences, teach-ins, and rallies were being held with support from union, religious, environmental, women's, peace, consumer rights, and other citizen groups. In the United States the backlash gained sufficient strength that by November 1997 President Clinton was denied a renewal of so-called fast track legislation. This measure, which would have enabled the president to negotiate new trade agreements with the expectation that they would be confirmed by Congress with no amendments and limited public debate, had been supported by virtually every major corporation and editorial page in the country.

It became evident, however, that to do more than merely slow the consolidation of power by the corporate juggernaut, it is necessary to create broad public awareness of attractive alternatives. I began to turn more of my attention to this need and became involved in establishing the Positive Futures Network (PFN), which publishes *YES! A Journal of Positive Futures*. *YES!* is dedicated to identifying and sharing the ideas of people who recognize the seriousness of our situation, are responding with initiatives that attack the problem at its core, and contribute to building a positive future. It helps people committed to creating a just, sustainable, and compassionate future link with one another. PFN and *YES!* continue to be a major focus of my attention because they provide answers to those who ask, "What can I do to make a positive difference?"

When Corporations Rule the World made the case that it is within our means to create life-centered societies in which our economic institutions serve life with the same dedication our present institutions devote to the service of money. I was quite certain at the time that the creation of such societies must be guided by principles derived from a deep understanding of living systems. Yet the work on living systems with which I was familiar seemed too limited, mechanistic, and removed from the richness of the living world as I experienced it to take the process of defining such principles where it needed to go. Thus I felt unable to take my statement of the alternatives beyond what I had presented in *When Corporations Rule the World*—until a chance meeting in May 1997.

During a break at the World Conference of the Society for International Development in Santiago de Compostela, Spain, one of the participants, Dr. Mae-Wan Ho, introduced herself to me as a biologist interested in how the wisdom embodied in living systems might help us create life-friendly economic institutions. I was intrigued but unaware that the woman I had just met is a respected researcher on molecular genetics and one of biology's most creative and visionary thinkers. Though we did not speak further during the conference, we happened to sit together on a departing flight from Santiago de Compostela to London. Her insights into the nature of living systems and the lessons they hold for our economic life enthralled me. It struck me that her articulation of these lessons pointed directly to the principles on which a life-centered post-corporate world must be built and were critical to the rethinking of human purpose and institutions that I hoped the approaching millennium would stimulate.

By the time Dr. Ho and I arrived in London, I knew I must set about writing this book. On the next leg of my journey home to New York I read the papers she had shared with me and worked out the initial outline for this volume. Once in New York, I began immediately clearing my schedule for the next year and a half so I might devote myself fully to the project.

A few weeks later I found myself on a panel with Elisabet Sahtouris, another deep thinker from the field of biology who was applying insights from the study of living systems, and in particular life's evolutionary processes, to the creation of a more functional economy. Her book *Earth-Dance* and a manuscript of *Biology Revisioned,* which she had coauthored with Willis Harman shortly before his death, further advanced my understanding of what some call the new biology and the insights it offers into the resolution of our present human crisis.

The insights into living systems that these two women were articulating provided exactly the underlying principles for the restructuring of our economic institutions and relations for which I was looking. Were these two meetings purely chance? Or evidence of some deeper intelligence at work? I will always wonder. Either way, they were key to my taking up the challenge of writing the book you are now reading.

The Big Story

One of the first of Dr. Ho's papers I read on the trip back to New York from London set forth her thesis that we are in the midst of a basic paradigm shift in science, from the metaphor of the machine to the metaphor of the living organism. It proved to be one of those ideas that triggers a rush of intellectual insight during which myriad bits and pieces of data and insight suddenly coalesce in a way that gives them new power and coherence. If our stories make a difference in the way we live, our collective choice of the *big* story by which societies define the nature of reality and their relationship to it makes a *very big* difference in how societies organize themselves and define their goals. The difference Dr. Ho articulated between the machine metaphor and the organism metaphor (see Chapter 5) jumped out as a key to sorting out the difference between the society we are and the society we have the potential to become.

For nearly three hundred years Western societies, and increasingly societies the world over, have been living out a deadly tale inspired by the basic precepts of Newtonian physics. According to this tale,

> The universe resembles a giant clockwork set in motion by a master clock maker at the beginning of creation and left to run down with time as its spring unwinds. In short, we live in a dead and wasting universe. Matter is the only reality, and the whole is no more nor less than the aggregation of its parts. By advancing our understanding of the parts through the reductionist processes of science, we gain dominion over the whole and the power to bend nature to our ends.

Consciousness is an illusion; life is only an accidental outcome of material complexity. We evolved through a combination of chance genetic mutations and a competitive struggle in which those more fit survived and flourished as the weaker and less worthy perished. Neither consciousness nor life have meaning or purpose. People are just extremely complicated machines, whose behavior is dictated by knowable natural laws.

Competition for territory and survival is the basic law of nature. We cannot expect humans to be or become more than brutish beasts driven by basic instincts to survive, reproduce, and seek distraction from existential loneliness through the pursuit of material gratification. A primary function of the institutions of civilized societies is to use the institutional control structures of hierarchy and markets to channel our dark human instincts toward economically productive ends.

This story has had numerous positive effects. It liberated Western societies from the stultifying intellectual tyranny of the church and gave legitimacy to learning through empirical observation. It brilliantly focused attention on mastering the material world and gave rise to extraordinary advances in scientific knowledge and technology that brought previously unimaginable affluence to some 20 percent of the world's population and propelled our species into new levels of planetary awareness and communication.

The story's negative effects, however, are now putting us on a path of self-destruction. It has led to the embrace of money as the defining value of contemporary societies and given birth to a hedonistic ethic of material self-gratification; the hierarchical, control-oriented megainstitutions of the state and the corporation; and an economic system that rewards greed and destroys life. This deadly tale gives us no reason to live beyond using our technology to create ever more perfect distractions. It tells us we have nothing higher to which to aspire than to indulge ourselves in material luxury, while absolving us of moral responsibility for the consequences of our actions—thus setting the stage both logically and emotionally for our embrace of capitalism.

To explore the story's mythic power, I've experimented with opening myself to it—getting into a relaxed state and embracing its worldview as my own. I recite the mantra. The universe is a lifeless machine. Life is an accident, consciousness an illusion. All being is in a slow process of decay. We have nothing to which to aspire beyond material gratification.

As I open my mind to the story's message, I find the material world begins to lose its mystery. It seems more readily knowable, and even controllable. This feels empowering, though with an ultimate sense of futility. Since my own consciousness is an illusion and death the only reality, surely any such sense of power or control is itself only illusion. It then hits me. My fate is to live out my life in terrible loneliness—hopelessly and inevitably. I feel in turn fear, anger, and futility. The questions flow into consciousness: What have I done to deserve this curse? Why do I experience an illusion of consciousness only to know and suffer this damnation? I long for something—anything—to dull my consciousness and distract my mind from such questions. I ponder the possibilities. Such is the power of this story.

Although our stories shape our images of reality, the story itself is not reality. It is merely a particular and partial interpretation of a reality far more complex than any individual mind can comprehend.

Science unfolds through the continuing articulation and testing of stories that we call *theories.* As old stories are discredited by their failure to predict and explain new evidence, new story elements begin to emerge until by successive approximations a new story takes shape that is more successful in prediction, explanation, and application. It is the way we learn to relate to our world. It is the way of science, and of an intelligent culture.

Ironically, physics, the field most responsible for crafting the dead-universe story, has itself been forced by its encounter with the mysterious world of quantum mechanics, in which the rules of mechanical causality seem not to apply, to recognize that the old story is at least incomplete. We must take the obvious next step of acknowledging that the dead-universe story deals only with those aspects of our world that can be described in terms of mechanics and the entropic processes of death and decay. It cannot provide satisfactory explanations for the pervasive processes of creation that demonstrably lead not to disorder but to ever more complex levels of organization and capacity for conscious self-direction. Our embrace of the old story's prophecy of death is leading our species inexorably toward self-destruction. The time has come for a story that acknowledges life's creative power and inspires us to strive for new levels of consciousness and function.

This is the powerful message of theologian Thomas Berry, who argues eloquently in *Dream of the Earth* that our future depends on a new cosmic story that restores sacred meaning to life and draws us to explore life's still-unrealized potentials. Such a story is taking shape and drawing inspiration from many sources, including findings from the modern physical and life sciences and the world's richly varied spiritual traditions. Though it remains both partial and speculative, the new story goes something like this:

> The universe is a self-organizing system engaged in the discovery and realization of its possibilities through a continuing process of transcendence toward ever higher levels of order and self-definition. Modern science has confirmed the ancient Hindu belief that all matter exists as a continuing dance of flowing energies. Yet matter is somehow able to maintain the integrity of its boundaries and internal structures in the midst of apparent disorder.

> Similarly, the cells of a living organism, which are in a constant state of energy flux, maintain their individual integrity while functioning coherently as parts of larger wholes. This ability implies some form of self-knowledge in both "inert" matter and living organisms at each level of organization. Intelligence and consciousness may take many forms and are in some way pervasive even in matter. What we know as life may not be an accident of creation but rather integral to it, an attractor that shapes the creative unfolding of the cosmos.

> To the extent that these premises are true, they suggest we have scarcely begun to imagine, much less experience, the possibilities of our own capacity for intelligent, self-aware living. Nor have we tested our potentials for self-directed cooperation as a foundation of modern social organization. Evolution, although it involves competitive struggles, violence, and death, also involves love, nurturance, rebirth, and regeneration—and is a fundamentally cooperative and intelligent enterprise.

> There is substantial evidence that it is entirely natural for healthy humans to live fully and mindfully in service to the unfolding capacities of self, community, and the planet. Yet in our forgetfulness we have come to doubt this aspect of our own being. Nurturing the creative development of our capacities for mindful living should be a primary function of the institutions of civilized societies. It is time that we awaken from our forgetfulness and assume conscious responsibility for reshaping our institutions to this end.

Unlike the dead-universe story, this story beckons us to deepen our understanding of the potentials of life and consciousness and to master the art of living at both individual and societal levels. It calls us to embrace life as the defining value of society and recognize that we have the freedom and the capacity to make this choice.

Some may argue that the new story is hardly new at all. Rather, it is one of the most ancient of stories, a rediscovery of the wisdom of traditional cultures that see evidence of the hand of conscious intelligence at work in all of creation and stress the integral relationship of the individual to the community. This is partially true. What is new is the way in which this story integrates the ancient wisdom with modern scientific findings, insights, and methods of observation to achieve new understanding and potentials for growth to higher levels of individual and community function.

Not surprisingly, I find that when I focus on making this story my own and recite its mantra in my mind, the effect is completely different from that of the dead-universe story. The power of death gives way to the living power of creation in all its splendor, unity, and diversity. I gaze in awe at every object, rock, flower, insect, animal, and person—each engaged in the dance of life, constantly re-creating its every atom and molecule, each an integral participant in an epic journey of discovery by which a living universe seeks to know itself through renewal and transcendence. Gazing into the eyes of another person I encounter a window into the soul of the creative universe, with its limitless potential for love and creativity. I rejoice in the gift of consciousness by which I am privileged to experience with awe and wonder the beauty of life's sacred miracle. I live, therefore I am inseparably a part of the process of creation. I feel joyful, expectant, confident, loved, and filled with life's possibilities. I realize I can make this story my own. It is my choice.

Then I wonder. What would happen if we were each to take conscious responsibility for choosing the big story by which we will live our lives? What sort of societies might our species create if a substantial number of us were to embrace a living-universe story as our collective story? What might be the implications for how we think about and organize our economic lives? Might a new story open the way to social and spiritual progress that is now blocked by a modern equivalent of the dogmatic intellectual tyranny once imposed by the church?

Our modern understanding of life and consciousness remains prim-itive compared with our knowledge of the physical world. As my encoun-ters with Mae-Wan Ho and Elisabet Sahtouris helped me realize, the great scientific challenges of the third millennium lie in a deepening of our understanding of life and its potentials. As the science of a dead universe defined our past, our future depends on advancing our understanding of ourselves as beings that exist as part of the living processes of our planet.

New lines of inquiry into the nature of living systems are beginning to influence the world of science. Perhaps one day, much as the science of the twentieth century looked to the physical world for explanations of the living world, we may come to draw on our knowledge of the living world for insight into how the structures of the physical world maintain their form. A transition from dead science to living science seems already to be under way, setting the stage for an epic shift in human consciousness and the transformation of our economic and institutional lives.

We now have the knowledge and the communications technology to function with a global-species intelligence—to anticipate the future con-sequences of our collective actions and make a conscious collective choice to act differently as we awaken to the reality that where we are headed is not where any sane person would want to go. Perhaps it is more than sim-ple coincidence that we now find ourselves faced with both the necessity and the opportunity to accept responsibility for our impact on the con-tinuing evolution of life and consciousness on our planet.

In the past, it has been mainly biological determinists, such as sociobiologists and social Darwinists, who have turned to biology for political and economic insights, usually to justify existing structures of racism, gender discrimination, inequality, and capitalism's ruthless com-petition. Those efforts have been characterized by a limited and fatalistic view of the human condition consistent with the dead-universe story. It is radically different to look to the function and evolution of living sys-tems for insights into our as yet unrealized potentials. This is the chal-lenge before us to which I hope *The Post-Corporate World* may make some small contribution.

In *When Corporations Rule the World* I spoke of a "market tyranny that is extending its reach across the planet like a cancer, colonizing ever more of the planet's living spaces, destroying livelihoods, displacing peo-ple, rendering democratic institutions impotent, and feeding on life in an insatiable quest for money."[2] At that point, I was using the term *cancer* simply as a metaphor.

In *The Post-Corporate World* I refine the analysis to argue that the problem is not the market as such but more specifically capitalism, which is to a healthy market economy what cancer is to a healthy body. Cancer occurs when genetic damage causes a cell to forget that it is part of a larger body, the healthy function of which is essential to its own survival. The cell begins to seek its own growth without regard to the consequences for the whole, and ultimately destroys the body that feeds it. As I learned more about the course of cancer's development within the body, I came to realize that the reference to capitalism as a cancer is less a metaphor than a clinical diagnosis of a pathology to which market economies are prone in the absence of adequate citizen and governmental oversight. Our hope for the future is to restore the health of our democracies and market economies by purging them of the pathology.

When dealing with a cancer of the body, containment is rarely an adequate strategy. To become healthy, one needs a curative regime designed to remove or kill the defective cells. Some combination of surgical removal with measures to weaken the cancer cells and strengthen the body's natural defenses is likely to be appropriate. There is a strong parallel to the task now before us. Curing the capitalist cancer to restore democracy, the market, and our human rights and freedoms will require virtually eliminating the institution of the limited-liability for-profit public corporation as we know it to create a post-corporate world through actions such as the following:

- End the legal fiction that corporations are entitled to the rights of persons and exclude corporations from political participation;
- Implement serious political campaign reform to reduce the influence of money on politics;
- Eliminate corporate welfare by eliminating direct subsidies and recovering other externalized costs through fees and taxes;
- Implement mechanisms to regulate international corporations and finance; and
- Use fiscal and regulatory policy to make financial speculation unprofitable and to give an economic advantage to human-scale, stakeholder-owned enterprises.

I have no illusions that removal of the capitalist cancer will be easily accomplished. Rarely is cancer in any of its manifestations easily cured.

On the other hand, I see no realistic prospect for the amicable coexistence of life and capitalism. They represent ways of being and valuing as antithetical to one another as the coexistence of cancer cells and healthy cells. Any seeming accommodation between them is inherently unstable and most likely to be resolved in favor of the cancer. On a small and crowded planet with a finite life-support system, our choice as a species is basically between life after capitalism and severe global-scale social and environmental collapse.

Engaging This Book

In the prologue to *When Corporations Rule the World,* I invited readers to approach the book as if they were engaging in a conversation with a valued friend, to listen sympathetically but also actively and critically—to bring their experience and perspectives to bear as people concerned for the future we are leaving to our children. The subsequent feedback suggests many readers took the invitation seriously, and became deeply, personally engaged with the book and its subject matter. Many shared it with friends and formed discussion groups to engage in real conversations on its issues.

This approach is even more appropriate to *The Post-Corporate World* because of its more personal message. I wrote *When Corporations Rule the World* as a political wake-up call. In *The Post-Corporate World* I reiterate that call but add a call to a spiritual awakening centered on a very old theme: overcoming the temptation to sacrifice the spirit for a handful of silver. To this end I intend that it contribute to raising our shared consciousness of the sometimes profound implications of the big story that shapes our values and sets the direction of our lives.

I know well that many readers will finish this book with a question: "Okay, I've got the new story. Now what do I do?" The first thing is to recognize that in a world ruled by institutions that depend for their power on our forgetfulness, waking up is itself a revolutionary act. Political and spiritual awareness is our best immunological defense against invasion by the capitalist cancer.

"All right," readers may say, "enough New Age navel-gazing, I'm ready to change my life and make some waves. What next?" This is not a how-to book on the ten simple steps to creating a better world. It is a book about changing the way we perceive reality and think about its possibilities. That said, I do hope you will find both ideas and inspiration for personal action in the pages that follow. You will find many suggestions for policy reform initiatives, such as those listed earlier, in Part III. Where specific groups are mentioned, check the footnotes for contact information—including Web site addresses that will lead you to many other organizations and resources. Part IV tells about people who are creating the new story by living it. They embody many useful ideas and much inspiration. Chapter 14 suggests a wide range of possibilities for individual action you may wish to consider in developing your personal strategy for engaging in the creation of the post-corporate world.

There are countless ways to be usefully involved, and each of us must find our own path to translating these ideas into personal action. I do ask that readers not attempt to contact me directly for personal guidance or to discuss issues raised here because I can only refer you back to these same sources and do not have the personal time and resources to respond individually—as much as I wish I did. For a regular source of ideas and contacts, subscribe to *YES! A Journal of Positive Futures,* the journal described earlier. Useful assistance is also available on the *YES!* Web site at www.futurenet.org.

As for what you can expect in the pages that follow, *The Post-Corporate World* is divided into four parts. Part I, The Deadly Tale, tells how the story of a clockwork universe led ultimately to the triumph of money over life through the rise of capitalism at the expense of democracy, markets, and life itself. Its purpose is to build the case that deep change is imperative to the survival and prosperity of our species. If you can read Part I without feeling depressed, it probably means you missed the point. But don't despair: the rest of the book focuses on the good news that change is possible and that momentum is building behind forces that could carry us to a post-corporate, post-capitalist future.

Part II, Life's Story, is the larger story of life as revealed in the fifteen-billion-year cosmic journey that brought us to our present defining moment. It shares insights from the new biology that reveal life's inherent capacity to self-organize in ways that honor the needs, freedom, and coherence of both the individual and the community—suggesting potentials within ourselves yet unrealized.

Part III, Envisioning a Post-Corporate World, examines in greater detail the nature of the institutional and policy choices we must make to eliminate the economic pathology that plagues us and create truly democratic, market-based, life-centered societies. Part IV, Coming Home to Life, looks at the processes already building momentum behind a radical metamorphosis to a new civilization able to function in balance and harmony with itself and the living systems of the planet. The Epilogue, Planetary Consciousness, looks ahead to the emergence of a planetary intelligence.

I've written this book to stand on its own for the reader not familiar with *When Corporations Rule the World,* but it is in many respects a sequel to the earlier volume. Although it builds from the same basic arguments, I've tried to minimize the repetition of ideas, themes, and examples already presented there. For example, *When Corporations Rule the World* deals in more detail with the operation of the global financial system, mergers and acquisitions, international trade agreements, downsizing, the corporate corruption of democracy, events leading to capitalism's abandonment of the social contract that created the Western middle class in the post–World War II years, and the role of groups like the Council on Foreign Affairs, the Bilderberg, the Trilateral Commission, and the Business Roundtable in building elite consensus. It also gives more attention to population, natural-resource constraints, inequality, exclusion, and the role of the World Bank and the International Monetary Fund in deepening the postcolonial economic dependence of the Third World through development aid. These treatments are not essential to following the arguments of *The Post-Corporate World,* but they lend additional depth to the analysis and provide more extensive documentation on the causes and dysfunctions of corporate rule.

Bear in mind as you read ahead that this is a book about choices, not destiny. I have written it from a belief that we have reached a crisis point that presents us with the opportunity and the imperative to take conscious responsibility for our inevitable role in shaping both our own destiny as a species and the future evolution of life on planet Earth. There is no guarantee we will make a collective choice for life. Indeed, there is a great deal in our history and present situation to suggest we may not. The prospects of a positive choice are greatly enhanced, however, to the extent that we engage in active public dialogue on the options before us and make our choices with an informed awareness of the consequences. It is to the end of advancing this dialogue that I have written this book.

Part I

The Deadly Tale

Chapter 1

The Sirens' Song

Economic self-interest has always been central to the organization of societies and the advancement of individuals. But the defining characteristic of the postmodern political era is the absolute domination of money as the organizing principle of human and international relations. Some days there seems to be nothing else.
—JIM HOAGLAND[1]

The world of material mechanics, which still holds sway over most minds and is the official science "story" of the mass media, is a world of scarcity (because matter is finite, because it has a limited capacity to fulfill us). It spawns violence by telling us that we are separate: "I can hurt you without hurting the larger whole that includes myself—and since there isn't enough for both of us, we have a reason to fight each other."
—MICHAEL NAGLER[2]

IN THE EPIC GREEK POEM *The Odyssey,* Circe warns Odysseus about the dangers that lie ahead on his journey home from Troy:

First thou shalt arrive where the enchanter Sirens dwell, they who seduce men. The imprudent man who draws near them never returns, for the Sirens, lying in the flower-strewn fields, will charm him with sweet song; but around them the bodies of their victims lie in heaps. Therefore pass these Sirens by, and stop your men's ears with wax that none of them may hear; but if you like you can listen yourself, for you may get the men to bind you as you stand upright on a crosspiece halfway up the mast. If you beg and pray the men to unloose you, then they must bind you faster.

Overcome by desire, but having heeded Circe's instructions, Odysseus is saved only by the ropes that bind him to his ship.

Greek mythology goes on to tell us that Orpheus later vanquished the Sirens—not through physical force or restraint, but with a more beautiful and compelling song. Orpheus was sailing with Jason and the Argonauts on their quest for the Golden Fleece. When their ship passed by the infamous island, the Sirens sang their deadly song. Butes, son of Zelion, fell under their spell, leapt overboard, and was lost. Before the others could join him, however, Orpheus tuned his lyre and began to sing so divinely that their attention was turned to him. Vanquished by that song, the Sirens lost their power and turned to stone.

Two competing songs. One a call to death disguised as an alluring promise. The other a call to life. Although centuries old, it is an allegory for our times. Only in our case, the Sirens are not strange creatures of the sea but familiar institutions of the world of money, while Orpheus's song comes from life itself.

Competing Songs, Competing Worlds

As we are called by competing attractors to two very different futures, our present experience might be likened to that of the science fiction character who is pulled back and forth between parallel universes operating by entirely different rules and values. In our case, one of these realities, the living world, consists of all the things that are essential to life—air, water, soil, trees, people, communities, places, animals, insects, plants, sunlight, and so on. It also includes our material artifacts such as tools, buildings, and machinery that are useful in meeting our various needs and enhancing our quality of life. The living world is a creation of the life spirit that quickens all beings and has long-established imperatives for healthy function—balance, sufficiency, synergy, regenerative vitality, and respect for the integrity of parts and wholes. Although it includes our human artifacts, for the most part it transcends value as measured by price or other financial considerations, and its appetites are moderated in relation to the physical limits of its habitats. Unrestrained growth, as demonstrated by cancer cells and exploding populations, is a sign of malfunction. Life's song calls with a message of love and beauty, an entreaty to respect life's values, to live fully, and to participate in the actualization of its creative powers.

The second reality, the money world, consists of money and the institutions of money—primarily corporations, financial institutions, and those aspects of government that deal with the regulation, budgeting, and expenditure of money. This world is purely a creation of the human mind and has no meaningful existence beyond the confines of our consciousness. Yet it too has its own logic, values, and imperatives for healthy function. Its institutions are designed to collapse unless there is sustained growth in profits, stock prices, output, consumption, trade, investment, and tax receipts. Its appetites are insatiable and it acknowledges no physical limits. Whatever exists today, more is required tomorrow. Everything—even life—has its price. An absence of growth is a sign of stagnation and even decline. Its song calls us with promises of ease, personal power, and material prosperity; in return we must accept money as the mediator of all values and dedicate our lives to its reproduction.

The two songs call us to honor their values and serve their imperatives. Yet the values and imperatives of the one stand in stark conflict with those of the other. The two, it seems, are engaged in a mortal struggle for the soul of humankind.

The natural and institutional manifestations of this struggle are very real. Yet its origins lie within ourselves—a modern version of the eternal struggle between good and evil that has been a central theme of human experience since our earliest myths. From the dawn of human consciousness we have known the tension between the call to nurture our capacities for love and transcendence and the call to indulge our capacities for greed and the pursuit of personal power in disregard of the whole.

That the struggle is a product of our own psyche is evident in the fact that money itself has no volition or power of its own. Although it has been one of the most useful of human inventions and contributed greatly to our progress, money is nothing more than a simple number on a piece of paper or some form of electronic medium that offers a convenient means to facilitate economic exchange.

With time, however, we have come to imbue money with almost mystical significance. Some speak of the soul of money. Others speak of it as a form of energy. We accept it as a storehouse of wealth. Yet this is all illusion. Money has none of the attributes of real wealth. Although we can use it to buy many useful things, it will not itself nourish our bodies, protect us from the elements, educate us, transport us, entertain us, or enrich our spirits. Money is created out of nothing when a government prints a number on a piece of paper or a bank issues a loan and credits the amount to an account in its computer. It has no substance or inherent utility, and since President Richard Nixon took the U.S. dollar off the gold standard in 1971, the governments and banks that create it no longer back it with anything of real value.

Money's importance and utility depends entirely on our collective agreement to accept it in exchange for things of real worth, such as our land, labor, ideas, and the products created therefrom. To make this point abundantly clear, picture yourself alone on a desert island with nothing to sustain you but a large trunk filled with bundles of hundred-dollar bills. You might find them a poor substitute for tissues, or perhaps choose to burn them to keep warm on a cold night—if you have a match.

What has made us so vulnerable to money's song? How has a mere abstraction gained such power over us? Although the problem did not originate with Newtonian science, the assumptions underlying the scientific paradigm inspired by his work have contributed in substantial measure to the creation of a culture predisposed to accept as valid the false promises of the money world's siren song.

From Dead Universe to Materialistic Hedonism

The mechanistic worldview that became the underpinning of modern science, and ultimately of modernism and its values, grew out of the work of the sixteenth- and seventeenth-century scientists and philosophers who gave birth to the age of science and reason. It began with Polish astronomer and mathematician Nicholas Copernicus (1473–1543), who developed the argument in his treatise *On the Revolution of the Heavenly Spheres,* published in 1543, that the earth makes one rotation on its axis each day and one rotation around the sun each year. His challenge to the prevailing faith that the earth is the stationary center of the universe gained compelling support from the astronomical observations of Italian scientist Galileo Galilei (1546–1642), which ultimately convinced the majority of scientists that Copernicus's main conclusions were true.

Building from these findings, French philosopher René Descartes (1596–1650), an influential advocate of rationalism, taught that the various bodies that make up the universe move in predictable mechanical relationship to one another as they play out forces originally set in motion by God. Sir Isaac Newton's (1642–1727) mathematical description of the law of gravity and the extension of its application to the bodies of the solar system provided confirmation of Descartes' teaching and led to broad acceptance of the view that every event in nature is governed by universal laws that can be described in mathematical notation.

Backed by the theory of English philosopher John Locke (1632–1704) that the human mind is at birth a blank slate with nothing written on it—not even the idea of God or of right and wrong—science came to accept the idea that all knowledge originates from sense perception and that observation and reason are the only valid sources of truth. Together these ideas freed science from the obligation to pay homage to revelation as a source of knowledge.

> Gone was the medieval conception of a universe guided by a benevolent purpose; men now dwelt in a world in which the procession of events was as automatic as the ticking of a watch. Newton's philosophy did not rule out the idea of a God, but it deprived Him of His power to guide the stars in their courses or to command the sun to stand still.[3]

In the earlier stages of the scientific revolution many scientists made an accommodation to religious teaching in their effort to explain how this extraordinary machinery came into being. Lacking any better explanation, many accepted Descartes's basic position that it was all created and set into motion by a master inventor—God. In the eyes of science, if there ever was a God, however, he had long ago left the scene, leaving only mechanism behind.

Thus it was that science came over time to see the universe as a gigantic clockwork driven by a spring that is gradually running down to a state of exhaustion—a mere collection of material parts that interact according to fixed physical laws knowable through observation, measurement, and mathematical calculation. That which cannot be observed and measured, such as spirit and consciousness, came to be excluded from consideration by science—and therefore from the scientist's perspective does not exist. Although science could scarcely deny life, it worked from the premise that life is purely the accidental result of mechanical, chemical, and electrical processes and can ultimately be understood solely in terms of its component physical parts.

As it dismissed spirit, so too did science dismiss consciousness—an illusory artifact of material complexity. As astronomer Carl Sagan put it, "My fundamental premise about the brain is that its workings—what we sometimes call *mind*—are a consequence of its anatomy and physiology, and nothing more."[4]

Throughout the scientific-industrial era, this view of reality served effectively to focus our collective attention on understanding and mastering our material world. We unlocked countless secrets of matter, traveled beyond our own world, dramatically extended the average human life span, created vast organizations able to function simultaneously around the world, and installed a global system of communication that—if we choose to do so—could link every person on the planet in instantaneous communication with every other.

However, these accomplishments have come with a heavy price. The scientific premise that life is an accident and consciousness an illusion stripped our lives of any purpose or meaning. It was seventeenth-century philosopher Thomas Hobbes (1588–1679) who made the link between this premise and the moral philosophy of competitive self-interest and materialistic hedonism subsequently embraced by modernist culture, current mainstream economic thought, and contemporary capitalism.

Much like his modern counterpart Carl Sagan, Hobbes maintained that absolutely nothing exists except body, matter, and motion: "Every part of the Universe, is Body; and that which is not Body, is no part of the Universe: and because the Universe is All, that which is no part of it is Nothing."[5] Therefore, Hobbes maintained, mind is nothing more than motion in the brain. Even God, if God exists, must have a physical body.

Hobbes also argued that what we humans do is determined by our appetites (primarily a desire for power) and our aversions (primarily a fear of others). Without rule by an all-powerful king to restrain and channel these animalistic impulses, our lives would be "poor, nasty, brutish, and short." This Hobbesian theory of governance is now known as *Hobbism*, defined by *Webster's New Collegiate Dictionary* as "the Hobbesian theory that absolutism in government is necessary to prevent the war of each against all to which natural selfishness inevitably leads mankind."[6] The Hobbesian logic that leads from mechanism to a belief in a world without moral purpose in which pursuing material gratification is life's only source of meaning and the brutish impulses of man must be restrained by authoritarian rulers is summarized by historian Edward McNall Burns as follows:

> Hobbes contended that not only the universe but man himself can be explained mechanically. All that man does is determined by appetites or aversions, and these in turn are either inherited or acquired through experience. In similar fashion, Hobbes maintained that there are no absolute standards of good and evil. Good is merely that which gives pleasure; evil, that which brings pain. Thus did Hobbes combine with materialism and mechanism a thoroughgoing philosophy of hedonism.[7]

Modern economics turned the Hobbesian ideology of rational materialism into an applied science of human behavior and social organization that embraces hedonism as the goal and measure of human progress, assumes human behavior is motivated solely by material self-interest, and absolves the individual of responsibility for moral choice. Indeed, one might argue that the influence of Hobbes is more strongly revealed in the thinking and prescriptions of mainstream economics than that of Adam Smith, a man of deep ethical conviction and an intellectual crusader against any concentration of unaccountable power.

The moral detachment of rational materialism is also reflected in the argument that scientists properly bring to their work a single-minded commitment to scientific objectivity and a search for knowledge and bear no responsibility for the uses made of their discoveries. Thus, whatever their personal moral reservations, physicists lend their knowledge to the design of life-destroying nuclear weapons systems, chemists participate in the production and release of toxic chemicals, and biologists rearrange genetic structures and release new organisms into the environment with unpredictable consequences.

When the modern corporation brings together the power of modern technology with the power of massed capital, it also brings together the scientist whose self-perceived moral responsibility is limited to advancing objective instrumental knowledge and the corporate executive whose self-perceived moral responsibility is limited to maximizing corporate profits. The result is a system in which power and expertise are delinked from moral accountability, instrumental and financial values override life values, and what is expedient and profitable takes precedence over what is nurturing and responsible.

As Hobbes aptly demonstrated, it all follows logically from the premise that life is accidental and meaningless—a story that denies life meaning, denies life respect, and absolves us of responsibility for the harm our actions may cause. Yet this is not our natural predisposition, which leads to the stressful and morally disorienting psychological conflict Richard Tarnas describes in *The Passion of the Western Mind:*

> Our psychological and spiritual predispositions are absurdly at variance with the world revealed by our scientific method. We seem to receive two messages from our existential situation: on the one hand, strive, give oneself to the quest for meaning and spiritual fulfillment; but on the other hand, know that the universe, of whose substance we are derived, is entirely indifferent to that quest, soulless in character, and nullifying in its effects. We are at once aroused and crushed. For inexplicably, absurdly, the cosmos is inhuman, yet we are not. The situation is profoundly unintelligible.[8]

The issue is not with scientists or with scientific inquiry. It is with a culture of science that limits the boundaries of acceptable inquiry and interpretation and places both scientists and the rest of us in this troubling intellectual and psychological bind. We are caught between the belief system of our scientific culture and the conflicting data of our daily experience.

The Rise of Money and Materialism

Until some 150 years ago, the worldview of rational materialism was confined to the intellectual elites of Western science and academia. It remained at odds with the spiritual teachings of the religious establishment and the values of the popular culture. In the beginning, the advantage lay with the church, which reached deeply into the daily lives of ordinary people through an active institutional establishment with local congregations and controlled the rituals surrounding birth, marriage, and death.

The institutions and ideas of science were more distant and less persuasive. Similarly, money and the attention it tends to direct to more instrumental and materialistic values played a relatively incidental role in the economic affairs of those who owned the tools of their production, produced for their own needs, and engaged in barter with their neighbors.

Under such conditions money functioned in the role of servant for most people, a facilitator of those limited aspects of the community's life that involved exchanges outside of the household and beyond the traditional norms of reciprocity and barter.

Step-by-step, however, as money came to be an increasingly defining force in political and economic affairs, the ideas and values of rational materialism also grew in acceptance, eventually finding a central place in the popular consciousness. The shift came about through the convergence of a number of forces. Among the earliest was the rise of *mercantilism,* which reached its high point in the period from 1600 to 1700 and brought great power to those princes and merchants who successfully accumulated vast quantities of gold and other precious metals.

Mercantilism has been defined as "a system of government intervention to promote national prosperity and increase the power of the state . . . to bring more money into the treasury of the king, which would enable him to build fleets, equip armies, and make his government feared and respected throughout the world."[9] The doctrine of *bullionism,* the idea that the prosperity of a nation is determined by the quantity of gold and silver contained within its borders, was central in mercantilist theory. This belief drove a great quest for gold and silver through both conquest and trade on the theory that the more of these metals a country holds, "the more money the government can collect in taxes, and the richer and more powerful the state will become."[10]

When viewed objectively, it seems illogical that a country becomes prosperous and powerful in proportion to the quantities of particular metals it has locked away in great vaults. Yet Spain's power and prosperity at the time were well known and they seemed to be the result of a vast flow of precious metals pouring into its coffers from its American colonies. Thus the idea became established among persons of ambition that great power comes to those skilled in accumulating large quantities of the coin of the realm. This in turn led to the rise in power and prestige of those in the economics profession, who claimed knowledge of the ways of money and the arts of its accumulation—and who became carriers of the Hobbesian moral philosophy. As the use of money spread, so too did the moral philosophy of materialism.

Money has such obvious benefits over barter for enabling trade that the expansion of its use was entirely natural. Yet the greater the extent to which human transactions are mediated by money, the greater the power of those who create and allocate these privileged numbers. This fact was not lost on the empire builders who colonized the lands of Africa, Asia, and Latin America. Finding it difficult to control and extract the economic surplus from people whose economic relations were defined by tribal and kinship ties rather than by money, the colonizers quite consciously set about creating dependence on money.

Their method was to impose taxes that could be paid only with money that they issued and controlled. That simple requirement forced the colonized to sell their labor and produce to the colonizers on whatever terms the colonizers chose to set. The village heads had to collect the taxes, thus undermining their legitimacy. The men of the village had to seek cash income on the estates of the colonizers, breaking down family and community ties, substituting market relations for affective ties, and increasing the dependence on those who controlled the creation and allocation of money.

Colonialism is an apt metaphor for our current situation. We have all become the colonized in a modern society in which virtually every transaction for food, shelter, transportation, child care, and security in old age is mediated by money. With time, the institutions of money have come to hold the power of life and death over virtually everyone. The power and prestige of money and of the economics profession has risen in tandem.

The spread of secular public education and the study of science during the late 1800s and early 1900s also strengthened rational materialism's hold. It provided an outreach capability for the scientific worldview and made it a more significant competitor in the popular consciousness with the religious worldview. Furthermore, science's increasingly visible accomplishments—radio, television, air and space travel, and the computer, for example—brought prestige, stature, and credibility to science and, by association, the values of rational materialism.

The increasing power and prestige of the large corporation driven by the logic of finance was yet another contributor to rational materialism's rise to prominence. As corporations provided each new technological wonder to the masses, their names became synonymous with progress and prosperity. Less visibly, they came to have substantial influence over research funding, ownership of intellectual property, and the choice of which technologies would be advanced and which would not. Thus in ways both subtle and overt, they shaped the decisions that were reconstructing society. Would our cities be built around sidewalks, bicycle paths, and mass transit aimed at facilitating the flow of people, or around systems of flyovers and turnpikes to facilitate the flow of automobiles? Would we give priority to nuclear energy that leaves the earth burdened with deadly radioactive materials for thousands of years to come, or to environmentally friendly solar energy? Would our food be produced by small farms using organic methods that enhance the soil, or by global agribusiness corporations that use chemical and energy-intensive methods to subdue the soil and its natural processes? In each case, it seems the institutions of money stacked the deck in favor of those choices that used the technologies they controlled and made the largest contribution to their power and profit. The more power that corporations acquired, the more our lives seemed to depend on their money and technology—and the less they seemed to depend on the living earth.

Colonization of the Popular Culture

Perhaps the most overt and conscious of the processes by which the values of rational materialism found their way into the popular culture was the rise of marketing, which involved an intentional reshaping of the culture. The culture of a human society is much like what physical scientists call a *field,* a concept they developed to explain the coherence with which physical matter organizes itself. A field is a universal force that permeates space and exerts influence over matter, such as an electromagnetic or a gravitational field. Fields are by definition invisible and may be detected and measured only by their material effects.[11]

Similarly, cultures are the invisible organizing fields of societies. Though cultures permeate our social spaces, they are visible only in the observed behavior of the individuals who share their values and prescriptions. They are as essential to any explanation of the coherent function of a society as electromagnetic and gravitational fields are to explaining the organization of matter.

As social beings we have a strong impulse to respond to cultural fields—and for a good reason. Cultural fields enable human societies to function coherently without the coercive centralized institutional authority that Hobbesian philosophy maintains is necessary to contain our baser instincts. When a cultural field emerges as a consensual expression of the shared experience, values, and aspirations of the members of a society, it serves as a deeply democratic mechanism for achieving social coherence. But when a small group is able to manipulate the society's cultural symbols and values to serve its own narrow ends, the processes of cultural reproduction can become deeply undemocratic and destructive.

As extensively documented by historian William Leach, the U.S. retailing giants of the late nineteenth and early twentieth centuries decided that to increase their profits they must create a greater demand for their merchandise and set about to replace the popular culture of frugality that had prevailed since America's founding with a culture of self-indulgence.[12] They became increasingly skilled in the use of color, glass, and light to convey a sense of a this-world paradise. They put elegant models on display in fashion shows, sponsored museum exhibits depicting the excitement of the new culture, and used the media to surround the individual with messages reinforcing the culture of desire. Consumer credit made it all seem within the reach of everyone. Through such means retailers virtually invented the culture of consumerism, described by Leach as "the most nonconsensual public culture ever created."[13]

Corporations remain hard at work today converting the world's popular cultures to Hobbesian hedonism. In the United States advertising expenditure equals 2.3 percent of the national product, nearly half the level of educational spending, and is growing by more than 6.0 percent a year.[14] Indeed, a major portion of corporate advertising is now aimed specifically at indoctrinating children in the values of consumerism and corporate rule—even to the point of bringing the corporate message into the public schools through the enforced viewing of television commercials through made-for-school TV broadcasts and exclusive marketing agreements. Channel One, a commercial venture, now brings televised advertising messages to eight million children directly in their school classrooms in the name of education.[15] In Evans, Georgia, high school student Mike Cameron was suspended for a day for wearing a Pepsi T-shirt on Coke Day and spoiling a school picture in which students spelled out the word Coke. During their most vulnerable formative years our children are exposed to the constantly repeated message that their personal worth is defined by the toys they own, the corporate logos on their clothing, and the brands of junk food they consume.

Global corporations are now reaching out to establish the hegemony of a culture of greed and excess in virtually every country in the
world in their relentless search for more customers. Global spending on
advertising—expected to reach as high as $437 billion in 1998[16]—is
rapidly coming to rival even global military spending expenditures—
$778 billion in 1994.[17] Indeed, we might well consider what corporations
are doing in as yet unconverted cultures to be a form of values warfare,
devaluing their cultures as backward, boring, and poor, and offering in
their stead promises of a material paradise of excitement, ease, and prosperity for all.

Television, which now reaches more than 60 percent of the world's
people, serves as the money world's most powerful tool of global cultural
and ideological indoctrination. Duane Elgin, author of *Voluntary Simplicity,* warns:

> By programming television for commercial success, we are program-
> ming the mindset of entire civilizations—perhaps even the species-civi-
> lization—for evolutionary stagnation and ecological failure. The use of
> television to promote exclusively materialistic values has become a massive
> mental health and public health problem for the United States and the
> world.[18]

Elgin isn't exaggerating. A thirty-year values study of nine million
freshmen on fifteen hundred U.S. campuses found a radical shift from
1966 to 1996 in student views of why college is important to them. In
listing what was essential or very important to their decision to attend college, 83 percent of entering freshmen in 1968 chose "Develop a meaningful philosophy of life" as essential or very important; only 43 percent
chose "Be very well off financially." By 1996, the desire to be financially
well off had become essential or very important for 74 percent, and developing a meaningful philosophy of life was down to 42 percent. The statistical variable that seemed best to explain the switch was the number of
hours of television viewed before arriving at college: those who reported
having watched the most television were least likely to believe that values
other than money matter.[19] From a money-world perspective, television
has been a brilliant success. Indeed, we saw not only a shift in the values
of college freshmen during this period of rapidly increasing television
viewing but also a shift in the values of a nation from the significant social

commitment of the sixties to the cynicism, materialism, and greed of the eighties and nineties. Although television was not the sole cause, it was most surely a contributor.

Scarcity in the Guise of Plenty

False promises are the money world's stock in trade. Most often its Sirens sing not of greed but of a universal material paradise—a world in which modern technology will banish poverty, war, and violence by providing everyone with a life of material comfort and luxury. Yet behind the promise lies a disturbing paradox. Although money-world institutions profit from the mass production and distribution of goods and services and are leading proponents of growth in production and consumption, scarcity plays a central role in their global quest for profit.

Any economist will happily tell us that scarcity creates value. Intelligent people pay money only for goods that are scarce. Which has the greater real value: air or diamonds? Air is free, diamonds are pricey. *Life* says air, because we must have it to live, and provides it in abundance. *Money* says diamonds, because they are scarce, and its institutions limit supply to inflate the price.

That's the money world's little secret. Though it promises abundance, its preference is for scarcity—the source of its profits. If wastes contaminate our municipal water supplies and create a scarcity of potable water, the money world profits from the sale of bottled drinks. Where there is a scarcity of good public transit, it profits from cars, gasoline, and road building. When soil fertility declines, it sells us more fertilizer. Where jobs are scarce, it finds labor cheap. The money world thrives on scarcity, not abundance, and its greatest prize is a monopoly that allows it to restrict supply.

Even the system by which money is created is itself designed to create scarcity. Most of us casually assume our money is created and issued by government. In fact, most of it is created by banks lending it into existence. Herein lies a seldom-noted problem.

Say a bank provides me with a $100,000 mortgage. It opens an account in my name and credits it with the amount of my loan. In so doing it creates $100,000 that I then spend into circulation. So far, so good. The catch is this: the bank expects to be repaid with interest, which on a long-term mortgage might require total repayments of $200,000 or more. Because all the other money in circulation was also created through lending by banks that also expect to be paid back with interest, there simply isn't enough money in circulation to pay the banks their due—unless the economy grows fast enough to expand borrowing at a rate sufficient to create the money required to repay the principal and interest on previous loans. Bernard Lietaer, international money manager and a designer of the single European currency, explains the implications:

> The bank expects you to pay back $200,000 over the next twenty years, but it doesn't create the second $100,000—the interest. Instead, the bank sends you out into the tough world to battle against everybody else to bring back the second $100,000. . . . So when the bank verifies your "creditworthiness," it is really checking whether you are capable of competing and winning against other players—able to extract the second $100,000 that was never created. And if you fail in that game, you lose your house or whatever other collateral you had to put up.[20]

In a debt-based money system bankruptcies and bank failures can be avoided only by continuous economic expansion. This is an important source of the money world's growth imperative. The system is designed to create winners and losers, with a bias in favor of the banks that make the money and against the working people and entrepreneurs who produce the real wealth. It is also a system designed to be unstable, because it must either grow or collapse.

For most people, the resulting life-and-death struggle for a means of living creates a pervasive fear of scarcity that triggers a mass impulse, even among the very rich, to acquire and hoard beyond real need. The hoarding of money in turn increases the scarcity of money in circulation and further escalates the fear. It becomes a vicious cycle of escalating fear and scarcity.

There is another way in which money creates scarcity, which we will visit more fully in Chapter 3. The insatiable demand it makes on corporations to produce ever greater profits creates a powerful pressure on corporate management to destroy real productive capital, the source of all real wealth, to generate quick profits. In contrast to the scarcity of money, which is to a large extent artificial, the loss of real capital creates real scarcity.

As a species, we face a fateful choice between the song of life and the song of money. Both promise life, but only one can deliver.

Life's song calls us to engage fully the wonder, joy, and love of life inherent within our being. It makes life the measure of value and progress and calls us to fulfill the prophecy of a story in which life itself is the defining reality.

The song of money calls us to experience life through the pursuit of material diversions—all so real, so attractive, and so immediate. Why not give it a try? Life will always be there.

But to follow money's song we must make money our measure of value and progress. Once we yield to its temptation, its imperatives become our imperatives. We find ourselves fulfilling the prophecy of death. But the Siren soothes our fears: "My way is natural, right, inevitable. The pain will soon be over—and from here there is no return."

We yearn to believe the promises, even to give ourselves completely to her service, in an effort to banish from awareness the glimmerings of a terrible truth: the Siren who hides her true nature behind a false cloak of democracy and market freedom has laid claim to our soul and is feeding on our flesh. Her name is capitalism.

Chapter 2

The Naked Emperor

For we are all capitalists now, are we not? These days the victory of the market over state is quite taken for granted.
—THE ECONOMIST[1]

Although members of other species trick one another, humans are the expert self-deceivers: as the best symbol users, the most intelligent species, and the only talkers, we are the only beings accomplished enough to fully fool ourselves.
— LYNN MARGULIS AND DORION SAGAN[2]

WE ARE SUBJECTED to a constant refrain: the victory of capitalism is the triumph of the market and democracy. Capitalism is an engine of wealth creation. Freed from the oppressive hand of public regulation, market forces will cause the world's great corporations to bring prosperity, democracy, a respect for human rights, and environmentally beneficial technologies to all the world. If some must suffer temporarily to make way for greater progress for all, it is only capitalism's creative destruction at work on the path to a better tomorrow.

The mantra continually propagated by our most powerful institutions brings to mind the human capacity for self-deception immortalized in the story of the emperor's new clothes. Many of us are like the emperor's subjects. We see the truth, but lack the courage to speak. The time has come to speak the truth that so many of us know in our hearts. Though the Siren known as capitalism wraps herself in the cloak of markets, democracy, and universal prosperity, she is the mortal enemy

The Emperor's New Clothes
Once upon a time a vain emperor who fancied himself a stylish dresser sent forth word that he would give a great prize to the tailor who sewed him a cloak woven of the finest cloth. A clever rogue came forward with an offer to make him a cloak from a cloth so fine that it could be neither seen nor felt against the skin. The emperor was elated. When the cloak arrived, his terrified aides could only express their admiration for the emperor's fine taste. As the emperor ventured forth on his great horse to display his new finery to his subjects, they dared only to applaud—until the voice of a small and innocent child was heard, "Why doesn't the emperor have any clothes?"

of all three. We tolerate her triumph to the peril of nearly all we truly value.

In this chapter we will examine the ways capitalism actively erodes the conditions necessary to the market's efficient social function. Understanding the extent to which markets and capitalism are mutually exclusive forms of economic organization is the key to answering those who maintain there is no alternative to global capitalism. Indeed, a market economy is the most obvious and promising of the alternatives.

Capitalism Against the Market

The theory of the market economy traces back to the Scottish economist Adam Smith (1723–1790) and the publication of his *Inquiry into the Nature and Causes of the Wealth of Nations* in 1776. Considered by many to be the most influential economics book ever written, it articulates the powerful and wonderfully democratic ideal of a self-organizing economy that creates an equitable and socially optimal allocation of a society's productive resources through the interaction of small buyers and sellers making decisions based on their individual needs and interests.

Market theory, as articulated by Smith and those who subsequently elaborated on his ideas, developed into an elegant and coherent intellectual construction grounded in carefully articulated assumptions regarding the conditions under which such self-organizing processes would indeed lead to socially optimal outcomes. For example,

- Buyers and sellers must be too small to influence the market price.
- Complete information must be available to all participants and there can be no trade secrets.

- Sellers must bear the full cost of the products they sell and pass them on in the sale price.

- Investment capital must remain within national borders and trade between countries must be balanced.

- Savings must be invested in the creation of productive capital.

There is, however, a critical problem. As international financier George Soros has observed: "Economic theory is an axiomatic system: as long as the basic assumptions hold, the conclusions follow. But when we examine the assumptions closely, we find that they do not apply to the real world."[3] Herein lies the catch: the conditions of what we currently call a *capitalist economy* directly contradict the assumptions of market theory in every instance.

Bear in mind that the optimally efficient market exists only as a theoretical construction. No economy has ever fully satisfied its assumptions and probably none ever will. The challenge facing those of us who would create an economy that approximates the market's promised outcomes of fair but modest returns to capital, full employment at a living wage, and socially optimal allocation of society's productive resources is to establish a framework of rules that create as closely as possible the conditions that market theory assumes.

It is in contemplating this task that we encounter the reality of capitalism's true relationship to the market economy. Historians have traced the first use of the term *capitalism* to the mid-1800s, long after Adam Smith's death, when it was used to refer to an economic and social regime in which the ownership and benefits of capital are appropriated by the few to the exclusion of the many who through their labor make capital productive.[4] This, of course, describes with considerable precision the characteristics of the current global capitalist regime, which bears no discernible resemblance to the concept of a market economy as envisioned by Smith and those who followed in his tradition. Those who rejoice at the triumph of capitalism are rejoicing at the triumph of the few over the many.

Indeed, capitalism's claim to the mantle of the market has no more substance than the rogue's claim that he has cloaked the emperor in a fine gown. In selectively culling out bits and pieces of market theory to argue that the public interest is best served by giving globe-spanning megacorporations a license to maximize their profits without public restraint, capitalism has distorted market theory beyond recognition to legitimate an ideology in the service of a narrow class interest.

Wearing the mantle of the market, capitalism's agents vigorously advance public policies that create conditions diametrically opposed to those required for markets to function in a socially optimal way. Table 2.1 provides an overview of some of the major differences that are examined in greater detail in this and subsequent chapters.

Like the cancer cells that attempt to hide from the body's immune system by masking themselves as healthy cells, capitalism's agents attempt to conceal themselves from society's immune system by masquerading as agents of a healthy market economy. Capitalism has become so skilled in this deception that we now find our economic and political leaders committed to policies that serve the pathology at the expense of the healthy body. To restore health we must recognize the diseased cells for what they are and repair their damaged DNA, destroy them directly, or deprive them of the body's nutrients.

The nature of capitalism as a market pathology can be readily demonstrated by examining how it vigorously and systematically eliminates the five conditions earlier noted as basic to market theory. What follows is a grim picture of our collective affliction. To exorcise our affliction, we must be willing to look it squarely in the face.

COMPETITION: SMALL FIRMS VERSUS MEGACORPORATIONS

Beginning with Adam Smith, market theory has been quite explicit that the efficiency of the market's self-organizing dynamic is a consequence of small, locally owned enterprises competing in local markets on the basis of price, quality, and service in response to customer-defined needs and values. No buyer or seller may be large enough to influence the market price individually.

By contrast, what we know as the global capitalist economy is dominated by a few financial speculators and a handful of globe-spanning megacorporations able to use their massive financial clout and media outreach to manipulate prices, determine what products will be available to consumers, absorb or drive competitors from the market, and reshape the values of popular culture to create demand for what corporations choose to offer. The alleged anticompetitive practices of Microsoft Corporation in its systematic domination of the software industry and the Internet

Table 2.1. Capitalism Against the Market

	Capitalism	Healthy Markets
Dominant attractor	Money	Life
Defining purpose	Use money to make money for those who have money	Employ available resources to meet the basic needs of everyone
Firm size	Very large	Small and medium-size
Costs	Externalized to the public	Internalized by the user
Ownership	Impersonal, absentee	Personal, rooted
Financial capital	Global with no borders	Local/national with clear borders
Purpose of investment	Maximize private profit	Increase beneficial output
The role of profit	An end to be maximized	An incentive to invest productively
Coordinating mechanisms	Centrally planned by megacorporations	Self-organizing markets and networks
Cooperation	Among competitors to escape the discipline of competition	Among people and communities to advance the common good
Purpose of competition	Eliminate the unfit	Stimulate efficiency and innovation
Government role	Protect the interests of property	Advance the human interest
Trade	Free	Fair and balanced
Political orientation	Elitist, democracy of dollars	Populist, democracy of persons

make it only one of the better known examples. Furthermore, the mega-corporations and financial houses continue to concentrate and consolidate their power over markets, technology, and capital through mergers, acquisitions, and strategic alliances—even as they shed their responsibility for people by downsizing and contracting out. The statistics are sobering.

In 1995, the combined sales of the world's top two hundred corporations—which employed only 18.8 million people, less than one-third of 1 percent of the world's population—equaled 28 percent of total world gross domestic product. The total sales of the Mitsubishi corporation were greater than the GDP of Indonesia, the world's fourth most populous country and a land of enormous natural wealth. The annual sales of Wal-Mart, the twelfth largest corporation, made its internal economy larger than the internal economies of 161 of the world's countries—including Israel, Poland, and Greece.[5]

Meanwhile, the consolidation of unaccountable corporate power is accelerating. In the United States the total value of corporate mergers and acquisitions increased at a rate of nearly 50 percent a year in every year save one from 1992 through 1998, with no end in sight. Most of these mergers and acquisitions have been accompanied by large-scale layoffs.

The greatest concentration is taking place in the financial and telecommunications sectors, with deeply ominous implications for the future of democracy. In the United States alone, from the beginning of 1993 to the end of 1997, there were 2,492 commercial bank mergers worth more than $200 billion, 5,114 deals worth a total of $110 billion in the insurance industry, and 1,435 radio and television mergers worth $162 billion.[6]

The increasingly arrogant defiance of law and the public interest embodied in these mergers was epitomized by the 1998 announcement by Citicorp banking corporation and Travelers Group insurance corporation of the largest merger in history to create the world's largest financial institution. It signaled that the titans of the money world no longer intended to be bound by the laws of the land—in this case the Glass-Steagall Act, a legal restriction passed by the U.S. Congress during the Great Depression that prohibited banks from owning insurance corporations and brokerage houses to prevent a repeat of the disastrous financial collapse of 1929.

Other industries in which concentration has moved at a rapid clip include health services, investment brokers, utilities, oil and gas refining, and hotels and casinos. In the United States there are now only three large military contractors and one producer of large commercial airliners.[7]

Though the United States led the world in merger mania during the 1990s, mergers worldwide totaled $1.63 trillion in 1997, up 48 percent over 1996.[8] Merger activity is rapidly accelerating in Europe as Wall Street investment banks become more active there, aggressively promoting hostile takeovers that advance the concentration of European industry and the shift of wealth from workers to managers, investment houses, and shareholders. European mergers and acquisitions set a record of $400.6 billion in 1996, double the level of just two years earlier. American investment banks were involved as advisers in two-thirds of these deals.[9] The move of eleven European countries to a single currency at the beginning of 1999 is expected to unleash a further wave of mergers and acquisitions.[10]

New agreements fashioned under the auspices of the World Trade Organization in Geneva plus terms imposed by the International Monetary Fund (IMF) following Asia's 1997 financial meltdown opened Asia's financial markets to greater intervention by Wall Street investment houses to the same end. The U.S. financial press referred to it as a great "fire sale" opportunity.[11]

Trends in the accountancy industry may be the harbingers of things to come. In the 1980s, the world had eight large international accountancy firms. Four mergers in 1997 reduced the number by half. With these firms providing an increasingly diversified range of consulting and management services to large clients, interests become so intertwined that the concept of the independent audit is becoming nearly meaningless.[12]

The global cartel is another favored mechanism by which the largest global corporations avoid competing with one another in the global economy by agreeing on mutually protective pricing formulas. In July 1998, the U.S. Justice Department had twenty-five grand juries investigating international price-fixing cases in industries as diverse as vitamins, glass, and marine equipment. It is estimated that cartels are transferring billions of illegal dollars from consumers to corporate coffers.[13]

Competition is key to the self-organizing dynamics of a market economy. In contrast, capitalism loves monopoly with a passion equaled only by its abhorrence of the competition that limits its ability to extract monopoly profits.

COMPLETE INFORMATION: SHARING VERSUS MONOPOLIZATION

Market theory stipulates that information should be freely available. Adam Smith condemned trade secrets as a form of monopoly power that prevents market entry by competing producers. Market efficiency requires that such artificial barriers be removed and relevant knowledge and expertise be freely shared. It also requires that buyers and sellers enter into each transaction fully informed about the nature and quality of the product and the current market price of comparable items. This is possible only to the extent that market participants freely share the information available to them.

Capitalism functions under quite different norms. Its corporations presume a right to withhold information about dangers posed by their products, deny consumers access to information that would allow them to make informed choices about the products they buy, and aggressively pursue the creation of government-enforced monopolies over critical technologies, including those essential to life.

In one of the more notorious examples of industry attempts to deny consumers their right to accurate product labeling, the United States Department of Agriculture (USDA) on December 16, 1997, released a six-hundred-page technical document proposing changes in federal regulations regarding organic standards. Backers of the proposed changes included the National Food Processors Association, the Grocery Manufacturers of America, and the Biotechnology Industry Organization. The changes would have significantly lowered the organic standards maintained by an association of forty nongovernmental and state organic certifiers. In their place it would have introduced a mandatory standardized "USDA Organic" label that would permit the use of genetic engineering, nuclear irradiation, toxic sewage sludge, intensive confinement of farm animals, and other conventional factory farm practices in the production of organically certified products. Furthermore, the rule change would have given the USDA a monopoly over use of the word *organic* and prohibited any organic certifiers or producers from setting a standard higher than those it established.

The response from consumers was strong and unanimous. The USDA received 220,000 citizen comments, twenty times greater than to any previous USDA proposal, and nearly all denounced the proposed rule change.[14]

On a related front, corporations have pushed through food libel laws in a number of states that make it a crime to make a statement not backed by conclusive scientific evidence that might cause people to doubt the safety of their food. By appropriating and redefining the term organic, the agents of capitalism seek the right to mislabel their own products and deny others the right to accurately inform the public that they are holding themselves to a higher standard. Through what are sometimes called the *veggie libel* laws, they seek to silence those who would raise critical issues of food safety for public discussion and debate.

With regard to trade secrets, corporations have been engaged in an increasingly intense campaign to strengthen and extend government protection of technology and information monopolies in the name of intellectual property rights. In response to the demands of global corporations, governments wrote strong safeguards for intellectual property rights into the North American Free Trade Agreement (NAFTA) and into the General Agreement on Tariffs and Trade (GATT) that created the World Trade Organization. The corporate goal is to establish an international intellectual property rights system that makes a patent granted in one country immediately enforceable in all countries to give the holder a strictly enforced global monopoly.[15]

Currently, biotech corporations are engaged in a vigorous campaign to gain monopoly control over life itself through the patenting of genetic materials and processes. One favored strategy is to force farmers into dependency on patented genetically engineered seeds that give the holder of the patent virtual monopoly power over a commodity such as soybean or cotton. Other biotech companies are in a race to patent every human gene they can identify. It is increasingly common for individuals to learn that without their knowledge or permission a corporation has acquired exclusive ownership rights to genetic material extracted from their bodies.

A brief segment in a television documentary I viewed some years ago on overpricing in the drug industry illustrates the extent to which some academic economists are revising economic theory to defend monopoly pricing. The documentary looked into a case in which a drug company was charging a price far above its costs for a patented drug that a small number of desperate patients depended on for their lives. An economist who was invited to comment argued that because the patients who used the drug had no alternative, the drug company had a fiduciary responsibility to its shareholders to raise the price to the highest level the users considered their lives to be worth. Because the drug's current high price was clearly below this amount, the company was in fact underpricing the product. Adam Smith, a staunch foe of monopoly pricing, must have been turning in his grave.

Full access to information and absence of artificial barriers to entry into the production of beneficial products are basic to the efficient function of the market and to meeting the needs of a troubled and resource-scarce world. Yet capitalism is an ardent champion of the right to withhold relevant information from customers and the public and to establish government-protected monopoly control of critical technologies.

ACCURATE PRICES: FULL COSTS VERSUS PUBLIC SUBSIDIES

Another major difference between a capitalist economy and an efficient market economy lies in the way they deal with subsidies and other externalized costs. Market theory explicitly states that for the market to allocate resources efficiently, the costs of a product must be borne fully by its producer and passed forward in the price charged to the consumer. Similarly, investors must bear the risks of their investments. Any subsidy, direct or indirect, distorts the incentives of the market's self-regulating pricing mechanisms and reduces the social efficiency of resource allocation.

By contrast, the institutions of capitalism are unabashed proponents of corporate subsidies. Using mechanisms that range from threatening to move jobs elsewhere to political contributions and fabricated grassroots lobbying campaigns, they convince those who control public expenditures to provide them subsidies for research, extraction of resources, advertising products in foreign markets, insuring overseas investments against political risks, and an endless range of other activities. Banks and investment houses regularly run to government to save them from the costs of bad investment, as in the savings and loan bailout and the repeated IMF and U.S. bailouts of bad loans to countries such as Mexico, Thailand, Indonesia, Malaysia, and Korea.

Corporations are constantly upping the ante on what they demand from state and local governments to bring jobs to their jurisdictions. For example, the incentive package given by the state of Virginia to Motorola to entice it to locate a research and manufacturing facility there included a $55.9 million grant, a $1.6 billion tax credit, and a reimbursement package worth $5 million for employee training. In New York City, investment banks threatened to leave the city for the suburbs, to which the cash-strapped city responded with ever greater tax breaks and other public subsidies. By 1998, $439 million in tax abatements had been granted to eighteen financial institutions—including the New York Mercantile Exchange, New York's largest commodity market—by the administration of Mayor Giuliani.[16] Big corporations now increasingly expect states to pick up a portion of their wage bill, commonly by returning to the company a portion of the state taxes withheld from qualified employees. In Tulsa, Oklahoma, the county sales tax for one year was diverted from public purposes to pay for construction of a new Whirlpool factory. In addition, the state would reimburse Whirlpool 4.5 cents for every dollar paid in wages to eleven hundred workers for ten years.[17]

Corporations have been especially aggressive over the past twenty years in seeking to avoid paying a fair share of taxes to cover the public services and infrastructure they demand, including roads and port facilities, the protection of their assets by the U.S. military, and the public education of their workers. In the 1950s, corporate income taxes accounted for 39 percent of all federal income tax revenue. From 1990 to 1995, that was only 19 percent. During that same period the share of federal income tax revenues coming from individuals rose from 61 percent to 81 percent.[18] If in 1996 corporations had paid taxes at the same effective rate as during the 1950s, it would have produced an additional $250 billion in federal revenues and wiped out the federal deficit for that year.[19]

It has been much the same story at local levels. In 1957, corporations provided 45 percent of local property tax revenues in the United States. By 1987, their share had dropped to about 16 percent.[20]

The Cato Institute, a conservative Washington, D.C.–based think tank, estimates that the U.S. government each year provides corporations $75 billion in direct cash subsidies plus another $60 billion in industry-specific tax breaks.[21] Worldwide, government subsidies for energy use—the majority for fossil fuel and nuclear sources—are estimated to be from $235 billion to $350 billion, a clear case of using public funds to encourage environmentally destructive practices.[22] Business analyst Paul Hawken has compiled data suggesting that corporations in the United States may now receive more in direct government financial subsidies than they pay in taxes.[23]

Then there are the costs of straightforward corporate crime such as overbilling by defense contractors of some $25.9 billion,[24] and by Medicaid contractors, primarily insurance companies, of an amount estimated by federal auditors at $23 billion in 1996.[25]

Still another type of subsidy takes the form of unreimbursed costs imposed on society by the products that corporations sell. These include health costs of $53.9 billion a year from smoking cigarettes, $135.8 billion for the consequences of unsafe vehicles, $141.6 billion for injuries and accidents from unsafe workplaces, and $274.7 billion for deaths from cancers caused by toxic exposures in the workplace.

In *Tyranny of the Bottom Line,* CPA Ralph Estes compiles an inventory of those public costs of private corporations that have been documented by authoritative studies—not including direct subsidies and tax breaks—and comes up with a conservative total for the United States alone of $2.6 trillion a year in 1994 dollars. This is roughly five times the corporate profits reported in the United States for 1994 ($530 billion) and the equivalent of 37 percent of 1994 U.S. GDP of $6.9 trillion. If we were to extrapolate this ratio to a global economy that had an estimated total output of $29 trillion in 1997, it suggests that the annual cost to humanity of maintaining the corporate infrastructure of capitalism may be upward of $10.73 trillion.

In short, although capitalism claims to be an engine of wealth creation, in fact its primary vehicle, the corporation, is more accurately described as a powerful engine of wealth extraction—its profits dependent on imposing enormous costs on the rest of society so that a few top executives and large shareholders may enjoy unconscionably large financial rewards. If market rules were applied, most of the dominant corporations would have long ago found themselves unable to cover their own costs and gone bankrupt or been restructured into smaller, more efficient firms.

BALANCED INTERNATIONAL ACCOUNTS: ROOTED VERSUS GLOBAL CAPITAL

Market theory's requirements that trade be balanced and capital be national (that is, be nationally owned and remain within national borders) are fundamental to classical economist David Ricardo's *theory of comparative advantage,* a cornerstone of market theory.[26] Much cited by capitalist interests pushing to remove barriers to the free flow of international trade and

Consequences of Foreign Debt

When a country spends more on imports than it earns from its exports, it incurs a foreign debt that must be covered by some form of foreign loan or other portfolio investment. In the end, whatever has been loaned or invested must be repaid with interest and profits in foreign exchange. Because there is rarely a reason to borrow or attract portfolio investments from abroad except to generate foreign exchange to pay for imports beyond what can be purchased with export earnings, the net amount of foreign exchange a country receives from foreign lenders and other portfolio investors generally equals the difference between its import expenditures and its export earnings.

It is much the same as for an individual. If you wish to spend more than you earn, you have to borrow money from someone to cover the difference. The person or bank making the loan is investing in you by acquiring a stake in your future earnings. You, of course, would be foolish to mortgage your future earnings simply for the pleasure of having the money sitting in your account. Normally people borrow only when they have in mind something they wish to buy beyond the means of their current savings and income. Of course, you will eventually have to increase your income or reduce your expenditures so you will have surplus income to repay the bank.

When a bank makes a foreign exchange loan to a government or business in another country, it is essentially providing that country with money that can be used to buy something from abroad it could not pay for from current export earnings. To repay its foreign obligations, the borrowing country must either earn the money for repayment by making more on the sale of its exports than it spends on imports or by borrowing still more from abroad and thereby compounding its foreign debt. This makes it very difficult to pay off a major foreign debt once incurred because to do so, a country must shift its whole economy from an export deficit to an export surplus and find a trading partner willing to incur a deficit. So long as trade between countries is balanced, there is no need for one country to borrow from another and thus no need to mortgage its assets and future production to foreigners.

investment, Ricardo's theory makes the case that open trade between two nations is beneficial to the national interests of both—so long as a number of very specific conditions are met. Among other required conditions, trade must be balanced between the two countries, both countries must have full employment, and investors must not be able to transfer their production facilities from one to the other. In typical fashion, those of the capitalist persuasion take no note of these conditions. For them it is enough that the free movement of money and goods increases profit opportunities for global capitalists. National interests are not their concern.

Ricardo's reasoning is quite straightforward. If trade between countries is balanced, labor is fully employed, and investors are unable to transfer their assets abroad, the investor who finds she cannot compete against foreign imports in one industry will shift her investment and the related jobs to another industry in which her country has some natural comparative advantage. For example, if for reasons of climate Portugal has an advantage in growing grapes and producing wine, and if for reasons of climate, technology, cheap energy, and labor skills England has an advantage in growing wool and producing woolen cloth, both countries stand to benefit if Portuguese woolens producers shift to wine production and English wine producers shift to production of woolen cloth, and the products are then exchanged through trade. Workers and capital remain fully employed in both countries, the British are able to enjoy more wine, and the Portuguese are able to enjoy more woolen clothing.

It's an entirely different matter if both investments and goods are free to flow where they will—which is the goal that the new global capitalists are advancing through international trade and investment agreements and organizations with names like NAFTA, GATT, WTO, OECD, APEC, and the MAI. Negotiated without public discussion and ratified by legislative bodies with limited debate and no opportunity for amendment, these agreements are used to eliminate economic borders and regulatory restraints on the power of the institutions of capitalism to move goods and capital freely, without regard to national interests or trade balances, wherever they see prospects for quick profit.

Assume under a regime of completely open borders that Portugal has both a more favorable climate and a substantial labor surplus that keeps wages deeply depressed, and that the retail prices of both cloth and wine tend to be higher in England. In this instance British investors will find it profitable to move their looms and wine presses to Portugal and ship both cloth and wine back to England.

Unable to compete with the lower-cost imports, the remaining British wine and textile producers will likely be driven out of business—depressing wages, increasing unemployment, and ultimately substantially reducing the British market for Portuguese wine and cloth. In the meantime, the Portuguese may find their economy increasingly controlled by British investors intent on keeping Portuguese wages low and repatriating as much profit as possible back to England to finance purchases of Portuguese textiles and wine by the remaining elite. This may result in additional wage employment in Portugal, but with wages low and much of the output exported to a narrow market, Portuguese workers may find they are unable to afford to buy the products of their own labor. The only winners are the investor classes, who point out that the Portuguese workers should be happy to have any kind of job at all given the sad state of both the British and Portuguese economies. It is toward this latter world that capitalism has moved us.

CAPITAL ACCUMULATION: PRODUCTIVE VERSUS EXTRACTIVE INVESTMENT

The fifth market condition discussed here addresses the question of whether savings are directed to productive investment or diverted to unproductive speculation. One of the most basic axioms of market economics is the simple equation: personal savings equals investment. In other words, market theory assumes that when people save, they defer current consumption in favor of investing in future productive output. As in the previous example, the winemaker might invest some of his earnings in a new wine press to increase future production.

The most advanced stage of capitalism's pathology is known as *finance capital* or *finance capitalism*. At this stage, the ownership of capital becomes increasingly separated from its application to production as power shifts from the entrepreneurs, inventors, and industrialists who are engaged in actual productive activity to financiers and rentiers who live solely from the income generated from the ownership of financial or other assets. The financial markets and the owners of capital become "increasingly purified in purpose—detached from social concerns and abstracted from the practical realities of commerce" and develop expectations regarding the returns invested saving ought to earn that increasingly "diverge from the underlying economic reality."[27]

The focus at this point is on using money to make money by expanding bank lending, creating financial and real estate bubbles, and speculating on fluctuations in the prices of currencies and other financial instruments. Consumed by their own illusions, capitalism's foremost proponents and practitioners come to pride themselves on having accomplished the equivalent of the ancient alchemists' dream of turning baser metals into gold. The financial excesses we are now witnessing on a global scale are much like those that preceded the Great Depression of the 1930s.

They are all a part of the *new global capitalism,* and virtually every country and person on the globe is to some extent subject to the resulting economic dysfunction and instability.

The mechanisms employed by finance capitalism to make money from money, without the intervening necessity of engaging in productive activity, allow those with money to increase their claims against society's stock of real wealth without contributing to its production. Although the activities involved make a few people very wealthy, from a societal perspective they are extractive rather than productive. Finance capitalism's inability to tell the difference between productive and extractive investment seems almost to be one of its defining attributes.

The process of making money without creating wealth starts with banks' creating money out of nothing each time they issue a loan. When I studied economics some years ago I was taught that banks are financial intermediaries. They take in money from those who have savings and make it available in the form of loans to those who invest it in productive activities. It is rather like one individual making a loan to another, except that as intermediary the bank translates the short-term savings of one group into long-term loans for another, does the paperwork, and takes the risk—or so I was led to believe.

In truth, there is another and more basic difference. If I loan $1,000 to another person—call her Alice—I no longer have the use of that money until Alice repays me. If, however, I deposit my $1,000 in a bank and the bank loans the $1,000 to Alice, Alice has her money and I still have mine. Between Alice and me we now have access to $2,000 in ready cash rather than $1,000. The bank did not in fact loan Alice "my" money. Rather it created the second $1,000 out of nothing, simply by opening an account in Alice's name and typing in $1,000.[28]

Clearly the bank has something more going on here than simply playing the role of intermediary between savers and borrowers. It is in the literal sense *making money*—creating it, putting it into circulation, and collecting interest on it—simply by posting a number to an account. Furthermore, the only thing of value that stands behind that money is the willingness of the rest of us to exchange our labor and other property for it. In a very real sense, the bank makes or creates the money and we guarantee its value with our labor and whatever other forms of real wealth we agree to exchange for it.

Another way to make money out of nothing without contributing to the creation of any real wealth is to create a financial bubble, which is a sophisticated version of the classic pyramid or Ponzi scheme. The fraudulent investment scheme that created a national crisis in Albania in the mid-1990s is an example. People were invited to participate in investment funds that promised returns as high as 25 percent a month. Impressed by the good fortune brought to them by the triumph of capitalism, some people handed over their savings. Though the investment scheme was not backed by any productive activity, with so much money pouring in it was easy for the promoters to use a portion of the money from new investors to pay the promised interest to the earlier investors. These payments established the credibility of the scheme and convinced still more people to invest. Soon the country was caught up in a speculative frenzy. Farmers sold their flocks and urban dwellers their apartments to share in the promised bonanza of effortless wealth. The inevitable collapse sparked widespread riots, arson, and looting when the Albanian government failed to make up the losses.

The speculative financial bubble, which involves bidding up the price of an asset far beyond its underlying value, is little more than a sophisticated and less obviously fraudulent variant of such pyramid scams. One of history's more famous financial bubbles occurred in seventeenth-century Holland when it was found that certain tulip bulbs, when attacked by a particular virus, produced flowers of brilliantly variegated colors. These bulbs came to be highly valued by collectors. Then speculators began acquiring them, pushing prices higher. Others came in to profit from the bonanza of prices that seemed to rise without limit. Soon everyone, from nobles to chimney sweeps, was in on the action, bidding up the price of a single bulb of a particularly prized variety to the equivalent of $60,000 in current dollars. The inevitable bursting of the bubble came in 1637.

Those of us inclined to laugh at the innocence of the Albanians or the seventeenth-century Dutch speculators should first consider our own participation in the world's stock markets. We operate on the mistaken belief that the money we use to buy stock or mutual fund shares goes into financing future productive output. However, in all but the rare instance in which we are buying shares sold in an initial public offering, not a penny of our money goes to the company whose shares we are buying.

According to 1993 Federal Reserve figures, equity financing raised through the sale of new shares contributed only 4 percent of the total financial capital of U.S. public corporations. The rest came from borrowing (14 percent) and retained earnings (82 percent). Furthermore, from 1987 to 1994, corporations paid out more to buy back their own shares than they received from new stock issues.[29] In early 1998, what is loosely called *investment capital* was flowing from corporations to the stock market at an annual rate of $110 billion.[30]

We live in an era in which, even as billions of dollars in new "investment" flow into the stock market and pump up prices at record rates, the net flow of funds from the stock market to the corporations in which we are in theory investing is actually negative. In truth, the stock market is a sophisticated gambling casino with the unique feature that through their interactions the players inflate the prices of the stocks in play to increase their collective financial assets and thereby their claims on the real wealth of the rest of the society.

So when I buy stock shares through my broker, not a penny goes to the company I'm presumably buying. After the broker takes a commission, what is left goes to the person who sold the shares. When I make my purchase, I'm simply betting that in the future someone else will be willing to pay me more for that piece of paper than I've just paid for it. If I were a really sophisticated investor, I would be betting on future price declines as well as future price increases, and I would be borrowing money to leverage my bets. No matter how I go about it, however, it has no more to do with real investing than betting on a number on a Las Vegas roulette wheel.

The Asian financial crisis provides a fascinating window into how the game works and how the resulting gyrations in the world's stock markets have an impact on the lives of real people. In 1997 Asia's much-touted financial miracle suddenly turned into the Asian financial meltdown. The meltdown began in Thailand and rapidly spread like falling dominoes through Malaysia, Indonesia, South Korea, and Hong Kong. Although specifics differed, we see in each instance a similar pattern. (See "Thailand's Encounter with Global Finance Capitalism," below.) During the miracle phase, large inflows of foreign money fueled rapidly growing financial bubbles in stocks and real estate and a rapid increase in the importation and sale of luxury consumer goods—creating an illusion of economic prosperity unrelated to any increase in actual productive output. The growing bubbles attracted still more money, much of it created by international banks issuing loans secured by the inflated assets. Because returns on productive industrial and agricultural investments could not compete with the returns to stock and real estate speculation, the faster foreign investment flowed into a country, the faster money actually flowed out of its productive sectors to join the speculation. In the meltdown phase, investors rushed to pull their money out in anticipation of a crash, stock and real estate prices plummeted, banks and other lending institutions were left with large portfolios of uncollectible loans, and financial collapse threatened, as liquidity dried up.

Like the losers in the Albanian pyramid scheme, the Wall Street bankers and investment houses that created the crisis through reckless lending—inveterate champions of the free market when the profits were rolling in—responded in typical capitalist fashion. They ran to governments for public bailouts. The IMF, with strong support from the Clinton administration, rushed to the aid of the bankers with emergency loans backed by public guarantees from its member governments. *The New York Times* reported, "One thing is clear: Whatever it takes, the Clinton administration will push to make sure that the size of the bailout is large enough to persuade investors to return."[31] In translation, this means the U.S. government intended to put up sufficient public money so that the private speculators would be attracted back into the market to restore the financial bubbles and get finance capitalism's party going again.

The IMF provided South Korea with a $57 billion bailout in December 1997. The Korean stock market rebounded smartly for a brief time. Then the speculators took the IMF money and ran. Korea's stock market suffered a 50 percent drop to an eleven-year low. Korea's taxpayers were left with an IOU to the IMF for $57 billion plus interest to be paid in foreign currency.[32]

We see in the Asian experience an all too common reality of capitalism's ability to create an illusion of prosperity by creating a speculative frenzy while actually undermining real productive activity. The U.S. financial collapse in 1929 and savings and loan crisis in the late 1980s, the gradual collapse of Japan's financial bubble that began in 1989, the Mexican collapse that followed the introduction of NAFTA, the Brazilian crash that followed the Asian meltdown, and the subsequent Russian crisis all share the characteristic that they involved the crash of financial bubbles created by financial speculation and reckless bank lending.

Still, it seems, the members of capitalism's inner circle remain impervious to the difference between productive investment—that is, using savings to increase the base of productive capital—and extractive investment—making money through speculation to establish claims on the existing real wealth of others. A 1996 *Foreign Policy* article titled "Securities: The New Wealth Machine" is unusually revealing of the mindset behind this blindness and the willingness of governments to align themselves behind finance capitalism's destructive power. The following are excerpts:

> Securitization—the issuance of high-quality bonds and stocks—has become the most powerful engine of wealth creation in today's world econ-

Thailand's Encounter with Global Finance Capitalism

Through the 1980s the Thai economy was fueled by direct investment flows from Japanese corporations building production facilities there to produce goods destined for export to the United States. As the inflow of direct investment began to level off, Thai economists came up with a scheme to keep foreign money flowing in to maintain the nation's high economic growth rate. They set a domestic interest rate above that of the U.S. dollar and guaranteed a fixed exchange rate between the Thai baht and the U.S. dollar. This created a powerful incentive to borrow in dollars to invest in baht for a profit guaranteed by the Thai government.

Just as the Thai technocrats intended, foreign money poured in. The country's foreign debt escalated from $21 billion in 1988 to $89 billion in 1997—$66.2 billion of it private. Most of the money found its way into the purchase of real estate, existing stock shares in Thai companies, and increased consumer spending on imported goods. As the economy boomed and real estate and share prices headed for the sky, fortunes were made and the money poured in even faster as U.S. and other foreign banks eager to profit from the Thai money machine competed with one another to create new dollars by lending to anyone who wanted to borrow dollars to convert to baht. The Thai government even invited the foreign banks to open branches in Bangkok to speed the process.

The agricultural and industrial sectors, Thailand's real productive sectors, couldn't compete for funds against the quick and easy high returns being generated by investments in stocks and real estate. Instead of upgrading their production facilities to maintain their international competitive position, industrialists diverted the cash flows from their industrial plants to more lucrative real estate or portfolio investments. This resulted in the seeming

omy.... It has broadened the market for income-producing assets by separating ownership from management and is creating wealth rapidly.

Historically, manufacturing, exporting, and direct investment produced prosperity through income creation. Wealth was created when a portion of income was diverted from consumption into investment in buildings, machinery, and technological change. Societies accumulated wealth slowly over generations. Now many societies, and indeed the entire world, have learned how to create wealth directly. The new approach requires that a state find ways to increase the *market value* of its stock of productive assets [emphasis in the original].[33] ... Wealth is also created when money, foreign or domestic, flows into the capital market of a country and raises the value of its quoted securities.[34]

paradox that the faster foreign money flowed into Thailand, the faster money flowed out of the productive sectors and into speculation. The country's actual productive base began to decline, and exports, which previously had grown vigorously, began to level off—undermining the country's ability to repay its rapidly growing foreign debt.

In the early stages, payments due on foreign loans had been easily covered by new inflows. In its *1996 World Development Report,* the World Bank cited Thailand as "an excellent example of the dividends to be obtained through outward orientation, receptivity to foreign investment, and a market-friendly philosophy backed up by conservative macroeconomic management and cautious external borrowing policies."

The financial pyramid began to crumble at the beginning of 1997, when the consequences of the real estate overbuilding and a glut of unoccupied buildings and uncollectible loans forced two of Thailand's premier finance companies to default on interest payments to foreign lenders. The more astute portfolio investors started pulling out. Concern turned to panic and stock prices plummeted. The Bank of Thailand stepped in to cover the demand to convert baht to dollars with $9 billion of the country's foreign reserves. Currency speculators stepped in to profit from the inevitable devaluation. The government announced that as many as a million Thais would lose their jobs in three month's time, negotiated a $17.2 billion emergency loan from the IMF, and announced that the IMF funds would be used to guarantee the foreign debts of the Thai finance companies, local banks, and enterprises that were in default, thus providing a public bailout of the speculators, both foreign and domestic, at the expense of the Thai public.

Based on Walden Bello, "The Rise and Fall of Southeast Asia's Economy," The Ecologist 28, no. 1, January/February 1998, pp. 9–17; and Walden Bello, "The End of the Asian Miracle," The Nation, January 12–19, 1998, pp. 16–21.

> Nowadays, wealth is created when the managers of a business enterprise give high priority to rewarding the shareholders and bondholders. The greater the rewards, the more the shares and bonds are likely to be worth in the financial markets.[35] . . . An economic policy that aims to achieve growth by wealth creation therefore does not attempt to increase the production of goods and services, except as a secondary objective.[36]

In translation, the author is telling governments that they should no longer concern themselves with increasing the national output of goods and services that have real utility. Instead, they should favor policies that provide incentives for: (1) owners of productive assets to convert their ownership rights into freely tradable securities; (2) managers to give exclusive attention to short-term shareholder interests; and (3) investors to bid up share prices.

Note that none of these actions make any net addition to the output of any product or service, nor do they result in the investment of a single penny in the creation or enhancement of a productive asset. The sole objective is to increase the total *market value* of traded securities, which serves only to create a temporary financial bubble that increases the claims of those who hold these securities against the society's real wealth. Forget production and the interests of working people, communities, and nature. Such is the flawed logic of finance capitalism that now drives policy making in the global economy and is bringing financial collapse to country after country.

As the logic serves their interests brilliantly, it is not surprising that the money world's insiders find it difficult to see its flaw. In 1997, the year of Asia's financial crash, securities brokerages in the United States—firms that specialize in the trading of financial securities—yielded their investors a total investment return for the year of 83.6 percent, the highest of any industry category. Also in 1997, the senior partners of the Wall Street investment houses received annual bonuses of $5 to $7 million each. Even junior partners garnered on the order of $4 million for their year's labors. For the three years 1995 through 1997, U.S. diversified financial services corporations produced an average return of 51 percent a year.[37] The large money center banks averaged 47.1 percent a year. There can be no mistaking that under finance capitalism the rewards go to those who make the money, not to the wage laborers who actually make the things the moneymakers hope to buy.

In a market economy investment is about creating and renewing productive capacity to meet future needs. In a capitalist economy investment is about making money. Whether productive capacity is created or destroyed in the process is purely incidental. Falsely equating the making of money with the creation of wealth and oblivious to the consequences of their actions for the rest of society, capitalists have proclaimed a new era of finance capitalism and congratulated themselves for having found the secret of creating wealth without the inconvenience of participating in any intervening productive activity. Far removed from the living world, the world of money has become their sole reality.

From Self-Organization to Central Planning

We have long been told of the self-organizing market's superiority to the stultifying central planning of socialism. It seems to follow, therefore, that to reap the full benefit of the market's invisible hand we must eliminate the barriers of regulation and economic borders to allow the market's free function. Only then, or so we are assured, can the market work its magic, allowing consumers to express their preferences and rewarding those producers who are most responsive to them.

Indeed, the last twenty to thirty years have seen major movement in the direction of deregulation and the opening of economic borders. How-

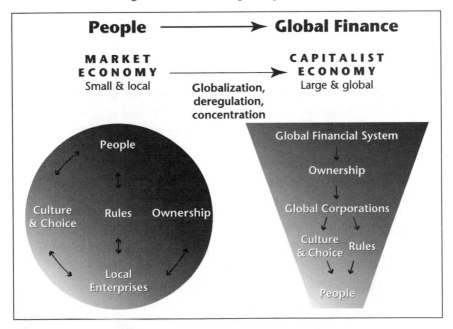

Figure 2.1. Power Shift

ever, we are coming to see that the result bears little resemblance to Adam Smith's ideal of a socially efficient self-organizing market. What we have instead is a global economy centrally planned by corporations larger than most states that march to the tune of financial speculators. It is yet another mark of capitalism's triumph over the market.

Figure 2.1 sketches what happens as capitalism consolidates its hold over a market economy, shifting power and the lines of accountability away from people to the impersonal and detached institutions of global finance. In a functioning market economy made up of small and medium scale locally owned enterprises, power is broadly distributed among local people who engage in reproducing the cultural values that shape their community, make purchasing decisions, set the rules of local commerce through their democratically elected governments, and participate directly in the ownership of local enterprises. It is a dynamic and interactive system in which people participate in many roles and bring their human sensibilities to bear on every aspect of economic life.

In contrast, what deregulation and economic globalization free is not the market, but rather the institutions of global capitalism. As the constraints of regulation and national borders are removed, financial markets become merged into a single electronic trading system, and global corporations consolidate and concentrate their power through mergers, acquisitions, and strategic alliances beyond the reach of any state. Savings are aggregated into professionally managed retirement, trust, and mutual funds with a fiduciary responsibility to maximize financial returns commensurate with risk.

The result is a capitalist economy in which the power to exercise ownership rights passes to the impersonal institutions of global finance. Money's power becomes delinked from human sensibility and people become captives of a system with no allegiance to their needs.

The financial institutions that act as owners are themselves blind to all but the financial consequences of their actions. Expecting those responsible for the corporations they own to take a similarly narrow view, they send a powerful message to corporate management. A solid profit is not enough. Annual profits must be constantly increased at a rate sufficient to produce the 20 to 40 percent annual increase in share price the markets have come to expect. The CEO who fails to produce such increases risks losing credibility with the financial community and may invite a takeover bid or risk ejection by large shareholders. How it is done isn't the market's concern. As they say at the Nike corporation, "Just do it." The global corporation responds by using its great power to reshape cultures, limit consumer choice, pass costs on to the public, and press governments to provide subsidies and rewrite the rules of commerce in their favor.

Perhaps the most ironic twist is that the economy internal to a corporation has far more in common with a centrally planned economy than with a self-organizing market economy. In the U.S. system of corporate and financial libertarianism, which is rapidly infecting Europe, Japan, and the rest of the world, no matter what authority a CEO may delegate, it may be withdrawn at any time. CEOs can virtually hire and fire any worker, open and close any plant, change transfer prices, create and drop product lines almost at will—with no meaningful recourse by the persons or communities affected. Such centralized power and control would surely have been the envy of any central planner in the Soviet Union.

The scale of central planning under capitalism is also impressive. For example, if we take the gross sales of a corporation to be roughly the equivalent of the GDP of a country, we find that of the world's one hundred largest economies, fifty-one are economies internal to corporations. In addition, the largest corporations are actively engaged in planning relations among themselves through industrial associations, strategic alliances, and cartels; influencing economic policies through aggressive lobbying; and reshaping the rules of the global economy through their participation with their governments in the negotiation of trade and investment agreements. Step-by-step, through institutions such as the World Trade Organization and the IMF, corporations have forged the instruments of a wholly undemocratic central economic planning process on a global scale.

In one critical respect, however, capitalism's central planners are quite unlike the Soviet planners, who at least in theory sought to plan for the interests of all their country's citizens. The corporate central planners are legally obligated to devote their attention solely to maximizing the returns to their shareholders. Of course, they may reassure themselves and the public that the market's invisible hand will translate this self-seeking into a public good, but unfortunately they are operating not in a market economy but rather in a capitalist economy whose hand is neither invisible nor benevolent.

Of course we are also reassured that so many people now hold shares in pension and mutual funds that virtually everyone benefits directly from the increase in shareholder value that is capitalism's proud accomplishment. Again myth triumphs over reality. Of all the world's countries, the United States probably has the broadest participation in stock ownership. Even so, 5 percent of U.S. households own 77 percent of U.S. shareholder wealth.[38] Seventy-one percent of households own less than $2,000 in stocks, including ownership through mutual funds and defined contribution retirement funds in which the employee benefits from stock appreciation.[39] Globally, the world's population that has a consequential participation in corporate ownership is most certainly far less than 1 percent.

This leads to a rather shocking conclusion. The triumph of global capitalism means that more than half of the world's one hundred largest economies are centrally planned for the primary benefit of the wealthiest 1 percent of the world's people! It is a triumph of privatized central planning over markets and democracy. Even more, it is the triumph of the extremely wealthy over the remainder of humanity.

Markets are a remarkable human institution for aggregating the choices of many individuals to achieve an efficient and equitable allocation of productive resources to meet human needs. Their function, however, depends on the presence of a number of critical conditions. Recognizing the power of the market ideal, capitalism cloaks itself in market rhetoric. It is intent only on its own growth, and so its institutions set about systematically to destroy the market's healthy function. They eliminate regulations that protect the human and environmental interest, remove economic borders to place themselves beyond the reach of the state, deny consumers access to essential information, seek to monopolize beneficial technologies, and use mergers, acquisitions, strategic alliances, and other anticompetitive practices to undermine the market's ability to self-organize.

Step-by-step, the institutional agents of the money world erode the conditions of healthy market function, using their control of the money-creation process to concentrate the powers of the ownership of productive assets in their own hands. They in turn use this power to reshape cultures, rewrite the rules of commerce, and limit consumer choice. The purposes and the lines of accountability of a healthy market economy are thus turned upside-down, leaving money as the master to demand that its own reproduction be the defining purpose of economic life. People, who created economic life and institutions to serve their needs, are reduced instead to serving the needs of capitalism and the institutions of money for cheap labor and compliant consumers.

We next turn to a discussion of perhaps the most chilling outcome of capitalism's triumph: the creation of a powerful and unfeeling global economic machine dedicated to the conversion of life into profit by depleting living capital.

Chapter 3

The Midas Curse

In the history of capitalism's long expansionary cycles, it is finance capital that usually rules in the final stage, displacing the inventors and industrialists who launched the era, eclipsing the power of governments to manage the course of economic events. . . . Since returns on capital are rising faster than the productive output that must pay them, the process imposes greater and greater burdens on commerce and societies.

—WILLIAM GREIDER[1]

We are seeing a worldwide pattern of decapitalization. Capital, whether it be natural capital in the form of resources, or human capital in the form of low-wage workers, or local capital in the form of functional and healthy local economies, is being extracted and converted to financial capital at an increasingly accelerated rate.

—PAUL HAWKEN[2]

IN GREEK MYTHOLOGY a king named Midas ruled over the people of Phrygia, an ancient nation in Asia Minor. In return for a favor, the god Dionysus offered to grant Midas a wish. Midas asked that all he touched might turn to gold. His wish was granted, but when his touch turned his food, drink, and even his beloved daughter to gold, he realized that his assumed blessing was in fact a curse. He now had gold without limit, but at the price of life—both his own and that of those he loved.

The story has a profound but still-neglected message. Trading life for money is a bad bargain because it is life, and life alone, that gives money its

65

value. Forgetful of life and obsessed with the pursuit of money, we have invited the Midas curse upon ourselves and our children for generations to come, establishing a human relationship to the planet that has reversed the creative and productive processes of billions of years of evolution.

Though the origins of economic exploitation predate capitalism and the invention of the corporation by several thousands of years, capitalism and its institutions have greatly accelerated the process in the last century. Indeed, designed to be blind to all but financial values and shareholder interests, capitalism's primary agent, the public, for-profit corporation, has proven to be ideally suited to amassing the financial, political, and technical resources that are now destroying evolution's product with great efficiency. This chapter describes and explains the workings of the Midas curse as it is played out in the modern context—illuminating the ways in which the institutions of capitalism are programmed both to deny and to deepen our environmental and social crises.

Evolution in Reverse

The problem is well captured in a simple story with a chilling message told by Karl-Henrik Robèrt, a Swedish cancer researcher and founder of The Natural Step, an organization concerned with identifying and addressing the root causes of the environmental crisis.

Billions of years ago our earth consisted of a toxic primeval atmosphere, toxic liquids, and a desolate and disordered surface. The transformation of this useless stew of disordered inorganic compounds into the wealth of mineral deposits, breathable air, drinkable water, soil, forests, fish, and animal life that provided the habitat from which the human species and its civilization emerged and flourished began with the green plant cell. These wondrous cells had the ability to capture surplus solar energy beyond their own growth and maintenance needs, an ability they used over a period of billions of years to create the many structured and concentrated compounds on which all human life and activity depends.

Because animals lack the capacity to directly capture and convert solar radiation to useful energy, all activities of animal species, including humans, have the consequence of dissipating the order created by green plant cells. This was not a consequential problem so long as these activities fell within the bounds of the ability of earth's green plant cells to convert animal wastes back into usable ordered matter. So long as the wastes of one species provide

nutrition for another, the creation of ever more complex and ordered structure through life's self-sustaining cycles can go on indefinitely.

Then about a hundred years ago humans began to make significant
use of concentrated energy sources—first coal, then petroleum, and eventually nuclear—to process natural resources in a linear direction. We were
soon turning ordered matter into visible as well as molecular garbage far
faster than the earth's remaining green cells could reprocess it. This allowed
us to expand our dominion over ecological space with such speed and force
that we literally began to reverse earth's evolutionary process. Indeed, a consequential portion of human waste now consists of toxic metals and stable
unnatural compounds that cannot be processed by green cells at all—an
enduring monument to our technical mastery and biological ignorance.[3]

According to Robèrt, what we have chosen to define as progress is
actually the reversal of four billion years of evolution. The money attractor and its growth imperative are calling us not forward to the future, but
rather backward toward a distant past before the earth became vibrant
with life.

The highly respected Worldwatch Institute notes in its *State of the
World 1998* report that the last half of this century has been in many ways
a remarkable success for humanity. Total global economic output
increased from $4.9 trillion in 1950 (1995 dollars) to more than $29 trillion in 1997—a sixfold increase. In the same period, worldwide, life
expectancy climbed from forty-seven years to sixty-four years and on
every continent literacy levels increased.

However, human demands on the environment increased apace.
"The use of lumber tripled, that of paper increased sixfold, the fish catch
increased nearly fivefold, grain consumption nearly tripled, fossil fuel
burning nearly quadrupled, and air and water pollutants multiplied several
fold." As a consequence of these growing demands on a finite ecosystem,
"Forests are shrinking, water tables are falling, soils are eroding, wetlands
are disappearing, fisheries are collapsing, rangelands are deteriorating,
rivers are running dry, temperatures are rising, coral reefs are dying, and
plant and animal species are disappearing."[4] Meanwhile, world population, already at nearly six billion persons, continues to grow at the rate of
eighty-eight million people a year, and global economic policies implicitly
assume that U.S. levels of consumption—and greater—are an achievable
and sustainable standard for the rest of the world to emulate.[5]

Waves of Extractive Development

What we are now experiencing is a culmination of wave after wave of extractive development that continues to reshape local economies the world over. Alan Durning, founder and head of Northwest Environment Watch, captures the process brilliantly in his historical account of resource extraction in the Pacific Northwest region of North America.[6] For me it is an especially poignant story, as this is the land of my birth and childhood to which I returned in early 1998.

Durning recounts that in the late 1700s and early 1800s the fur traders arrived. Sea otter and then beaver populations were wiped out, rearranging hydrology and nutrient recycling patterns with a resulting reduction in species diversity from headwaters to the ocean floor.

Then came mining, beginning in the mid-1800s and growing to a juggernaut until it too collapsed from exhaustion shortly before World War II. The region had not only been stripped of its extractable minerals but was left with a deadly legacy—holes in the ground from which river-killing acids continued to drain, mountains of toxic-laced tailings, and sulfur-deadened landscapes downwind from the once-active smelters. Even into the 1990s, the heavy metals continued to kill fish in the region's major rivers.

Next came fishing. Stories of the abundance of the Northwest salmon runs are legend. On sites where Native Americans once plucked salmon from the Columbia River with their bare hands, huge fish wheels erected by white settlers scooped as much as fifty thousand pounds of chinook from the river on a good day. By 1915 the catch in most of the Northwest's major fisheries had started its sharp decline. The current catch is a fraction of what Indian tribes once brought in each year.

Agriculture, the next wave of depletion, thrived on the extraordinarily fertile soils deposited in the region during the Ice Age by receding glaciers, in some places to a depth of as much as two hundred feet. The soil was so productive that an enterprising farmer could earn the price of his land from a single crop, but the intensive cultivation methods used lost six pounds of soil for every pound of wheat grown. As soils were depleted, productivity was maintained by increasing the use of chemicals, which now contaminate groundwater supplies. The livestock industry also thrived, until overgrazing reduced rich grasslands to impoverished scrub. These practices turned agriculture into an extractive industry.

The abundant and wild rivers were dammed for irrigation and cheap power. Irrigation opened more land to extractive agriculture, and cheap power attracted smelters that turned imported bauxite into aluminum. The combination of abundant water and cheap power attracted the Hanford, Washington, reactors that produced the plutonium for America's nuclear arsenal. Wastewater used for cooling the reactors was dumped into the Columbia River, raising levels of radioactivity to three times that allowed for drinking water. The low cost of electricity encouraged its extravagant use and discouraged conservation measures such as insulating homes. The dams and related pollution have devastated much of the region's flora and fauna.

Logging crested in 1988 and has declined ever since. Some believe the forests that stretch from southeast Alaska to northwest California were once the heaviest accumulation of living matter in the history of our planet. Supported by government subsidies, the stripping of trees from the land progressed almost as though the removal advanced some holy cause. By the 1990s most of the accessible old-growth forests were gone, replaced by a spotty patchwork of timber industry plantations based on fast-growing species that produce a fraction of the output and jobs of the old-growth cuts.

Running Backwards

Economists assure us that such unpleasant realities represent only temporary sacrifices on the road to universal prosperity. Through economic growth we will expand the economic pie to create more for everyone. Plausible as it sounds, the argument is based on two false premises: first, that making money is the same as creating wealth, and second, that an increase in the gross domestic product (GDP) represents an increase in the wealth and well-being of society.

We demonstrated the fallacy of the first premise in the previous chapter. The premise that GDP is a valid measure of the wealth and well-being of society is equally false. Indeed, the substantial distortions embodied in our measures of GDP are an important reason for our failure to see more clearly the real costs of economic growth.

GDP is a measure of gross domestic product, meaning it is an index of the gross market value of a nation's monetized transaction for goods and services. Productive work done for self or love is not counted, no matter how beneficial to well-being. But even the most grossly harmful trans-actions *are* included so long as they are monetized.[7]

A mother who bears and rears her own children as a labor of love counts for nothing. But if a single woman contracts to bear another's child for a fee as a surrogate mother, the fee counts as an economic contribu-tion—as do the commissions and fees charged by lawyers, doctors, semen donors, and other intermediaries. An increase in divorce rates increases GDP by generating lawyers' fees and requiring one party to establish a new home. An increase in crime stimulates demand for alarm systems and security guards. The costs of producing and using weapons of war all count as positive contributions, as do the costs of rebuilding after the mayhem.

Ironically, many of the expenditures that contribute to economic growth, such as sales of bottled water, are compensating responses to the social and environmental decline that economic growth has created. In this respect economic growth is a lot like heroin. In the beginning a little produces an exhilarating rush, but soon more and more is needed to avoid the terrible pain that results from its gradual destruction of the user's physical and psychological health.

Economists rationalize this anomaly by explaining that to adjust GDP figures by subtracting harmful production would require making value judgments about which products are harmful. To maintain their value-free objectivity as scientists, they rely on market prices and transac-tions as objective measures of value, neglecting the fact that this is itself a significant value judgment. The idea of a value-free economics is a con-tradiction in terms. Values—whether ethical or unethical, spiritual or materialistic—are central to every aspect of economic life.

For most people it is obvious that any meaningful index of wealth creation needs to take account of the amount and condition of a nation's real productive capital, making appropriate deductions for depreciation and depletion. The economists who calculate the GDP, however, work by a different logic. First, they completely ignore all forms of productive cap-ital except human-made physical capital, such as buildings and equip-ment. Then, instead of deducting its depreciation, they add it in as a pro-duction cost, thus counting it as a positive contribution to gross productive output. As a consequence, the faster physical human-made capital depreciates, the faster GDP grows.[8] It's the same for consumer durables. The faster we junk and replace our cars, computers, TVs, and appliances, the faster GDP grows.

With similar illogic, the economists who calculate GDP take no note whatever of the depletion of living capital, the sum total of the self-renewing human, social, institutional, and natural capital that serve as the foundations of life and civilization. When we lay waste to a forest or a fishery, we count the sale of the timber and the fish as an addition to wealth but make no adjustment for the productive potentials and ecosystem services lost. It is the same when we take nonrenewable petroleum and mineral resources from the ground. The cost of extraction counts as a contribution to GDP, but nothing is subtracted for the depletion of our available natural physical capital.

It is thus quite possible by an economist's measure for a country's economy to be growing briskly even as it is suffering rapid erosion of its future productive potential and the well-being of its citizens. And in many countries that is exactly what is happening.

Fortunately, a few economists have the courage to make the value judgments that more orthodox economists are wont to avoid. These pioneers have reconstructed the GDP indices for the United States, Germany, the United Kingdom, the Netherlands, and Australia. Adding beneficial but uncompensated work, and deducting items that represent a net loss of well-being, they arrived at a per capita Index of Sustainable Economic Welfare for each.[9]

Their conclusions confirm what a number of people have come to suspect. While all five have enjoyed robust economic growth over the past fifty years, trends in sustainable per-capita economic well-being are in each instance on a downward slope or have been stagnant. In the United States the reversal from improving to declining came in 1968 and the level has subsequently fallen by more than 40 percent to a point below what it was in 1950. In the United Kingdom the peak came in 1974. By 1990 sustainable economic well-being was only 3 percent higher than it had been in 1950 and was still falling. The Netherlands peaked in 1980. In Germany, where there were rapid positive gains in economic well-being following World War II, the peak came in 1981 and fell by 40 percent in just seven years. Australia peaked in the same year.[10]

There is substantial evidence that a decline in economic well-being is not confined to the high-income countries of the North. Consider the miracle economies of the Third World that have supposedly been lifting themselves out of poverty with growth rates of 7 to 9 percent. As noted in the previous chapter, one by one—first Mexico and then Thailand, Malaysia, Indonesia, and the Philippines, followed by Hong Kong, South Korea, and Brazil—they have experienced financial meltdown that exposes the shaky foundations of their seeming success. But the bursting of financial bubbles is only the more internationally visible symptom of their pain. The disruption of the cultural and social fabric, significant increases in inequality, disruption of agricultural sectors, and devastating environmental damage all remain as legacies of their fleeting moments of economic glory.

One of the more dramatic manifestations of Southeast Asia's environmental crisis was the dense plume of smoke larger than the continental United States that blanketed the region in 1997. The primary culprits were large corporations engaged in clearing natural forests to establish pulp, palm oil, and rubber plantations. The fires spread to at least two million hectares of forest and peat lands in Malaysia and Indonesia. Tens of millions of people, some as much as a thousand kilometers away, were sickened and hundreds died. Others died from car and plane crashes caused by the loss of visibility and from health complications.[11]

Brazil also suffered record forest fires during 1997 and 1998, by some accounts even larger than those in Indonesia but less publicized because they were in more remote areas. The main perpetrators were the same as in Indonesia, large commercial interests clearing land for plantations.

China, with a fifth of the world's population, is yet another example of the Midas curse. Independent estimates credit it with an average annual economic growth rate of 6.8 percent from 1978 to 1995. In 1996 its growth rate of 9.7 percent was the highest in the world. During his 1998 visit, President Clinton touted it as a major economic success story. Here again, the distortions in growth measures mask the underlying reality. In a 1997 *Nation* article, China expert Carl Riskin warned that widespread bankruptcies, deepening inequality, and soaring unemployment threatened China's social stability. He further noted that China, which generates some 18 percent of the world's ozone-depleting substances and is the largest producer of greenhouse gases after the United States, is one of the most polluted countries in the world.[12] A World Bank study estimates that 2.03 million people die annually in China from the effects of air and water pollution.[13] The acid rain produced by sulfur emissions from burning Chinese coal causes an estimated $5 billion in forest and crop damage each year.[14] Overall, about 8 percent of China's GDP is lost each year in damage to life, health, and property from air and water pollution. As Riskin notes, "Subtract that from the real economic growth rate and virtually none of it is left."[15] If adjustments had been made for resource depletion and the enormous costs of rampant crime and corruption brought on by China's transition to capitalism, the net growth would surely be negative.[16]

Looking beyond the illusions of the so-called miracle economies, even an appearance of success is hard to find. Since 1980 some one hundred Third World and Eastern European countries have suffered absolute economic decline or stagnation even by conventional GDP criteria. At an individual level it is estimated that 1.6 billion people, a quarter of the world's population, have been suffering long-term reductions in income.[17] In many instances the disastrous social and environmental consequences of earlier periods of growth deepen the human pain from the fall in monetary incomes.

Making Money, Growing Poorer

The Midas curse of capitalism is presently playing itself out on a global scale, enriching the money world by impoverishing the living world. The growing gap between prosperity of the one and the decline of the other is illustrated by the simple graph in Figure 3.1.

The top upward sloping line represents a rapid growth in financial assets and the second line a slower growth in GDP. In Chapter 2 we looked at how finance capitalism creates money out of nothing by creating financial bubbles that inflate the value of financial assets. Recall the excerpt from a *Foreign Policy* article calling on governments to focus their energies not on production but on enlarging the pool of inflated financial assets. In the logic of finance capitalism, money is wealth and the goal of economic activity is to make as much of it as possible.

The extent to which finance capitalism has already shifted the emphasis from the production of real goods and services to the inflation of financial assets is revealed in a study by McKinsey and Company. The study reports that from 1980 to 1992, financial assets in the Organization for Economic Cooperation and Development (OECD) countries—

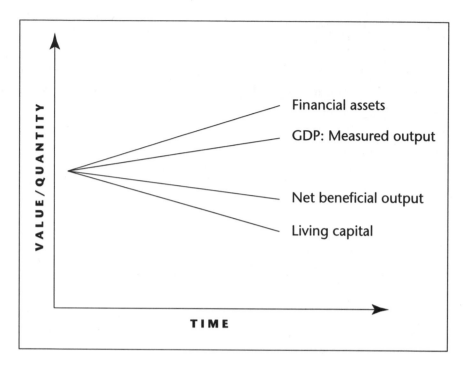

Figure 3.1. Making Money and Growing Poor

twenty-nine major industrial countries—grew twice as fast as growth in their GDP. This means potential claims on economic output grew at twice the rate of the output itself. Such an inflation of financial assets, like the financial bubbles that led to Asia's financial collapse, represents a major economic distortion, a shift in economic power to those who make money from those who create real wealth. Apparently steeped in the logic of finance capitalism, the McKinsey researchers took this asset inflation to be a sign of success, as they bullishly predicted that the total value of financial assets would be three times the value of GDP by the end of the millennium.[18]

The distortions go far deeper, however, because as we noted earlier an important portion of the output that GDP currently measures represents a decrease, rather than an increase, in well-being. When GDP is adjusted to remove such distortions, we find a progressive decline in the resulting index of sustainable economic welfare, shown in Figure 3.1 as a downward sloping line.

Even the index of sustainable economic welfare, however, is incomplete because it does not fully reveal the rate at which we are depleting the underlying base of living capital on which our future well-being depends. There is substantial anecdotal and statistical evidence that we are depleting our forests, soils, fresh water, and fisheries; disrupting our climatic systems; unraveling our social fabric; experiencing the breakdown of family structures; allowing educational standards to decay; and losing faith in the legitimacy of our major institutions, but there are no systematic efforts to create a unified index giving us an overall measure of the state of our living capital. Obviously, this would involve significant technical difficulties. However, the accumulated evidence points to a sharp and likely accelerating decline, represented in Figure 3.1 by the sharply downward sloping line.

It is striking that the two primary indicators our leaders rely on to assess their economic policies—stock market performance and the GDP—are both money-world indicators that tell us a good deal more about how fast the rich are getting richer than about the real quality of our living. The two important prospective indices not monitored by policy makers—the index of sustainable economic welfare and the status of the planetary stock of living capital—are both indicators of how things are going in the living world. So when the money-world indicators are rising, we are told we are doing well when in fact we are growing poorer. Indeed, it is probable that the faster stock prices and the GDP rise, the faster the things we should really care about are deteriorating.

The Corporation as Agent

As we look for the driving forces behind the destruction of life for money to enrich the few, our attention is inexorably drawn to the institution of the corporation. As the systems of finance have globalized and institutionalized, the corporation's ties of accountability to people and the interests of the living world have steadily weakened. Because the corporation is populated by the people who work in its employ, there is a tendency to think of the institution almost as a living person—an illusion cultivated by corporate public relations and given legal standing by court rulings. Yet the corporation is not a person and it does not live. It is a lifeless bundle of legally protected financial rights and relationships brilliantly designed to serve money and its imperatives. It is money that flows in its veins, not blood. The corporation has neither soul nor conscience.

We who serve in the corporation's employ, even the powerful and well-paid CEOs and money managers, are hirelings paid to embrace the corporation's values and do its bidding. In preparation for our corporate roles we are trained in the language of finance and the methods by which a price can be assigned to everything and every choice can be evaluated in financial terms. Eventually we come to accept it as right and natural that we ourselves be evaluated on financial performance and motivated by financial incentives.

It is instructive to recall that the modern corporation is a descendant of the chartered corporations, such as the British East India Company and the Hudson's Bay Company, that were formed by the British crown as monopolies to exploit colonial territories by extracting their labor and resources and monopolizing their markets. Some claim the American Revolution was as much a revolution against the crown corporations as against the crown itself. As a consequence, corporations were treated with great caution by both citizens and politicians in the early days of the new American republic. The few corporate charters issued were generally for a limited duration to serve a carefully delineated public purpose, such as constructing a canal system. The crown has since been replaced by the modern shareholder and access to corporate charters has been democratized, but our current experience with the global megacorporation suggests its role has not changed.

As we noted in Chapter 2, the only way most corporations can produce the profits the financial system currently demands is by passing off ever greater costs to the society. This includes expropriating and selling off the living capital of human societies and the planet at such a rate that, in the words of ecological economist Herman Daly, "It looks as though we are holding a going-out-of-business sale." We need scarcely look beyond the daily reports of *The Wall Street Journal* to find examples of the world's largest corporations profiting from the

- Depletion of *natural capital* by strip-mining forests, fisheries, and mineral deposits, aggressively marketing toxic chemicals, and dumping hazardous wastes that turn once-productive lands and waters into zones of death;

- Depletion of *human capital* by maintaining substandard working conditions in places like the Mexican *maquiladoras,* where they employ once-vital and productive young women for three to four years until failed eyesight, allergies, kidney problems, and repetitive stress injuries leave them permanently handicapped;

- Depletion of *social capital* by breaking up unions, bidding down wages, treating workers as expendable commodities, and uprooting key plants on which community economies are dependent to move them to lower-cost locations—leaving it to society to absorb the family and community breakdown and violence that are inevitable consequences of the resulting stress; and

- Depletion of *institutional capital* by undermining the necessary function and credibility of governments and democratic governance as they pay out millions in campaign contributions to win public subsidies, bailouts, and tax exemptions and fight to weaken environmental, health, and labor standards essential to the long-term health of society.

Take the case of the Benguet Mining Company in the Philippines, documented by Robin Broad and John Cavanagh in their book *Plundering Paradise.*[19] In the quest for gold, Benguet Mining cuts deep gashes into the mountains, strips away trees and topsoil, and dumps enormous piles of rock into local rivers. With their soils and water sources depleted, the indigenous Igorot people who live in the area have difficulty growing their rice and bananas and have to go to the other side of the mountain for drinking water and to bathe. The cyanide used by the Benguet corporation to separate the gold from the rock ends up in streams that carry it into the lowlands, where it kills cattle and reduces rice yields, and into the ocean, where it kills the coastal fish and coral reefs, destroying the livelihoods of thousands of people along the way.

Tragically there is nothing at all special about the Benguet case. It is much the same with Shell Oil in Nigeria, Texaco in Ecuador, Freeport-McMoRan in Indonesia, and countless other less publicized cases of corporations that profit from the destruction of natural capital while devastating the lives and habitats of people.

Consider the report cited by Bob Herbert in *The New York Times*[20] on conditions endured by young women ages fifteen to twenty-eight working at factories that make Nike shoes in Vietnam, where three meals of rice, a bit of vegetable, and perhaps some tofu (bean curd) costs the equivalent of $2.10. Renting a room costs at least $6.00 a month. Yet the workers making Nike shoes that may sell for more than $100.00 a pair must cover these and all other expenses out of a paycheck of $1.60 a day.

Those interviewed complained that since starting work at the factory they have suffered frequent headaches, general fatigue, and weight loss. Workers are allowed one bathroom break and two drinks of water per eight-hour shift. Again, Nike is unfortunately not all that special. It just happens to have become a symbol for the many corporations that profit from the exploitation of Third World workers. It has also made Nike founder and CEO Philip Knight—my former business school classmate—the seventeenth wealthiest person in America with $5.4 billion in assets.[21]

Meanwhile, corporations pay legions of lawyers, trade associations, and public relations firms to change the laws to allow the conversion of living capital to money at an even faster pace. They have pushed rulings through the European Commission making it legal to dispose of radioactive and other toxic wastes by diluting them for recycling into consumer products, use as "fertilizers," or disposal by normal landfill or incineration.[22] They place toxic incinerators next to poor communities and fight efforts to set and enforce emissions standards that would limit the release of deadly substances.[23] They spend millions on TV and print advertising to undermine public support for essential action on global warming.

The reality of corporations as agents of the modern Midas curse has been slow to register in the public mind, perhaps because the same corporations spend millions of dollars on public relations campaigns presenting themselves as leaders in environmental protection.

> A corporate leader in ozone destruction takes credit for being a leader in ozone protection. A giant oil transnational embraces the "precautionary approach" to global warming. A major agrochemical manufacturer sells a pesticide so hazardous it has been banned in many countries while implying that it is helping to feed the hungry. A petrochemical firm uses the waste from one polluting process as a raw material for another, and boasts this is an important recycling initiative. A logging company cuts timber from a natural rain forest, replaces it with plantations of a single exotic species, and calls the project "sustainable forest development."[24]

General Motors, Monsanto, Mobil, Royal Dutch/Shell, Dow Chemical, Westinghouse Electric, and the Mitsubishi Group are among the better known of the global corporations engaged in such duplicity, as documented by Jed Greer and Kenny Bruno in their book *Greenwash: The*

Reality Behind Corporate Environmentalism.[25] A whole industry of public relations firms, like Burson-Marsteller, specialize in cleaning up these firms' public images through skillful use of the media to create what journalist and media analyst Murray Dobbin calls "the myth of the good corporate citizen."[26]

The reality behind the public relations images is that of the corporation as an institution of extraordinary power and little accountability driven by the very nature of its structure and ownership to expropriate and sell off the world's living capital for quick profit, concentrate wealth in the hands of the very rich, control public communications to limit public awareness of the consequences of capitalist rule, and undermine reform initiatives. It is the engine of our undoing.

Paid to Be Blind

The truth our leaders find it so difficult to see is painfully evident to the billions of people who exist at or beyond the margins of the capitalist system. I regularly observed the fate of the excluded during the fifteen years I lived in Asia, where each year several million people are displaced from their homes and means of livelihood by development projects that expropriate their lands, waters, and fisheries for uses such as dams, plantations, industrial estates, prawn farms, highways, golf courses, tourist resorts, and military installations. Many such projects are financed at least in part with foreign aid money and World Bank loans. In most cases those displaced are pushed from simple poverty into desperate deprivation. Those who reap the benefits are invariably already better off than those displaced. In most instances the expropriated resources are converted from sustainable to unsustainable uses.

This is a part of the larger pattern in which the great majority of the benefits of global economic growth have gone not to the poor but to those who already have more than they need—often far more. According to the 1997 *UNDP Human Development Report,* in 1960 the share of global income enjoyed by the wealthiest 20 percent of the world's people was thirty times the amount shared by the poorest 20 percent. The ratio more than doubled during thirty years of official development efforts. It reached sixty-one to one in 1991 and rose to seventy-eight to one in 1994.[27] The more successful capitalism becomes in the consolidation of its triumph over democracy and the market economy, the faster the gap grows.

The most telling picture of all is found in the pages of *Forbes* magazine, the self-proclaimed "capitalist tool." Each year *Forbes* publishes an annual inventory of the world's billionaires, heralding the growth in their numbers as the ultimate index of capitalism's success. In 1996 the magazine identified 447 billionaires whose fortunes it attributed to capitalist enterprise, up from only 274 in 1991. Their total assets were roughly equal to the total combined annual income of the poorest half of humanity. By 1997 the number of billionaires was growing so fast that *Forbes* could no longer afford to keep track of them all.

The Philippines: Making Way for Progress

Poverty in Manila's inner city seems more extreme because—unlike the shanty towns on the "septic fringe" of many mushrooming cities—here the poorest families live wedged into the faults and crevices of conspicuous wealth, much of it controlled by foreign corporations. One of our first field visits in Manila was to a central-city area with many high-rise hotels and industrial buildings. Neon signs and sumptuous window displays deck the storefronts. But the alleys between the buildings look like human beehives, or termite colonies, with thousands of tiny cellular dwellings plastered precariously against the high brick walls. In each alleyway, a narrow central path, about two feet wide, separates the shacks on either side. Made of bamboo slats and cardboard, most of the shacks consist of a single room, about six by eight feet square. Each shack lodges a whole family. On top of the first layer of shacks balances another layer of similar shacks, then another and another. In some alleys the shacks are stacked precariously five or six stories high.

"Don't these crowded settlements ever catch fire?" I asked. "Oh yes! Sometimes the managers of the industrial buildings and hotels on either side of the shacks start a fire to clear out the alleys. They see the squatters only as a nuisance. You can't imagine the human disaster caused by such fires—the deaths, severe burns, new disabilities, homelessness for hundreds!"

The Dole Fruit Company of U.S.A. now owns the majority of high-quality land in the southern islands of the Philippines. And as its land holdings keep expanding, the poor are crowded into the remaining, poorer-quality land. The best fruit is exported. The lucrative profits, taxed at absurdly low rates, leave the country to fill coffers in the United States. As multinational agribusiness increases its profits by replacing farm workers with fossil fuel-guzzling machines, more and more people become jobless. As competition for jobs rises, wages fall. Destitute peasants migrate to the slums and crowded alleys of the cities where, in turn, job competition drives wages down and rent up.

Quoted from a field report by David Werner in Newsletter from the Sierra Madre *#37, May 1998.*

We can, however, continue to track capitalism's success by the financial gains of the richest among us. For example, from 1996 to 1997, the world's richest person, Bill Gates, CEO of Microsoft, increased his net worth by $17.9 billion, roughly equal to the total annual economic output shared by the eleven million people of Zimbabwe in southern Africa. By 1998, Gates was up to a total of $51 billion in assets as he moved to increase his control over Internet access and more broadly into telecommunications in general, giving new meaning to the question, "How much is enough?"[28]

Although other corporate CEOs are not doing as well as Bill Gates, they are doing a great deal better than those who work for them. According to *Business Week's* annual survey of CEO compensation, CEOs of the largest U.S. corporations enjoyed an increase in total compensation of 35 percent in 1997 over 1996, bringing them to an average annual compensation, including stock options, of $7.8 million—326 times the earnings of an average factory worker. Sanford Weill, CEO of Traveler's Group, won the sweepstakes for the year with $223.3. million.[29] An analysis by the two organizations United for a Fair Economy and the Institute for Policy Studies found that many of the highest-paid executives were the ones who had eliminated the most jobs.[30] U.S.-style CEO pay packages are now moving into Europe, pressing European CEOs to focus on shareholder return to the neglect of other goals in the same manner as their American counterparts.[31]

It doesn't take special genius to see a direct relationship between the shift in policy focus from creating real wealth to encouraging the inflation of financial assets, the unconscionable and growing gap between rich and poor, the accelerating depletion of real wealth, and the blindness of those who hold the levers of power in money-world institutions. The one-tenth of 1 percent or less of the world population that constitutes the super rich can afford to make generous political contributions to reward politicians for advancing policies favorable to finance capitalism, such as capital gains tax cuts that shift the tax burden from financial speculators to working people. The greater the gains from speculating on financial bubbles, the greater the resources the speculators command to reward friendly politicians and the more willing they are to offer corporate CEOs a substantial share in the gains as an incentive to do whatever is required to keep their stock price rising.

By the rules of global capitalism, real wealth rightfully goes to whomever is able to bid the most money. Since the speculators, politicians, and corporate top managers to whom the levers of power are entrusted are doing exceedingly well in financial terms, they find that their claims to the real wealth of society are expanding at a most satisfactory rate—creating for them an illusion that the world's real wealth is expanding in proportion to their financial wealth.

The wealthy can afford to fly over the congestion and pollution in their private jets and helicopters, live in the most luxurious and secure communities, work in penthouse suites in grand office towers, enjoy the finest designer clothing and gourmet foods, and vacation in the most pristine of the world's remaining wilderness areas. In their eyes, life for the human species surely has never been so good. They are well paid to be blind to the real consequence of their money-world service and suffer no consequences of the depletion of real wealth. The more global the economy, the easier is their access to whatever of the world's wealth remains.

A two-page culinary article in *The New York Times* titled, "Despite the Bad News, the Fishing Is Good," exemplifies the mindset. It began by noting the bad news that in the northeastern part of the United States the once-abundant Atlantic coastal fisheries have been fished to exhaustion. The article hastened to assure readers, however, that abundant supplies of the world's most delicious fish are being flown in each day from as far away as Chile and Thailand by overnight air express—$6.7 billion worth in 1996. And, the article crowed enthusiastically, because the labor is cheap, the price of these delicacies is even lower than local varieties.[32]

So worry not about the loss of a local fishery and the fishermen left with no work. Never mind the ballooning U.S. trade deficit, the contribution to global warming of air freighting fish, or the poor of Chile and Thailand who no longer have fish on their own tables. Let the good times roll as the tables of the rich overflow with the world's bounty.

The detachment from reality is much the same among the elites of the Third World. A few years ago while visiting Malaysia I had a brief encounter with the minister responsible for Malaysia's forests. Seeing that I was Western and assuming I was probably an environmentalist, he wasted no time in explaining to me that Malaysia would be better off once its forests are cleared away and the money from the sale stashed in banks to earn interest. The financial returns would be greater. The image flashed into my mind of a barren and lifeless Malaysian landscape populated only by branches of international banks, with their computers faithfully and endlessly compounding the interest on the profits from Malaysia's timber sales. It is a metaphor that sums up all too well the future we are creating.

Such is the insanity that drives the capitalist pathology. King Midas traded life for real gold and was quick to recognize the folly of his greed. We of the capitalist era are slower to grasp the folly of ours. In heeding the siren song of capitalism it is as if we made a collective decision to treat life as an unwanted infestation it is our mission to banish from the planet. We have embraced money as our reality, our source of meaning, the object of our veneration. Born into the culture of the great forgetting, we remember only dimly the primordial truth that we exist and prosper only as one with life.

A useful servant but evil master, money gains our loyalty by promising what only life can deliver. Life is the source of all that nurtures our bodies and our souls. It is to her inspiring and epic story that we now turn as she calls us to awaken from our forgetting, hear her song, rejoice in the wonder of her journey, and respect her wisdom.

Part II

Life's Story

Chapter 4

The Incredible Journey

Pure chance, absolutely free but blind, is at the very root of the stupendous edifice of evolution. This central concept of modern biology is no longer one among other conceivable hypotheses. It is the sole conceivable hypothesis.

—JACQUES MONOD[1]

The evidence for the goal-directedness or purposefulness of life processes at every level of organization within the hierarchy of the ecosphere is so great that its denial to normal people seems quite inconceivable.

—EDWARD GOLDSMITH[2]

HOW DID IT HAPPEN that a planet barren of life became a living jewel in the vastness of space? A product of chance or of purposeful striving? Dumb luck or a deep intelligence? These two widely differing interpretations of life's story suggest sharply contrasting approaches to our future. Do we trust our future to a role of the dice by global currency speculators and get on with pursuing the sources of our distraction? Or do we take responsibility for attuning ourselves to a deeper purpose and set a conscious course toward our future so informed?

Science has in general come to the study of life with a lens honed by the study of a universe presumed to resemble a vast clockwork. It has thus sought to explain life in terms of chemical reactions and mechanistic processes that exclude spirit and meaning. There is, however, another interpretation of life's story, gleaned from the same scientific data, that leads to a very different view of life's possibilities—and of our own destiny. The following is an abbreviated version of this story as it is being told by such thoughtful and inspired raconteurs as theologian Thomas Berry and scientists Lynn Margulis, Dorion Sagan, Elisabet Sahtouris, and Brian Swimme. Listen closely, as a fateful choice hangs in the balance.[3]

In the Beginning

Most of what modern science claims to know of the story of creation begins fifteen billion years ago when a great flash of energy—simply named the Big Bang—brings into existence the vastness of space and all it contains. To give a meaningful time perspective to the ensuing drama, I've compressed the period from then to now to the scale of a twenty-four-hour clock. Mark the flash as midnight and start the clock. When we again reach midnight, it will be the year 2000 A.D.

For several billion years, scattering particles carrying the energy of billions of future suns form themselves into atoms. The atoms swirl in great clouds that eventually form into galaxies, which coalesce into stars that grow and die and are reborn again elsewhere as new stars, star systems, and planets. Through the interplay of the nuclear and gravitational forces, ever more complex elements and molecular compounds are continuously being created as by-products of these cataclysmic events.

Some ten and a half billion years after the great flash, our own sun comes into being. We are already more than sixteen hours into our twenty-four-hour day. Morning has passed, and it is 4:48 P.M. in the afternoon. Night is fast approaching.

As our sun establishes itself, the gases spinning off its surface coalesce to form a system of planets. Among them is the planet Earth, a gaseous body of violent turbulence. Over a period of fifty million years Earth's gases gradually cool to form a solid surface. For a time Earth remains as barren as our moon is today, until the heat from the pressures of its own mass and the energy of its highly radioactive contents forces out the gases and water vapors that form into oceans and create a predominantly carbon dioxide atmosphere—much like the atmospheres of present-day Mars and Venus. It is now 4:53 P.M.

These processes leave Earth with two essential conditions for the emergence of life: the right temperature and large bodies of water. Earth's active processes also release a vast supply of salts as rocks are worn down.

Meanwhile, large, complex sugar and acid molecules are being created by the violent lightning storms that cover the planet. Together the rock salts and complex molecules serve as the basic building blocks from which the lightning storms ultimately bring to life the first living cells—roughly seven hundred million years after Earth's formation. They are simple single-celled bacteria with no cell nucleus, too small to be seen with the naked eye. Scientists call them *monera*. It is now 5:46 P.M. The stage is set for a new phase in the planet's physical transformation.

The Age of Invention

The next 2.9 billion years of our story, from 5:46 P.M. to 10:24 P.M., belong exclusively to single-celled organisms. Thanks in substantial measure to the work of biologist Lynn Margulis, who collaborated with James Lovelock on the Gaia thesis, which describes the earth itself as a self-organizing, living organism,[4] we are learning of the incredible ingenuity and accomplishments of these seemingly simple life forms during one of the most fascinating periods in the planet's history.

As with all living things, single-celled bacteria live in dynamic relationship to their environment, absorbing materials and energy and excreting waste products—ultimately reshaping their environment as the environment reshapes them. And herein lies their fascinating tale.

The earliest forms of self-organizing organisms obtain their energy directly by absorbing hydrogen sulfide molecules. Soon thereafter, they learn the art of fermentation to break down sugars and other organic compounds to release energy for their own use. Let's call these early bacteria *fermenters*. They also learn to store the freed energy as adenosine triphosphate (ATP) molecules. To this day, every living thing on the earth depends on the production and storage of ATP for its energy, using the same technologies these bacteria developed.

The bacteria cells, which most commonly reproduce by duplicating their DNA and then splitting themselves down the middle or budding to the side, turn out to be highly inventive creatures. Some learn to reproduce by producing tiny spores with tough shells surrounding a copy of their DNA and a bit of protein. These are then released to float with the winds or tides in an inert state until they come into contact with more plentiful food supplies. Some of these eventually float onto land, where they begin the process of breaking down rocks into soil.

The planet's first chemists, the bacteria learn to build new kinds of proteins, including new enzymes, and to invent new molecules. They also learn to divide into distinct strains with different lifestyles in order to exploit new ecological niches, including new niches of their own creation. Some of the new strains specialize in living off the acid and alcohol wastes of other strains. Some learn to use and fix nitrogen from the air. Still others learn to propel themselves through the water by inventing the equivalent of an electric motor drive, complete with rings, tiny bearings, and rotors.

Early on they discover how to share new learning with one another by touching and temporarily dissolving the adjoining portion of their cell walls so that bits of DNA can be exchanged. As Margulis and Sagan express it, these "bacteria trade genes more frantically than a pit full of commodity traders on the floor of the Chicago Mercantile Exchange,"[5] but in a far more cooperative spirit of sharing newly gained advantages. In the aggregate these cooperative exchanges mean that each new bit of learning gradually becomes available to every bacterium on the planet. Credit for the creation of life's first global communications system thus goes to the bacteria.

There comes a time, however, when the success of the fermenters becomes their undoing. Their population expands to the point that their consumption exceeds the rate at which the earth's processes are creating new supplies of freely available food molecules. In their drive to replicate themselves, the fermenters have created the first global-scale population crisis. They respond with yet another round of innovation based on the capabilities now in place.

The breakthrough discovery is *photosynthesis*. A new strain of bacteria, call them photosynthesizers, emerges with the ability to capture the energy of sunlight and use it to split molecules of carbon dioxide and water to form oxygen and the sugars from which DNA, ATP, and cell structures are formed. This represents a major step for life—from the mining of a limited energy supply that takes eons to renew to relying on an abundant and continuously renewing energy source, the precursor to green plant life and life's sustainable presence on the planet. It happened about 3.5 billion years ago. It's 6:24 P.M.

Because the atmosphere is bathed in sunlight and filled with carbon dioxide, the photosynthesizers living in shallow waters now have seemingly limitless possibilities for expansion. Indeed, they turn out to be

Earth's most successful creatures for some two billion years, multiplying wherever there is water and mud—and making ever more oxygen. Unfortunately, their success is not without consequence. The world's first pollution crisis is in the making.

The chemical processes of photosynthesis release into the atmosphere large quantities of free nitrogen and oxygen as waste products. Indeed, over time the photosynthesizers convert an almost oxygen-free atmosphere into an atmosphere comprising 21 percent oxygen. In so doing they accomplish what is known in science fiction as *terra-forming* the planet—they create and maintain an atmosphere suited to the needs of larger, multicelled animal life.[6] At the time, however, it did not seem such a positive development.

Oxygen is a highly volatile gas and its production in large quantities makes the planet's atmosphere unstable, almost combustible. Furthermore, when oxygen comes in contact with the giant food molecules favored by the fermenters, it changes the molecules' chemistry and renders them useless as food. Oxygen is directly toxic to both the fermenters and the photosynthesizers that come in contact with it too, as it breaks down the fragile outer wall essential to the coherence of the cell's life processes, leaving the components of the cell to expire in dispersing droplets. The emergence of an oxygen-rich atmosphere thus results in a massive dieback—a new life-threatening crisis that in turn spurs a new round of innovation.[7]

Some fermenters survive by remaining underwater or buried in mud deposits to avoid contact with the air. Some photosynthesizers begin developing enzymes that protect them from the oxygen they produce. They also find ways to protect themselves from the sun's ultraviolet rays by making protective screens or joining together in dense colonies in which those on top burn to death, leaving their bodies to shield the rest.

The most significant response, however, comes from those photosynthesizers that turn the crisis into opportunity by inventing the process of respiration—call them *breathers*, the forerunners of animal life. By learning to use oxygen to break up food molecules to free energy and matter for their own use, they gain access to ten times the energy available to previous cell forms. In the words of Brian Swimme and Thomas Berry, "That which had been killing life now enabled life to burst with energy."[8] The simple single-cell organisms now have three ways to fuel themselves—

fermentation, photosynthesis, and respiration. It has been nine hundred million years since the first fermenters came to life. It is now 7:12 P.M.

Sahtouris describes this as a period in which the physical matter of the living earth was virtually re-created.

> The raw materials of Earth's interior spew or well up as new rock to be transformed into living matter, while old living matter, dead and compressed back into rock, sinks back into the soft mantle at the edges of tectonic plates. . . . Virtually all of the atmosphere and all of the rocks [on and near Earth's surface] have been through at least one phase in which they were living matter. The same is true of the soil and the seas. It is easier to distinguish between life and death than between the domains of life and nonlife we have assigned to biologists and geologists. In fact, virtually every geological part or feature of Earth we can find is a product of our planet's life activity.[9]

Life Gets Complicated

Long before the emergence of multicelled life, another food shortage drives hungry breathers to begin invading the fermenters to dine on their molecules—eating them alive from within. The invaders, however, encounter the problem of all parasites: they become dependent on the hosts they are killing and in the end doom themselves. A remarkable thing then happens. The enemies find life-saving benefits in binding themselves into an alliance in which both give up a degree of independence for a mutual gain. The breathers find that by limiting themselves to consuming only the wastes of the fermenters they gain a permanent food supply. They also come to benefit the fermenters by positioning themselves just within the fermenters' cell walls. Here they consume the oxygen molecules that come into contact with the cell before the oxygen can do damage. By sharing in the additional energy produced by the breathers, the fermenters come to enjoy powers they could never have achieved on their own. What began as an ugly competition leads to the mutual benefits of synergy.

With time, some of these hungry fermenter/breathers begin ingesting photosynthesizers. Again an accommodation is reached. Rather than digesting the photosynthesizers, the fermenter/breathers incorporate them into their own cell structure. Thus the capabilities of fermenters, photosynthesizers, and breathers are melded into a giant cell with a complex internal recycling system able to produce ATP energy in all three ways. This vastly increases the collective efficiency of the composite cells both in using food molecules ingested from the environment and in photosynthesizing their own food, a significant advantage during periods of food shortage.

A further capability is added when other types of breathers, shaped like small whips with the ability to propel themselves through the water, attach to the outside of giant cells to tap their energy. The attachment creates yet another symbiotic relationship in which in exchange for the energy they consume, the whips give the host cell a means of moving to where food is most plentiful.

The formation of these *super cells,* which occurred some two billion years ago (8:40 P.M.) at many different places on the earth, presents a fascinating example of a successful cooperative enterprise that grew out of desperate competition. In the words of Margulis and Sagan, "These new cells were ultimately the result of hunger, crowding, and thirst among teeming bacteria. . . . Curbing their viciousness and surrendering independence, they explored new ways to persist and reproduce."[10]

The formation of the composite cells prepares the way for yet another breakthrough. Recall that bacteria cells have no nucleus. Scientists call such cells *prokaryotes.* Their DNA strands float freely within the cell. Initially the same is true of the composite cells. Eventually, however, the partners fully unite into a self-directing entity by clustering some of their DNA into a nucleus, which serves as a sort of central information storage and processing center for the whole of the cell. The result is a single nucleated cell a hundred to a thousand times the size of the original individual bacterium cells of which it is composed.

The step from nonnucleated prokaryotes to nucleated cells, known as *eukaryotes,* marks what some consider the most significant dividing line in the history of life on planet Earth. The eukaryotes are the building blocks of all complex multicelled forms of life. It has taken nearly 2.2 billion years to create the eukaryote, but once accomplished it opens the way to a bold new phase in the evolutionary process. It is 9:19 P.M.

The next step is taken when some of the duplicated cells created by reproducing eukaryotes fail to separate. Colonies of connected algae cells begin to form seaweed and thereby create the first multicelled life. This is followed by the first multicelled animal life—jellyfish and flatworms—six hundred million years ago. It's 11:02 P.M. The first land-based plant life emerges and begins to evolve some 150 million years later. Things move into high gear from there as each species finds and adapts to its own ecological niche in the evolving ecosystem and develops capabilities specific to its own needs. The early development and subsequent refinement of sight was one such capability.

At about 11:11 P.M. (ninety million years later) the first vertebrate animals appear. By 11:37 dinosaurs are roaming the earth. Birds discover the art of controlled flight at 11:39, and monkeys are demonstrating the advantages of the prehensile hand and tail at 11:57.

Twenty-Three Seconds to Midnight

The hominids, early ancestors to modern humans, appear on the scene four million years ago, at 11:59 and 37 seconds. At fifteen seconds to midnight—a mere 2.6 million years ago—they are followed by *Homo habilis,* with a larger brain, more refined physical features, and smaller teeth. These creatures develop skills in hunting and the use of stone tools. *Homo sapiens,* the first modern humans, arrive about four hundred thousand years ago, slightly more than two seconds before midnight. Unimpressive to the eye, the humans carry a new capacity of cosmic import. As Brian Swimme and Thomas Berry explain:

> In its beginnings, and in its early development, the human was so frail, so unimpressive, a creature hardly worth the attention of the other animals in the forest. But these early humans were on a path that would in time explode with unexpectedly significant new power, a power of consciousness whereby Earth, and the universe as a whole, turned back and reflected on itself. Earth's community of life would never be the same, for here was a development with such consequences that it can only be compared to the emergence of oxygen within Earth's early communities of life, a development that carried both the destructive and the creative significance of that earlier event.[11]

The potentials of this new creature are embodied in the combination of innovative physical characteristics that include "increase in brain size, upright posture, bipedal walking, frontal focus of eyes and countenance, development of the arm and hand in relation to the eye, [and] increased capacity of the hands for grasping."[12]

The full significance of these combined innovations is found in their meaning for the inner psychic development of this new species. Freeing the hands from the task of walking makes them available for "shaping and handling tools, throwing, hunting, and food gathering" as well as "for artistic expression and emotional communication."[13]

The species's long period of childhood creates the necessity for enduring social bonds of cooperation and mutual defense and sets the stage for the development of culture. Two and one-tenth million years after their arrival, our earliest ancestors are making clothing, building shelters, constructing hand axes, and using fire. It is now three seconds to midnight—only five hundred thousand years remain to the year 2000.

A significant step is taken when they develop the complex nerve system to the muscles of the tongue that gives them the capacity to form speech sounds—some four hundred thousand years ago.[14] The first spoken languages appear, enabling the formation of an articulated consciousness. Speech in turn becomes a tool to refine and deepen this consciousness and to speed species learning and the development of shared culture. As their consciousness becomes more refined and self-aware, they begin the practice of burying their dead, a response to the dawning of reflection on the line that separates the living from the dead, the nature of the "self" that lives, the mysteries of creation, and the relationship of humans to the cosmos.[15]

By 16,000 B.C. our ancestors are painting figures on cave walls, suggesting further development of an aesthetic consciousness and awareness of self. It is now 11:59 P.M. and 59.9 seconds. One-tenth of a second to midnight—and the rest is quite literally history.

In a Blink of the Cosmic Eye

Perhaps as much as forty thousand years ago, the first settled villages appear, probably in Southeast Asia, as some among the earliest humans begin forsaking the hunter-gatherer ways in favor of settling down and cultivating food. This begins a process of redefining the human relationship with plants and animals. The same pattern follows in due course in the Middle East and other regions of the world.

The new living pattern creates new needs, such as for more precise ways of tracking the seasons and determining the planting cycles. The calendar is invented. Settled agriculture brings the mystical sense of death and rebirth and human participation in a cosmic order of interacting spiritual forces. The introduction of irrigation heralds the invention of more sophisticated forms of social organization. Early religious beliefs center on the Great Mother deity, and women generally have the central roles in religious observance, governance, and artistic expression. According to the archeological record, towns were built without fortification and houses were of similar size, suggesting an absence of warfare and conquest, and indicating significant social equality.[16]

A major shift takes place at the end of the fourth millennium B.C. Against the larger backdrop of small villages and place-based cultures—many of which developed their own sophisticated bodies of knowledge around subjects such as botany, zoology, astronomy and cosmology, mapping, and watersheds—there emerges in selected locations a greater specialization between farming and nonfarming roles. With time, those working directly with nature become devalued relative to the warriors, who dominate by force of arms. Male deities usurp female ones. Priests or god-kings emerge in Egypt, China, and India both to rule their people and to mediate human relationships with the divine. Those men who acquire power through weapons and wealth form a worldview that assumes their own superiority.[17]

The imposition of dominator cultures sets the stage for the subsequent creation of institutional hierarchies, class stratification, and the exploitation of life for the benefit of a few privileged humans, often at the expense of the rest. In the complex ways of life's creative processes, the dominator culture as well brings a period of unusual technological, intellectual, and artistic achievement: "wheel transportation, brick making, stone cutting, sailing vessels, sewage systems, water mains, mining and metallurgy, grain and food preservation, weaponry, carpentry, and architectural design were all innovations of this period."[18] Grand architectural structures follow, along with the emergence of great cities and the classical civilizations such as Mesopotamia, Egypt, India, the Indus Valley, Crete, North China, Greece, and Rome. It is a time of the first great empires.

The cities become centers of intellectual reflection and inquiry into the nature of the cosmos, reality, ethics, and the good society. The beginnings of Greek philosophy in 600 B.C. are followed forty years later by Confucius in China and Buddha in India, and later the rise of Christianity in Europe and Islam in the Middle East.

The decline of the Roman Empire and the eventual conquest of Rome by the Goths in 410 A.D. combine with the deepening corruption and barbarism of the Christian church to lead Europe into a civilizational decline sometimes referred to as the Dark Ages. In the twelfth century the cities of Europe begin to free themselves from feudal control and re-emerge as civilized centers of thought and creativity. Some cities in Italy, France, and Germany eventually establish democratically elected governments with universal suffrage.

In 1543, Nicholas Copernicus initiates the scientific revolution with the publication of *On the Revolutions of the Heavenly Spheres*. It presents the revolutionary thesis that Earth and the other planets revolve around the sun—contradicting the religious teachings of the church and ultimately undermining its intellectual and political authority. Science flourishes in the 1600s as the methods and philosophy of physics and astronomy launch a challenge against superstition and religious dogma. This is the century of Kepler, Galileo, Bacon, Descartes, and Newton. In the pursuit of a mission to replace ignorance and superstition with objective knowledge, awe and reverence are gradually replaced by the analytic eye that accepts no reality that cannot be observed, measured, and described in mathematical notation. In the words of Swimme and Berry:

> The ancient mystical experience of the universe was dissolving, the universe that humans had long experienced, communed with, endured and adored, been nurtured and killed by. They had danced to its rhythms, listened to its winds, chanted their exaltation and their grief, wondered at the gorgeous display of the heavens at sunrise and sunset. They had observed the movements of the heavens, identified the planets, marked off the great time divisions, coordinated human celebration with the vast celebration which is the universe itself.[19] . . . [Yet in the scientific revolution] there was a feeling of awakening from the great metaphysical dream world . . . from the unjustified reverence for the earlier sources of human understanding, from the irrational subjection of experimental and observational sciences to the belief systems of the past.[20]

Meanwhile, the commercial revolution is displacing the static local economies of the Middle Ages. Voyages of discovery and colonization expand commerce from the narrow confines of the Mediterranean to create a thriving worldwide trading enterprise. The scale of individual commercial enterprises expands accordingly. The great chartered trading companies, precursors to modern corporations, are formed as powerful instruments of colonial extraction. The British East India Company virtually rules India as a private estate until 1858.

Various ideals begin to break down, such as a belief that trade should be an equal exchange, production and trade should be conducted for the benefit of society with only a reasonable charge for the service rendered, and loans should be free of interest. Financial speculation on the price of gold and silver, the unrestrained pursuit of profit, and growth in the respectability of banking are important features of this period.[21] Money takes on a new importance as a mediator of relationships between people and nations, and its successful acquisition becomes a measure of personal accomplishment.

Together the commercial and scientific revolutions prepare the way for the industrial revolution, which begins in Britain in the mid-1700s driven by the potentials of mechanization and the steam engine. The age of the machine is now under way, creating a vastly increased demand for raw materials to feed European factories and driving a search for markets to absorb the vast increases in production now possible. These demands give additional impetus to colonial expansion and consolidation.

Rule by powerful landowners and financial elites begins to give way to more populist forms of democracy in the newly formed United States of America. In the mid-1800s, similar forces take hold on a national scale in many European countries and democracy starts to come into its own as a major form of political practice.

Dramatic advances in transportation and communications technologies in the nineteenth and twentieth centuries increase the speed of human movement at an exponential rate, eventually eliminating distance as a meaningful barrier to human interaction. The first practical steam-powered locomotive is built in 1803. The first Atlantic crossing by a ship with a steam-driven side-wheel comes in 1819. The first commercial railway is established in 1825. The telegraph is invented in 1837 and the telephone in 1876. The first internal combustion automobile is constructed in 1885. The first successful transatlantic radio communication comes in 1901. The first flight powered by a gasoline engine is in 1903.

Regular commercial ship travel across the Atlantic is well established by the end of the century. Commercial airline service across the Atlantic is initiated in the 1930s. The first transatlantic commercial jet service follows in 1958. The first communications satellite is launched in 1960. Commercial jumbo jet service begins in 1970, and human travel at near the speed of sound becomes routine for millions of people. The first practical personal computer, the Apple II, is introduced in 1977, followed by the IBM personal computer in 1981. The Internet comes into widespread use in the 1990s. The industrial age has now been with us for 1.44 thousandths of a second on our cosmic clock.

Matter That Chooses

The story of life is the epic story of the incredible and improbable journey of a universe creating itself through never-ending cycles of death and rebirth, destruction and rebuilding, through which it learns to meld undifferentiated energy into ever more complex and highly evolved structures. Even in this abbreviated version, the cosmic story as revealed by the data of science unfolds in a manner exactly the opposite of that predicted by the story of a dead mechanical universe engaged in winding down into a state of disorder.

Theoretical physicist Lee Smolin poses yet another puzzle that science has yet to resolve. It just happens that our universe sprang forth with the particular combination of physical constants—such as those that define the strength of gravity and the quantum forces that bind atoms—necessary to produce stars of sufficient life span and molecules of sufficient complexity to support the emergence and evolution of life. Smolin calculates the probability of this happening purely by chance at about one in 10^{229}. The number of all the protons and neutrons in all the stars we can see from the earth is only 10^{80}—by comparison a trivial number.[22]

If indeed nothing more were involved than a roll of the cosmic dice, by far the most probable outcome of our Big Bang would be heat death—a vast space uniformly filled with a gas at a constant, uniform temperature in which life would be impossible—again, exactly what the law of increasing entropy would lead us to predict.[23]

What we experience, however, is a universe of infinite complexity striving always to transcend itself, to reach beyond the given to realize its as yet unactualized potentials. In the words of Willis Harman, "In some ultimate sense, there really is no causality—only a Whole evolving."[24] Pure energy forms into atoms, atoms join to form molecules, molecules join to form cells, cells join to create organisms, organisms join to form flocks, herds, and societies, and societies join to form a self-reflective planetary intelligence.

So we come back to our original questions about life's story: Pure chance or purposeful striving? Dumb luck or deep intelligence? The mainstream of science continues to maintain that it is a combination of pure chance and the mechanistic processes of natural selection. It is here that the scientific leaders of the new biology part company with the mainstream. Lynn Margulis and Dorion Sagan put it succinctly: "Life is matter that chooses."[25] Life remembers as well, as it strives constantly to maintain and re-create itself.

Critical to understanding the disjuncture between the view of formal science and the reality of our living world is the centrality of the ever present cycle of death and rebirth, degeneration and regeneration by which life, and perhaps even the cosmos itself, continuously recycles its basic elements to create ever more elegant and able wholes through self-directing processes that bear little resemblance to the working of machines. Science continues to struggle in its effort to explain a decidedly nonmechanistic reality in mechanistic terms. With the rapid rate of new developments in the field of biology this tension becomes increasingly intolerable. This is leading some biologists to seek an understanding of life on its own terms, an enterprise that holds promise of leading to a whole new sense of our own possibilities.

As I reflect on such wonders as the incredible inventions of the bacteria that terra-formed the planet and learned to live within their natural limits I come to wonder—not whether bacteria have a capacity for intelligent collective action, but whether we humans have yet achieved a comparable capacity.

Perhaps twenty-first century science may reach the point of concluding that, far from being accidental, intelligence, life, and consciousness are integral to and virtually inseparable from the existence and evolution of the cosmos and all within it. What we already know suggests that the true wonders of the cosmos and its creative power lie far beyond our current comprehension—frontiers of understanding yet to be plumbed as we free ourselves from a partial and misleading story that impedes our ability to take our next evolutionary step.

Will we continue mindlessly to pursue the siren song of money? Or will we adapt our organizational and technological powers to the logic of living systems and the cause of actualizing life's potentials on a living planet? Life is about choices. How well we respond to the choices now at hand will provide a revealing test of how well our collective intelligence compares with that of an ancient population of bacteria.

Chapter 5

Organism as Metaphor

The body is a complex thing with many constituent parts, and to understand its behavior you must apply the laws of physics to its parts, not to the whole. The behaviour of the body as a whole will then emerge as a consequence of interactions of the parts.
　　—RICHARD DAWKINS[1]

No organic being is a billiard ball, acted upon only by external forces. All are sentient. . . . Each is capable, to varying degrees, of acting on its own.
　　—LYNN MARGULIS AND DORION SAGAN[2]

AS THE PROLOGUE MENTIONS, a chance encounter with microbiologist Mae-Wan Ho on a flight from Santiago de Compostela, Spain, to London provided the impetus for this book. I was especially taken by a paper she shared with me entitled "The New Age of the Organism," in which she forecast an emerging shift in the basic paradigm of science from the metaphor of the machine to the metaphor of the self-organizing living organism. She also shared her thoughts on how such a shift in perspective might change the way we think about the design of our economic institutions. By the end of the conversation I was convinced that her insight into life's incredible capacity to self-organize in ways that maintain the integrity of both the individual and the whole holds a critical key to resolving humanity's deepening economic and social crises.

Let's pause for a moment to set the context. We have created an economic system that has put not only ourselves but also the living systems of the planet at peril by reversing the process of nearly 4.5 billion years of evolution. The problem arises from a set of reinforcing values and institutions that lead us to the systematic destruction of the living capital created through the living processes of both the planet and human civilization to create money, which in our forgetfulness we have come to confuse with real wealth.

The challenge before us is to reverse our present backward course and re-create ourselves as contributors to the advancement of life's epic journey. It starts with choosing life as our guiding metaphor and continues with deepening our understanding of life's ways in search of insights into the unrealized possibilities of our species.

Dead or Alive: Choosing a Metaphor

The metaphor by which science defines itself serves as the lens through which it views and interprets reality. To a significant degree our reality as a global society has come to be defined by the lens that science wears. A science that embraces the machine or clockwork as its model sees a world that is deterministic and composed of static and discrete elements. Viewed through this lens, reality is made up of individual parts, each of which is external to and can be isolated from the other parts without itself being changed. Taking a part out of a clock may keep the clock from working but the part remains unchanged, and if it is reinstalled the clock will operate normally.[3]

Ho observes that those who view life through the reductionist lens of the machine metaphor, as mainstream biologists continue to do, attempt to understand living organisms as collections of separable structures, chemical processes, and electrical currents that can be understood in isolation from their environments. This leads to the assumption of a nondemocratic hierarchy of control dictated by predetermined and unchanging genetic structures that deny life's consciousness, intelligence, freedom to choose, and capacity for intentional cooperation—which are among life's more important defining features. The mechanistic lens thus leads to a denial of the very essence of life and its possibilities. Ho suggests that as science opens itself to the study of life on its own terms we may find it opens our minds to seeing new possibilities not only in ourselves but also in our understanding of the material world.

One key to the shift in perspective is an idea introduced in Chapter 4—that life is matter that chooses. It not only chooses but is engaged in the continual conversion of the inert matter of its environment into itself, into matter with the ability to choose—in other words, at once re-creating itself and transforming its environment. The living organism is dynamic and evolving. It controls its own material substance and its internal clock. If we look through the lens of the living-organism metaphor, it opens our eyes to a whole new way of seeing and interpreting the nature of reality.

Take our own bodies. We are constantly re-creating our physical being through the internal processing of the food we eat, the air we breathe, and the water we drink, creating new cells and shedding the old in a dynamic ongoing exchange with our environment. Furthermore, every cell, every bacterium, and every organ in our bodies is engaged in the same process of self-re-creation, even as they respond to and influence the body's other cells and organs to maintain our identity as conscious physical and spiritual beings.

The whole self-organizing process is radically democratic and participatory as each of literally trillions of decision makers participate in a process that "has no bosses, no controllers, and no set points,"[4] yet through some inner intelligence evolves and maintains the coherence of the whole of our bodies and the form and substance of the membrane that defines the physical boundary between ourselves and our environment.

As Ho explained the prospective implications of shifting our metaphor from the machine to the living organism, my head was spinning with the possibilities. Suppose the underpinnings of modern intellectual life came to embrace the premise that consciousness, intelligence, and free will not only are real but permeate the fabric of the cosmos. What new potentials might this shift in metaphor lead us to discover in ourselves? How might it cause us to redefine our relationship to the planet? How might it influence the way we think about governance and the design of our institutions and economic systems?

Although science is still a goodly way from shedding the machine metaphor, several trends are creating an opening for new approaches. One is the continued failure of theoretical physics to find a new unified theory that reconciles conflicts between the theory of relativity and the theory of quantum mechanics. Relativity theory explains gravity, but only by ignoring quantum mechanics. Quantum mechanics cannot explain gravity. Thus, neither theory stands on its own and neither can be reconciled with the other. Frustration over the long-standing impasse that extends back to the early 1900s may be opening the way to more fundamental rethinking.

Another trend is the emerging interest in complex systems that is occurring at prestigious centers such as the Santa Fe Institute, where computer simulation technologies are opening the way to the rigorous investigation of phenomena that cannot be modeled by mathematical formulas. Yet another influential factor, as noted by Janine Benyus in *Biomimicry*, is that the field of biology is coming into its own.

> Our fragmentary knowledge of biology is doubling every five years, growing like a pointillist painting to a recognizable whole. Equally unprecedented is the intensity of our gaze: new scopes and satellites allow us to witness nature's patterns from the intercellular to the interstellar. We can probe a buttercup with the eyes of a mite, ride the electron shuttle of photosynthesis, feel the shiver of a neuron in thought, or watch in color as a star is born. We can see, more clearly than ever before, how nature works her miracles.[5]

Ironically, the implications of a shift in metaphor from mechanism to organism are nowhere more important than in the study of life itself and may prove to be as important to biology as to other sciences, because as Lynn Margulis and Dorion Sagan observe:

> Life is distinguished not by its chemical constituents but by the behavior of its chemicals. The question "What is life?" is thus a linguistic trap. To answer according to the rules of grammar, we must supply a noun, a thing. But life on earth is more like a verb. It repairs, maintains, re-creates, and outdoes itself.[6]

We know life not by what it is, but by what it does. To understand and learn from it we must come to terms with the fact that we cannot hope to understand it solely in terms of its chemical, electrical, and material components. We must open our minds to understanding it on its own terms even as we seek to maintain the rigor and discipline of our observation and analysis.

In this spirit, let us now take a deeper look at what life does at the level of the individual organism and the biological community to see what else we might learn of our own latent potential.

The Organism

Within the seed is the knowledge of whether it is to become a stalk of wheat, an oak tree, or a tomato plant. The fertilized ovum knows whether its destiny is to become a salamander, an eagle, or a human. When the conditions are right, the internal cells of the seed or ovum spring to life in a self-directing process of division and differentiation as they engage in a cooperative process of absorbing energy and nutrients from their environment, breaking down the elements of what they consume, and transforming them into their own living matter through the processes of cell growth and division.

Though each organism responds to its own destiny, the process of fulfillment is far from passive. Each germ of life awaits the right conditions, the right moment to spring into a full-blown quest to become what it was meant to be. The plant adapts its structure and internal processes to the conditions of its available space, nutrients, and changes in seasons; orients itself to shade or sunlight as suits its nature; and creates its own distinctive variations on the structure that defines its species nature. So too does the animal adapt itself and its diet to the conditions of its setting, finding novel sources of the nutrients it needs and adapting its internal functions to the sources available. Its internal processes repel and destroy dangerous alien organisms and repair damaged flesh with an intelligence and adaptability far beyond the capacity of even the most advanced human machines.[7]

Most remarkable of all, these processes are the self-organizing outcome of the self-directed choices of countless individual cells and symbiotic bacteria that have joined in the cooperative enterprise of creating a living being with capacities far beyond those of any of the individual participants. Our own bodies are an example. Each of us is a composite of more than thirty trillion individual living cells.[8] Yet even these cells constitute less than half of our dry weight. The remainder consists of microorganisms, such as the enteric bacteria and yeasts of our gut that manufacture vitamins for us and help metabolize our food. These symbiotic creatures are as necessary to our survival and healthful function as our own cells.[9] Each cell and microorganism is an individual self-directing being in its own right, joined together in a self-organizing, continuously self-renewing alliance that functions as, and by all outward and inward appearances is, a single being.

Throughout its life span the organism renews its physical structures through cell death and replacement. In the human body, approximately three billion cells die each minute—each reliably replaced by a living cell of like kind. The stomach lining replicates itself every five days, the liver every two months, and the skin every six weeks. Ninety-eight percent of the atoms in the body are replaced each year.[10] Yet the identity, function, and coherence of each organ and the body as a whole are actively self-maintained year after year. The same is true for all living organisms—powerful evidence that every living being possesses an inner knowledge and awareness of self.

Another of the fascinating qualities of living organisms is their seeming ability to defy the second law of thermodynamics by maintaining themselves in a constant internal state of active energy disequilibrium or flux. Mechanical heat-driven engines require a constant input of heat to perform work. As soon as the heat source is withdrawn they run down to a state of energy equilibrium and stop. By contrast, the living system maintains itself in a continuously "energized" state in which waste energy from one cell becomes an energy source for another. Energy flows from cell to cell with minimal loss. The organism is thus "able to work without a constant energy supply, and moreover, can mobilize energy at will, whenever and wherever required, and in a perfectly coordinated way."[11] Yet in the larger scheme, life does honor the second law, as it must from time to time tap into sources of energy from its environment to renew its internal energy stores, thereby reducing order in its environment to self-maintain its internal order.[12]

Although the whole plant or animal may compete with its own kind or other species for its external energy sources, its internal cells and organs freely share their available internal energy stores as required to support the healthy function of the whole on which they all depend. When a special need arises, such as in the case of an illness, injury, or need to flee from a potential predator, the available resources are instantly directed to the appropriate cells. When our body's energy reserves have been exhausted, muscle tissue will be broken down to supply energy to the brain and maintain basic metabolic processes until danger has passed and food may be sought to replenish them. It is perhaps the ultimate expression of life's capacity for cooperative teamwork. There is no hoarding or concentration to favor the selfish wants of one part of the organism over the more immediate needs of another. In some way each cell seems to know that need takes priority over want.

Ho describes the process by which living things maintain their coherent function:

> The stability of organisms depends on all parts of the system being informed, participating, and acting appropriately in order to maintain the whole. Organic stability is therefore delocalized throughout the system.... This is the radical nature of the organic whole (as opposed to the mechanical whole), where global cohesion and local freedom are both maximized, and each part is as much in control as it is sensitive and responsive.[13]

We have some knowledge of the body's central nervous system, genetic coding, chemical messengers, and energy fields, but we have scarcely begun to understand the complex and often subtle mechanisms that make life's unfolding and self-organizing coherence possible. We are, however, beginning to grasp the significance of the fact that at every level and at every step along the way, life's individual beings are constantly engaged in making billions of individual decisions based on sensitive responses to both internal and environmental data. Through these choices the whole of life takes form with coherence, competence, creativity, and intelligence through processes that no individual cell, organ, organism, species, or community is in a position to dominate or direct.

Much as we once looked to the central nervous system as the body's command and control system, DNA was once considered to work in a mechanistic fashion, with the cell's nucleus serving as a sort of preprogrammed command center. Except for rare mutations, the individual gene was presumed to be stable, to contain a discrete and additive bit of information, and to be passed on only to direct descendants.

But contemporary research is revealing a far more dynamic picture. Researchers are finding that genes are dynamic and interactive with other genes in the genome (the collection of genes in a given cell), they can change in direct response to their own or the organism's environment, and they can jump horizontally by infection from one organism to another—even between species that do not interbreed. The evidence that life is engaged in a continual reprogramming of its genetic coding reveals still more of life's capacity for creative self-direction. It also suggests how dangerously little we know of the potential consequences of releasing genetically engineered organisms into the environment.

It is beginning to look as though life's coherence cannot be explained by some mechanism of central control or even by the studied uniformity and disciplined self-suppression of a military drill team. Rather, life's coherence is the outcome of creative processes that bear a striking resemblance to a grand jazz band in which all players have their own parts, with scope for individual self-expression to enrich the melody and harmonics in ways that flow from a deep awareness of the whole and a commitment to its integrity. The result is "a seemingly paradoxical state that maximizes both global cohesion and local freedom."[14]

The more we know of what life does, the more difficult it becomes to explain its ability to maintain self-referencing coherence without assuming the presence of some sense of self at each level of organization—the cell, the organ, and the organism—combined with a capacity for instantaneous communication and self-directed mutual adaptation among all the organism's elements.[15] Thus, Elisabet Sahtouris concludes that a coherent sense of self is common to all living things and that consciousness may turn out to be, in some form or another, intrinsic to all of nature and its processes. Ho maintains that, far from being "a passive object at the mercy of random variation and natural selection," life is "an active participant in the evolutionary drama. In constantly responding to and transforming its environment, it partakes in creating the possible futures of generations to come."[16]

Biocommunities

In biology a community is defined as a group of plants and animals that live together in the same geographical area, each filling a specialized ecological niche defined by its distinctive function and physical location. Thus, the function of the American buffalo was that of grazer and its address was the North American grasslands.

Each biological community (or biocommunity) embodies the accumulated wisdom of millions of years of adaptive learning. Each functions in many respects like a large organism. Though the individual parts have a far greater scope for autonomous behavior than the cells of the familiar multicelled organism, the function of the whole ultimately depends absolutely on the cooperation and integration of the parts. In one type of biological community, for example, "Trees shelter birds and insects, bees pollinate flowers, mammals package seeds in the rich fertilizer of their feces and distribute them, funguses and plants exchange materials, sapotrophs from microbes to vultures recycle, birds warn of predators, etc."[17]

The food chain by which each community functions is a self-contained energy system in which plants live on sunlight, herbivores live on the plant life, and carnivores dine on herbivores. The destruction of life to maintain life is one of life's realities. Yet under normal conditions life consumes life only to live. Except for humans, rarely does it destroy other life for mere sport or convenience or kill another of its own species for vengeance.

The biological community takes the basic structures and processes of the organism to a new level of function. In particular, as we will elaborate in the next chapter, these structures and processes of the biological community reveal the following qualities:[18]

- They self-organize through complex systems of information feedback by which each component organism and community adapts its behavior to the condition and needs of the whole. There is no central control and no hierarchy of authority.

- They are grouped into multitudes of smaller, relatively self-contained multispecies subcommunities that sustain themselves on locally captured solar energy and function as integral parts of the larger community.

- They are inseparable from place as they are exquisitely adapted to the most intricate details of their geographical habitat. They keep supply lines short by positioning each organism near its food supply, and take optimal advantage of whatever opportunity the habitat offers to sustain life on a continuing basis—even under the most inhospitable circumstances.

- They generate virtually no waste beyond inevitably dissipated energy. Energy flows constantly through the system and materials are constantly recycled as wastes from one organism or species are consumed as food by others. The system maintains an internal balance between the energy dissipated into its environment and the renewing processes by which the system's plant life captures solar energy and converts it to useful forms.

- They nurture a rich diversity of species and cultures as a source of system resilience and creative potential.

The contrast between a healthy biological community and the global capitalist economy is starkly revealing. The latter is centrally planned by global megacorporations that have no attachment to place and neither knowledge of nor concern for the well-being of the whole. Its function depends on depleting the earth's stores of ancient sunlight (fossil fuels) and eliminating the energy and materials self-reliance of individual communities. It overwhelms the natural productive processes of local ecosystems with concrete and chemicals, and it depends on supply lines thousand of miles long. It systematically converts the differentiated energy and material resources of its environment into unusable and often toxic pollution and garbage. And it preserves only those elements of biological and cultural diversity useful in generating immediate profits for money-world institutions.

Self-Organizing Computer Simulations

Science began to take a serious interest in studying how living systems self-organize only recently, in part because of a lack of adequate tools for the rigorous study of such complex processes. The conventional mathematical tools of science are well suited to the study of causality, correlation, and probability. They have limited application, however, to the study of phenomena that involve the interaction of large numbers of individual decision makers—such as interlinked computer processors, living cells, social insects, or humans—each reacting independently to constant and generally unpredictable changes in its distinctive environment.

Advances in computer simulation techniques now make it possible to model such processes, often leading to outcomes impossible to predict simply from a knowledge of initial conditions. The most interesting of these simulations exhibit a capacity to learn from their experience and to develop and apply problem-solving abilities that have not been already programmed into them by humans.

Much of this work is being developed by a group of scientists clustered around the Sante Fe Institute in New Mexico. As documented by Mitchell Waldrop in his book *Complexity*, they are "forging the first rigorous alternative to the kind of linear, reductionist thinking that has dominated science since the time of Newton—and that has now gone about as far as it can go in addressing the problems of our modern world."[19]

An example of a simple simulation is that of the self-organizing flocking behavior of birds. Each simulated bird is programmed with three simple rules: (1) try to maintain a minimum distance from other objects in your environment, including other birds; (2) try to match your velocity with that of other birds in your neighborhood; and (3) try to move toward the center of the mass of the birds in your neighborhood.

The simulation program provides no master set of instructions for organizing the birds into a flock. Any such behavior has to emerge out of the purely individual decisions of each bird. Yet flocks form every time the simulation is run, irrespective of how the birds are scattered around the computer screen at the beginning of the session. Once formed, the flock flows past any obstacle in its path in a fluid and natural manner, sometimes dividing and flowing around both sides of the obstacle to re-form on the other side as if by a master plan.[20]

Such simulations have been used to understand increasingly complex systems. Although they do not explain life, they are proving to be an invaluable tool for understanding the creative power of systems in which many decision makers organize into wholes greater than their parts without the use of hierarchy. This work has great potential to deepen our insights into how life accomplishes its miraculous feats of self-organization, and in so doing to yield further insights into our own possibilities.

Parts, Wholes, and Whole-Parts

Generations of physicists have sought to reduce matter to its elementary particles on the theory that the parts explain the whole. The quest led to an unexpected discovery: the most elementary particles we have found are not truly things so much as interconnections between things. In the words of physicist Niels Bohr, a pioneer of quantum theory, "Isolated material particles are abstractions, their properties being definable and observable only through their interactions with other systems."[21] In contrast to the presumption of classical physics, parts can be understood only by their relationships to a large whole.[22]

Thus we come to suspect that the world of quantum mechanics may have more in common with the organic world of life than with the mechanical world of classical physics. Both are about relationships and the evolving interplay between parts and wholes, suggesting that perhaps developing our understanding of relationships is the key to understanding both matter and life.

A new perspective on whole-part relationships is taking shape around the concept of the *holon*—a term coined by Arthur Koestler to designate that which is simultaneously a whole in its own right and a part of a larger whole.[23] An atom is a whole in itself. When it is also part of a molecule it becomes a holon, or a whole-part. The molecule that is also part of a cell is a holon, as is the cell that is part of an organ, and so on. This hierarchy of relationships from the atom to the organism is known as a *holarchy*. The concepts of holon and holarchy are fundamental to understanding the healthy function of complex living systems, which requires that each of their whole-parts maintain its own identity and boundaries even as it functions as part of the larger whole.[24]

Indeed, life's continuing quest to achieve ever-higher forms of complexity and competence takes place through joining individual entities into new wholes with new capabilities. This has led Dorion Sagan to suggest that "evolution favors populations of individuals that act together to re-create individuality at ever higher levels."[25] The real key to evolution is not competition, but rather cooperation.

Theoretical physicist and philosopher of science Fritjof Capra has observed that two seemingly opposing tendencies—"the self-assertive and the integrative—are both essential aspects of living systems."[26] Through self-assertion the individual assures its own essential integrity and maintains the diversity essential to the creative potentials of the whole. Yet it is only through integration that these potentials are fully actualized. The dynamic tension between these two tendencies is essential to the evolutionary processes. Just as self-assertion may have an inherent competitive dimension, integration depends on cooperation in the interest of a common good.[27]

Mutuality is also a key principle in structuring healthy whole-part relations in living systems. Even as the whole exerts influence on the parts, the parts exert influence on the whole. When one holon within a holarchy acts as though it is the whole, as in the case of a cancer cell, it is a sign of pathology, and that holon must be rooted out to restore the whole to proper function.[28]

When Cells Turn Rogue

Dysfunctions of living systems offer another window into the complexity of life's ways. Cancer is especially instructive because unlike a virus, which is alien to the body, cancer occurs when the body's own cells turn rogue and become a threat to its survival.[29]

The healthy body has internal mechanisms to match the rate of cell reproduction with the rate of death of like cells through complex processes of intercell communication. Cancers develop when the critical genes that control cell growth become damaged and release a process of uncontrolled reproduction unmindful of the body's needs. This aspect of cancer underscores one of life's most remarkable qualities. The purely selfish gene popularized by writers such as biologist Richard Dawkins is a pathological anomaly. When a cell functions as part of a larger organism it curtails its "selfish" tendency toward indefinite propagation.[30]

DNA damage, including the types that may trigger uncontrolled cell division, is a fairly routine event for which the body has developed several lines of defense. The first defensive action comes from the cell itself, which will attempt to repair the damaged DNA. If repair is unsuccessful, the cell is programmed to commit suicide, a process called *apoptosis,* to maintain the integrity of the larger organism. As a further fail-safe measure, each cell has a mechanism built into its genetic structure that limits the number of times it can divide.

If these internal mechanisms fail, there remain at least two further lines of defense. One, of course, is the immune system, which attacks foreign intruders. Unfortunately, the immune system is handicapped in dealing with cancer, because cancer cells are created by the body itself. In their earlier stages cancer cells offer the immune system few clues as to their rogue nature.

As a last line of defense the body attempts to starve the rogue cells. As the initial tumor grows, more and more of the rogue cells become isolated from the blood capillaries on which they depend for the delivery of new supplies of energy and material. Eventually their growth stops, leaving a small and benign tumor.

Up to this point the cancerous cells are generally not a consequential threat to the health of the organism. Some cancer cells, however, aggressively seek to overcome the body's defenses in the pursuit of their own unlimited growth. They may learn to deactivate the gene that triggers apoptosis, break free of the original tumor and move through the blood-stream to establish new tumors in other organs, release a protein that activates growth of the capillary system, and confuse the immune system by actively masking their own nature. Unmindful of their dependence on the health of the body of which they are a part, the cancer cells move to colonize ever more of the body—expropriating the available nourishment and disrupting the coherent function of essential organs until they destroy themselves by killing their host.

As I noted in the Prologue, cancer is more than a metaphor for the relationship of capitalism and the global corporation to the market and democracy. It is a clinical diagnosis. Think of capitalism as a defective genetic coding in our economic system that causes individual enterprises to seek their own unlimited growth without regard to the consequences for society.

A shift from machine to organism as the guiding metaphor of postmodern societies holds promise of a transformation in human consciousness, understanding, and institutions as profound as that which resulted from the Copernican revolution's shift from an earth-centered to a sun-centered conception of the solar system. As the machine metaphor has led us to the brink of self-destruction, the metaphor of the organism holds the key to the ecological revolution through which we will discover potentials in our being and meaning in our lives essential to the task of creating societies that respond to life's call.

Among the many possibilities, one of the more fascinating and hopeful centers on life's evident capacity for self-organization through processes based on cooperative choice. Much as the machine metaphor tends to legitimate the organization of societies under the control of state and corporate bureaucracies to protect us from the Hobbesian war of all against all, the living-organism metaphor points to possibilities for the cooperative self-organization of human societies to release creative potentials far beyond what most of us dare to imagine.

Equally fascinating are the implications of life's ability to form itself into entirely new entities able to function as unitary beings without sacrificing the freedom and coherence of the individuals who constitute them. This poses a truly revolutionary idea for a species that spent much of the last hundred years tearing itself apart in the often violent struggles between those who called for the suppression of the individual in favor of community (communism) and those who rejected the obligations of community in favor of unrestrained individualism (capitalism). Life is telling us that these are both pathological extremes. In fact, life tells us, there is no conflict between community and individuality— indeed in a healthy living system they support and strengthen one another.

The metaphor of the organism also leads us to a new understanding of the nature and centrality of living capital as the source of all real wealth. The transformative power of the organism—both human and nonhuman—is the ultimate source of all that has value in the fulfillment of our own being. It includes not only the whole of the natural living capital, by which the planet's life support system is continuously regenerated, but also the human, social, and institutional capital by which we utilize the wealth of the living planet to serve our needs and by which we may ideally come to lend our own distinctive capacities to further life's continuing journey. Living capital is the whole of life's accumulated usable knowledge, its capacity for choice, and its store of embodied energy, life's active potential to create and sustain itself in yet more complex and able forms. The metaphor of the organism holds the key to our learning to live more fully and competently as one with life toward the fulfillment of its larger purpose.

As humans, we possess both the gift of life and the gift of reflective consciousness. If life has the power to choose, our capacity for choice is greater than that of any other species. We must use that power now to embrace life as our master teacher and develop our skills in the arts of living with a passion comparable to that which we are now devoting to the art of making money. Using our growing knowledge of life's wisdom to re-create our economic institutions to the service of life must be a centerpiece of that agenda.

Chapter 6

Embracing Life's Wisdom

We must draw our standards from the natural world. We must honor with the humility of the wise the bonds of that natural world and the mystery which lies beyond them, admitting that there is something in the order of being which evidently exceeds all our competence.
　　　—VÁCLAV HAVEL[1]

I sympathize, therefore, with those who would minimize, rather than with those who would maximize, economic entanglement between nations. Ideas, knowledge, art, hospitality, travel—these are the things which should of their nature be international. But let goods be homespun whenever it is reasonably and conveniently possible, and above all, let finance be primarily national.
　　　—JOHN MAYNARD KEYNES[2]

IN THE AFTERMATH of the 1997 Asian financial debacle, a *New York Times* editorial on Vietnam's economic policies chided those Vietnamese who "dream of some middle course that would allow them the benefits of capitalist development without increased foreign influence and a weakening of domestic political control."[3] In the view of the *Times*, "Such dreams are illusory, as other socialist countries trying to step halfway into the world market have discovered."

In a way the *Times* is right. When a country opens itself to capitalism, corporate rule comes with the package. Yet behind this truth lies a larger assumption, which is that Vietnam has no real options and that yielding to the forces of capitalism will prove more beneficial than resisting. In this assumption the *Times* is simply repeating a cant so common and unchallenged in mainstream discourse that one of global capitalism's leading boosters, Margaret Thatcher, gave it a name—TINA—an acronym for There Is No Alternative.

This brings to mind the fictional species the Borg, the most dangerous of all aliens encountered by the spaceship *Enterprise* on the TV series *Star Trek*. The Borg have their own mantra: "We are the Borg. You will be assimilated. Resistance is futile." Assimilation means being converted to a half-mechanical, half-biological entity to function as an expendable captive of the Borg collective, with no sense of individual identity and without capacity for independent thought or action.

In their arrogance, both Marxism and capitalism preached the inevitability of their triumphant assimilation of the human species. Marxism has fallen and the excesses of capitalism assure that it will follow. We should by now have learned two important truths: First, societies based on extremist ideologies of either the far left (rigid collectivization) or the far right (ruthless individualism) are inherently unstable. Second, there is nothing inevitable or immutable about the ways in which we choose to structure our economic lives. Choices as to the rules and structures that define our economies are human choices. Because those rules and structures play such a powerful role in expressing our values and shaping how we live, it is proper that they be subject to thorough public debate and dialogue informed by serious, critical, nonideological analysis.

Through a largely nonconsensual process we have created an economic system with characteristics that most resemble those of a cancerous tumor. The challenge before us is to create an economic system more conducive to our long-term survival and healthy function.

One approach is to mimic the characteristics of a healthy ecosystem. As we shall see in the chapters that follow, such a system would look much like a proper market economy with an overlay of an ethical culture and a framework of sensible rules established by a democratic government. Nothing radical. Nothing unfamiliar. Just the practice of basic values to which most of us already claim allegiance. Before turning to the details, however, let's reflect back on what life's story reveals of its ancient wisdom and consider in broad brush strokes how that wisdom might be translated into a framework for rethinking and restructuring the economic life of human societies.

Lessons of Life's Ancient Wisdom

Not surprisingly, life has learned a good deal since the first early bacterium sprang into being 3.9 billion years ago. Life's story is rich with insights into its remarkable abilities and potentials. For those of us who would learn to live, there is no greater teacher. Let's review a few of the lessons from life's story with special relevance to our search for life after capitalism.

LESSON 1: LIFE FAVORS SELF-ORGANIZATION

> **Lessons of Life's Wisdom**
> 1. Life favors self-organization.
> 2. Life is frugal and sharing.
> 3. Life depends on inclusive, place-based communities.
> 4. Life rewards cooperation.
> 5. Life depends on boundaries.
> 6. Life banks on diversity, creative individuality, and shared learning.

The most fundamental of life's lessons centers on life's capacity to self-organize toward ever higher levels of complexity, capacity, and consciousness. In the dance of life, each level of organization—cells, organisms, and communities of organisms—has the capacity for independent choice and action. Each retains its identity and volition even as it finds its place of sustenance and service within a larger whole. Each member organism functions simultaneously as a whole in its own right and as a part of a larger whole. Over and over the paradox is repeated: although life is matter with the freedom to choose, living beings exist only in relation to other living beings. Therefore, the freedom of the one depends on the responsible use of that freedom in relation to the needs of the many.

> Human economies can and should function as self-organizing systems in which each individual, family, community, or nation is able to exercise its own freedom of choice mindful of the needs of the whole, and no entity has the power to dominate any other.

LESSON 2: LIFE IS FRUGAL AND SHARING

Waste not, want not is one of life's favored mottoes, voluntary simplicity a key to its success. The amount of free and sustainable energy that is being constantly supplied to the planet in the form of sunlight places a strict constraint on life's ability to maintain otherwise inert matter in a living state. Energy and materials are continuously recycled for use and reuse within and between cells, organisms, and species with a minimum of loss.

Because the wastes of one become the resources of another, we might say that living systems have come rather close to being able to eat their cake and have it too. As Janine Benyus expresses it, "In ensemble, living things maintain a dynamic stability, like dancers in an arabesque, continually juggling resources without waste."[4] Life's rich abundance is a product of its ability to capture, use, store, and share as needed whatever energy is available to it with extraordinary efficiency.

> Human economies can and should be organized to contribute to life's abundance through the frugal use, equitable sharing, and continuous recycling of available energy and resources to the end of meeting the material, social, and spiritual needs of all their members.

LESSON 3: LIFE DEPENDS ON INCLUSIVE, PLACE-BASED COMMUNITIES

Physical habitats are the living places within which each species creates and defines its relationship to other species and to the resources on which its survival and prosperity depend. Because life exists only in relation to other life, species that share a particular habitat organize themselves into inclusive place-based biological communities within which they learn through mutual adaptation to optimize the capture, sharing, use, and storage of the energy sources available to them. As each individual being, species, and biome adapts itself to the most intricate details of its particular physical locale, life's web establishes a sustainable and balanced dominion over the physical spaces and resources of the planet. With grace, beauty, and consummate skill, each individual finds its place near to those on which it depends for food and those it feeds in turn.

> Human economies can and should be built around inclusive, place-based communities, adapted to the conditions of their physical space, adept at the collection and conservation of energy and the recycling of materials to function as largely self-reliant entities, and organized to provide each of their members with a sustainable means of livelihood.

LESSON 4: LIFE REWARDS COOPERATION

Shared spaces create shared destinies and interests—the imperatives of cooperation. Although the competitive aspect of life's evolution has dominated Western attention since the studies of Darwin, paradoxically, competition's most constructive contribution to evolution generally has been to create an imperative for cooperation.[5] As Sahtouris observes, "One can discern in evolution a repeating pattern in which aggressive competition leads to the threat of extinction, which is then avoided by the formation of cooperative alliances."[6]

In the interdependent world of life, unrestrained competition is generally self-defeating. Those who survive and prosper are invariably those who find a niche in which they meet their own needs in ways that simultaneously serve others.[7] Thus it is that in healthy systems the interests of part and whole—self and other—remain in exquisite balance. If each cell were dedicated solely to the pursuit of its own growth and reproduction, as neo-Darwinians such as Richard Dawkins assert, all life would be a cancer and would soon expire.[8]

As we saw in Chapter 4, it was only after the breather bacteria discovered the benefits of eating the wastes of the fermenters, while at the same time providing the fermenters with a propulsion system and protecting them from the destructive consequences of their encounter with free oxygen, that both the breathers and the fermenters were able to move to a new level of function. In the most fundamental sense, evolution is a progression toward ever greater cooperation.

> Human economies can and should acknowledge and reward cooperative behavior toward the efficient use of energy and resources in providing adequate livelihoods for all and enhancing the productive capacities of a shared pool of living capital.

LESSON 5: LIFE DEPENDS ON BOUNDARIES

Boundaries are also an essential feature of life—integral to the processes by which each living organism creates and manages its internal energy flows. Consider the importance of the cell's outer membrane to its integrity. As Smolin observes, "Were there no such barrier, diffusion and heat flows would quickly result in a mixing of the matter and energy between the inside and the outside of the cell, killing it. Instead, the cell is able to control exchanges between its interior and exterior to its own advantage, in order to maintain a high level of internal organization."[9]

For similar reasons, a multicelled organism must have a skin or other protective covering that establishes a boundary between itself and its environment. Biocommunities are bounded by oceans, mountains, and climatic zones that inhibit intrusions by potentially predatory species. The importance of boundaries holds at every level. Boundaries define life's individual identities, and the borders within which each being builds and maintains its energy flows are essential to its existence.

Even our living planet maintains boundaries by which it mediates its relationship with the rest of the cosmos. Smolin explains that our planet "is kept isolated from the rest of the universe by the action of the Earth's gravitational field, while the atmosphere and ozone layer serve partly to control its exchange of radiation with the outside universe."[10] Eliminate the planet's boundaries—for example, the ozone layer—and life as we know it will cease to exist.

Yet it is also true that life depends on relationships and therefore is never fully self-contained. Thus its borders are permeable, neither totally open nor totally closed. They are also necessarily managed. For example, the cell regulates its energy and material exchanges with its environment both to maintain its internal energy regime and to protect its physical space and being against hostile invaders. Paradoxically, borders are essential to cooperative and productive exchange with others. A cell without an outer membrane is a dead cell, and because a dead cell is unproductive, it isn't much use in a cooperative alliance. Only by maintaining its own bounded integrity can a cell maintain its own capacity to learn, to store active energy, and to cooperate with other cells in the sharing of energy and information.

> Human economies can and should have managed borders at each level of organization, from household and community to region and nation, which allow them to maintain the integrity, coherence, and resource-efficiency of their internal productive process and to protect themselves from predators and pathogens while cooperating to enhance the potentials of the larger whole.

LESSON 6: LIFE BANKS ON DIVERSITY, CREATIVE INDIVIDUALITY, AND SHARED LEARNING

Life knows well the innovative power of self-organizing systems composed of many individuals creating and testing new abilities in response to changing environmental conditions. The greater the diversity, the greater the potential for further innovation and the greater the resilience of the system in times of stress and crisis. Genetic and cultural diversity are life's storehouses of intellectual capital and the building blocks from which it melds itself into new and more capable forms.

Life's story presents powerful evidence that the desire to learn, innovate, and share knowledge for the benefit of the whole is integral to its nature. Successful living entities protect their individual physical space or territory, not out of selfishness or the desire to destroy others but simply as a measure essential to the integrity of their own function. Information and technical knowledge, being infinitely replicable, are freely shared.

The drive to learn, innovate, and share useful information is inherent in humans as well. Throughout history our most brilliant scientists, innovators, and teachers were driven not by the promise of financial rewards but by an inner compulsion to learn, to know, and to share their knowledge. Only the most repressive institutions have been able to thwart that drive. We must presume that in human systems as in other living systems, withholding useful knowledge for exclusive gain is appropriately regarded as unnatural—a sign of pathology that inhibits efficient system function. It is a lesson of special relevance to our time. As we confront the task of adapting ourselves to the limits of the global ecosystem while simultaneously learning to meet the needs of the whole of planetary life, our need for rapid innovation has never been greater. Success depends on engaging every locality in its own processes of innovation and the free and rapid sharing of beneficial knowledge and technology among them.

> Human economies can and should nurture cultural, social, and economic creativity and diversity and share information within and between place-based economies. These conditions are the keys to system resilience and creative transcendence.

Although applying life's lessons to human economies may seem an idealistic exercise, those lessons are backed by life's accumulated wisdom of 3.9 billion years. They are not beyond the means of single-celled bacteria and neither are they beyond ours. Their application does, however, require a major culture shift and retooling of our institutions.

System Design for a Post-Corporate World

Our current system is destined for social and environmental collapse. We thus face an imperative to create an alternative. Whatever that alternative may be, it will emerge only through intensive reflection and dialogue involving virtually every person on the planet. It would therefore be both inappropriate and foolish to attempt a prescriptive treatment here.

The list of system design elements that follows is intended only to present one possible framework. It represents a convergence of characteristics drawn from three sources: the lessons of life's wisdom listed in the preceding section; the work of systems modeler Hartmut Bossel of the University of Kasel in Germany[11]; and the values and practical visions of a great many extraordinary people from ordinary walks of life, whom we will be visiting in Parts III and IV, who are at the forefront of creating a life-centered postmodern civilization.

> **A Post-Corporate World: Design Elements**
> 1. Human-scale self-organization
> 2. Village and neighborhood clusters
> 3. Towns and regional centers
> 4. Renewable energy self-reliance
> 5. Closed-cycle materials use
> 6. Regional environmental balance
> 7. Mindful livelihoods
> 8. Interregional electronic communication
> 9. Wild spaces

Bear in mind that we are not at the moment concerned with the question of how we might get from where we are to the place described in this section. Nor is this list of design elements chosen with the intent of portraying a world that will have immediate universal appeal as an attractive alternative to the consumer society. Our concern in this chapter is simply to define a possible systems framework for a socially and environmentally viable society.

DESIGN ELEMENT 1: HUMAN-SCALE SELF-ORGANIZATION

Economic and political life in a post-corporate society is built largely around self-organizing processes based on the smallest feasible decision-making units. Thus, by preference the governmental functions are assigned to the lowest and smallest unit of government appropriate to that function—the one most accessible to direct citizen input. Similarly, economic affairs are organized on the basis of large numbers of relatively small production facilities and other enterprises owned by local stakeholders such as workers, managers, suppliers, customers, and members of the locality that is home to the business. Most individuals have an ownership stake in the enterprise from which they obtain their livelihood and a long-term interest in its viability.

Although economic relationships are structured primarily on market principles and use market competition to spur efficiency and innovation, firms also work within a larger framework of community cooperation and the sharing of resources and technology. Ethical standards in economic, as in other, relationships are highly valued, and those who violate these standards are held in low regard.

DESIGN ELEMENT 2: VILLAGE AND NEIGHBORHOOD CLUSTERS

The basic model varies by local circumstances, but human settlements are generally neighborhood-oriented, organized more on the pattern of a village than of the dispersed, auto-dependent suburban housing tract. Many of the layouts are modeled on successful ecovillage and cohousing experiments. A typical pattern involves modest row houses of varied designs, based on local materials and adapted to local climate, clustered around courtyards with lawns, playgrounds, and flowerbeds. Spaces between housing units are used for small gardens, composting, and raising small animals, such as chickens and goats, for food. Most living clusters bring together members of all generations, with older folks helping with housework, gardening, and child care and families sharing in turn with elder care. Basic food and convenience items are available from local shops owned and operated by local residents.

There may be cooperative office facilities with shared equipment and support staff for those who would otherwise work out of home offices—reducing the need for larger homes and individual office equipment. Some villages have small local industrial parks that offer shared support facilities for various kinds of small productive enterprises. Most villages have a local elementary school, a holistic primary health care facility, and a community arts and meeting center with a small library and public electronic research, reading, and communications facilities in easy walking distance of the residences.

Each village has its adjacent green spaces and agricultural enterprises. In more urbanized centers, most clusters consist of multistory, multifamily dwellings or apartments organized around parks and green belts interspersed with urban gardens. Each village cluster is a place for living, relatively self-contained with regard to more basic needs, and sufficiently small in total area that walking and bicycles are adequate to meet most transportation needs. The elderly and disabled get around easily on small electric carts. Pathways, parks, and public squares encourage informal socializing.

DESIGN ELEMENT 3: TOWNS AND REGIONAL CENTERS

Usually, there is a larger town center within bicycling distance of each village cluster that features a wider range of medical services and sports facilities, a high school, repair services, specialized shops, administrative offices, and a variety of public services. Shuttle buses link villages to their nearest town center, which are in turn linked to one another and to larger regional centers by bus and light rail public transit. Colleges and universities, more specialized hospitals, research centers, firms engaged in larger-scale production, and governmental offices responsible for serving the region are located in the regional centers. More difficult to produce, high-technology goods such as pharmaceuticals, medical and scientific equipment, machine tools, and computer chips are generally produced in these regional centers, with different regions specializing in different products to the extent that larger-scale production facilities are required.

DESIGN ELEMENT 4: RENEWABLE ENERGY SELF-RELIANCE

The basic model of village, town, and regional center clusters connected by efficient public transportation largely eliminates the need for private cars, resulting in significant energy savings and freeing up large amounts of space for human use. Most villages have a few commercially or cooperatively owned high-efficiency solar- or hydrogen-powered cars and trucks available for sharing or renting for special trips for which public transportation is not suited. Large garden and power tools needed only occasionally are owned cooperatively for use on a shared or rental basis. Housing units feature energy-conserving architecture, insulation, solar collectors, photovoltaics, and biogas generators that make each group of houses largely energy-independent. Biogas and solar hydrogen provide supplemental energy as needed. Each settlement grouping seeks to be as self-sufficient as possible in energy through the full development of its solar and biogas resources.

DESIGN ELEMENT 5: CLOSED-CYCLE MATERIALS USE

Each community is also relatively self-reliant in materials use. To the extent possible, necessary resources are harvested and processed locally and then maintained in a constant state of use, reuse, and recycling. All packaging materials are reused. Bottles are refilled locally. Products are designed to be repaired locally and ultimately recycled. Organic matter is composted in local vegetable gardens. Sewage is biologically processed, used to generate biogas, and recycled onto agricultural fields. Products such as appliances, vehicles, machines, and electronic equipment are leased rather than sold and returned to their local manufacturers at the end of their useful life to be repaired, upgraded, or broken down into their basic material components for recycling. Virtually no waste is dumped into the environment.

DESIGN ELEMENT 6: REGIONAL ENVIRONMENTAL BALANCE

Each region structures its economy to live in balance with the limits of the regenerative capacity of its biosystem and seeks substantial self-reliance in its use of environmental resources. Income and sales taxes have been eliminated in favor of resource, pollution, and land-use fees that encourage conservation and local self-sufficiency. High taxes on imported fuels limit the use of other than locally generated solar energy. Energy fees keep bulk transportation costs between regions relatively high, thus encouraging local recycling and a general reliance on regional resources and regionally produced goods.

To encourage economic efficiency and innovation, market competition is maintained within regions through rigorous antitrust enforcement and regulatory and fiscal tools that favor human-scale firms. There are also sharply graduated taxes on the value of the productive assets owned or controlled by a single firm to create a bias in favor of the small.

The fiscal and regulatory policies of national or interregional levels of government are designed to encourage each region to adjust to its natural carrying capacity. One of the more important functions of national and global governmental bodies is to facilitate the negotiation and mediation of agreements with regard to cross-border pollution and unbalanced trade relations between regions. Such agreements are designed to assure that one region cannot live beyond its own means by unfairly stressing the environment of another region.

DESIGN ELEMENT 7: MINDFUL LIVELIHOODS

Because work centers on providing the goods and services necessary to a good life and available paid employment is equitably shared, there is no need to encourage the production and consumption of harmful and unnecessary products simply to sustain the economy. Work is as much a source of fulfillment and an opportunity to participate in the life of the community as it is a source of income. Eliminating the production of harmful and wasteful products in turn eliminates most needs for large-scale production. There is also a flourishing of artistic and artisan craft production.

The benefits of increased productivity are shared through some combination of increased incomes and the sharing of available paid work by adjusting the hours that each individual puts into paid employment. This means people have much more time for recreational activities, sports, participation in the arts, intellectual and spiritual development, family life, and community service. As a result, family and civic life are rich. Many community services are maintained largely through volunteer labor. Most communities have local currencies to facilitate the monetized exchange of goods and services within and among the villages affiliated with a given town center.

DESIGN ELEMENT 8: INTERREGIONAL ELECTRONIC COMMUNICATION

Most investment and production are local, so the international movement of goods and materials is greatly reduced, as is the need for long-distance business travel. The pricing of energy at its true cost makes the physical movement of goods and people between regions costly and acts as a natural tariff barrier. There is serious attention to international and cross-cultural exchange to build human bonds that transcend one's own locality. An experience abroad is considered an essential part of a basic education, and most adults engage in some form of extended voluntary exchange activity to share ideas, friendship, and cultures—but the pattern of frenetic long-distance air travel for brief business meetings and resort tourism is a thing of history. Most long-distance travel is by energy-efficient public water and rail transport, which reduces its frequency but makes it more relaxed and meaningful. For reasons of energy efficiency and environmental health, air travel is infrequent and reserved largely for emergencies and high-level diplomatic exchange.

Most interregional communication is electronic and all individuals have ready access to electronic communications facilities through which they can interact almost without cost with other people and cultures anywhere on the globe. Easily accessible and high-quality videoconferencing virtually eliminates the need for long-distance travel to meetings.

Although the nine system design elements necessarily result in people's developing strong roots in communities of place, the electronic networks intensify communications among people beyond family, community, regions, and nations, for exchange of friendship, technology, literature, experience, ideas, and political initiatives. The combination of strengthened local autonomy and open communication supports substantial cultural diversity and differentiation, a well-developed appreciation of the ways in which such diversity enriches the whole, and a sense of common interest and destiny. It also creates the values, social structures,

Place-Based Versus Cybercommunities

Communities of place are the foundation of a living society. There are those who maintain that in the age of computer communication, communities of place are outdated and properly replaced with "communities" of cyberspace. Such thinking reveals a lack of recognition that we are living beings and our healthy function depends on our participation in a biocommunity, which by its nature is necessarily place-based.

Cybercommunities are electronic networks that in their more serious roles may function as emotional, political, and technology support groups. Communities of place comprise the people who share a place of living and whose destinies are thereby inextricably intertwined by the concerns and issues this involves. In a functioning community of places people come to depend on one another for their daily needs in a way that is not possible in a cybercommunity that knows no place, affords no physical contact, and includes none of the resources necessary to sustain life.

The networks of cyberspace can be an important adjunct to communities of place as a counter to tendencies toward isolation and xenophobia, and for that reason they are included as a design element in our model. On the other hand, a life confined to cyberspace is a life without roots, human touch, responsibility, mutual dependence, place, or permanence. When large numbers of people find their most satisfying sources of human connection are mediated by electrons through cyberspace with others with whom they have never sat together to break bread and for whom they have no enduring responsibilities, it is a sign of a serious social dysfunction. Like money, electronic communication is a powerful and useful tool but only so long as we use it as a tool—not as a substitute for the sustaining bonds of living relationships.

and technologies that support the emergence of a self-directing planetary intelligence.

DESIGN ELEMENT 9: WILD SPACES

The use of physical space honors the needs of other living creatures for wild spaces in which nonhuman life may flourish in its own way with minimal disturbance. Core wilderness areas are separated from core human populations by buffer zones of greenbelts and ecologically significant open spaces, intensive mixed-cropping organic agriculture, and sustainably managed forests, so that human communities merge seamlessly with surrounding natural communities. Wild spaces are connected by wildlife corridors that facilitate natural evolutionary processes, with appropriate mitigation measures taken where transportation corridors between settled patches cross wildlife corridors.[12]

The first reaction of those of us conditioned to the glitz, excitement, wanderlust, and gee-whiz technological distractions of the modern consumer society might well be that this sounds a bit dull. The point of these nine design elements is to define a system of living relationships that work to support a decent and environmentally sustainable living for the human population of a crowded and resource-scarce world.

Some of the hard-edged excitement of our current system would indeed give way to the benefits of living in a society that functions by the principles of democracy and a market economy; affords substantial economic security to all without extremes of wealth and poverty; has clean air, pure water, and abundant vegetation; is made up of caring communities with little crime or violence; moves at a slower pace, affording ample time and opportunity for recreation, sports, culture, and intellectual development; has strong families that function within a larger community support system with plenty of safe spaces for children to play with caring but unobtrusive adult supervision; offers interesting and meaningful work for all who need it and ready access to natural settings; and is a society of owners rather than day laborers. These are all outcomes that we might expect to be associated with a society that honors these nine design elements.

In reviewing these elements we begin to sense how decisions regarding our economic relationships are related to other choices, such as to whether we wish to

- Preserve or eliminate cultural and genetic diversity;

- Give priority to meeting the needs of the many or producing luxuries for the wealthy few;

- Make useful technologies freely available to all who can benefit from them, or restrict their use to those willing and able to pay royalties determined by corporate owners;

- Assure a meaningful and democratic role for individual citizens in economic and political governance, or give over the responsibility for shaping our future to a small global elite; and

- Link ownership rights to the communities of place that bear the consequences of their exercise, or create a system of absentee ownership that separates owners from the public consequences of their decisions.

You will also note that this framework for a living society is based on the principles of a market economy, a point that will be taken up more fully in Chapter 8. As I have already discussed in Chapter 2, the market economy and the capitalist economy define the ends of a continuum from service to life to the service of money. One is self-organizing and roots power in people, place, and community in order that life may flourish. The other is centrally planned and managed by corporate institutions to profit from colonizing living systems and extracting their embodied energy reserves. The challenge ahead is to move ourselves to the healthy end of this continuum.

In responding to the siren call of money we have created a global capitalist economy elegantly designed to serve money's needs and interests—and have sacrificed life in the process. In heeding life's call, we face the task of creating a post-corporate world designed with equal elegance to serve the needs and interests of the whole of life. To do so we must shift power from money to people through a change in our values and the reform of our public policies and institutions.

This chapter has sketched the broad outlines of an economic vision grounded in life's ancient wisdom. We now turn to Part III, Envisioning a Post-Corporate World, in which we will give practical definition to that vision.

Envisioning a Post-Corporate World

Chapter 7

Responsible Freedom

I slept and dreamt that life was joy.
I awoke and saw that life was service.
I acted and behold, service was joy.
　　　　—RABINDRANATH TAGORE[1]

Living systems evolve in complexity, flexibility, and intelligence
through interaction with each other. These interactions require
openness and vulnerability in order to process the flow-through of
energy and information. They bring into play new responses and
new possibilities not previously present, increasing the capacity to
effect change.
　　　　—JOANNA MACY[2]

WE HUMANS ARE THE ULTIMATE choice-making organisms, for far more than any other of life's creatures we have the ability to create a future of our conscious choosing. This freedom is both our blessing and our curse, however, as it means we bear the burden of responsibility to make our choices wisely. Capitalism's beguiling promise of freedom and prosperity *without* the commensurate burden of responsibility is perhaps the primary source of its deadly attraction. Hear this verse from its seductive song:

> We need only embrace the way of the free market and by the magic of the market's invisible hand our most self-aggrandizing behaviors will inexorably be translated into good works that contribute to the creation of just, prosperous, and harmonious societies. For this reason greed and the

competitive striving for self-advancement are in fact noble instincts, and we best serve humanity by giving ourselves over to them.

Through costly experience we are learning that the term *free market* is a code word for giving capitalism a free hand to colonize the living resources of the planet for short-term financial gain at the expense of human freedom, prosperity, and even of the market itself.

As we awaken to life and embark on the path to a post-corporate world, we come face-to-face with one of the most fundamental of life's lessons: we gain freedom only as we accept responsibility for using it with mindfulness of the needs of the whole. In the living world it is the cancerous cell that seeks freedom without responsibility, and its freedom is ultimately self-limiting. True freedom in either economic or political life comes only with mindful responsibility.

Mindful Choice

The quality of mindfulness plays a critical—even inescapable—role in the choices made by free men and women. Most of us know or have known individuals who seem unusually mindful in their thought and action. Neither self-effacing nor self-aggrandizing and often described as *centered,* they know their own needs and are comfortable with their own being. They are deeply mindful of their relationship and responsibility to the whole of life and society. Their thoughts and actions seem to flow from that awareness and reflect a balancing of their individual needs with the needs of the whole—much as the healthy cell balances its needs with those of the organism of which it is a part. Functioning in an advanced state of self–whole awareness, such individuals are relatively free of compulsions and illusions. In the words of Zen master Thich Nhat Hanh, "When you live in awareness, you also remain in control of yourself. Though your windows are open on the world, you are not compelled by it."[3]

Those who live in awareness have an inner freedom that transcends the limitations of their institutional setting. Their capacity to act with a critical consciousness renders them largely immune to the manipulations of propaganda, advertising, and the material incentives of money-world institutions. They have an inner freedom difficult for even the most tyrannical institution to suppress. They thereby acquire the power to change that which is not right with the world.

Others seem driven by their compulsions—to shop, to follow the latest fashions, to accumulate money and power, to adhere rigidly to political or religious dogma. They seem trapped by their obsessions and constrained in their freedom regardless of the state of their financial wealth or the democratic guarantees of the political system under which they live.

We are all mindful in some respects and compulsively unconscious in others. Both potentials lie within us. Although life draws us toward mindfulness and money draws us toward compulsion, it falls to each of us to decide which of our possible natures we will nurture.

It is a choice with far-reaching implications. By choosing mindfulness for ourselves, we more readily see the capacity for mindfulness in others and allow them to recognize more easily that capacity within themselves. The more of us who make that choice, the easier it becomes to place our faith as a society in institutions that honor and nurture the capacity for mindful action in the interests of both self and society. Thus, the first step toward re-creating society is a personal choice to awaken to the positive potential within.

Aristotle and the Ideal of Civic Consciousness

The ideal of a society grounded in the self-discipline of conscious living has deep historical roots in both Eastern and Western traditions. It was embedded in Chinese culture and philosophy for many centuries before its revival and revitalization by Confucius (551–479 B.C.). The distorted interpretations of modern Asian autocrats and the intrusion of Western capitalism notwithstanding, the ideal of conscious living continues to this day as a deeply valued cultural ideal throughout much of Asia.

In Western societies this ideal goes back at least to the early Greek philosophers who sought to define what distinguishes the just and noble society from a lawless state of nature. Aristotle (384–322 B.C.) articulated it in his conception of a *politike koinonia* (political society/community), later translated into Latin as *societas civilis,* or a civil society.

For Aristotle, the civil society is an ethical-political community of free and equal citizens who by mutual consent agree to live under a system of law that expresses the norms and values they share. The law thus becomes a codification of the values and practices of the shared culture and is largely self-enforcing.[4]

The requirement for coercive intervention by the state to maintain order is minimized because the coherence of the society is achieved primarily through self-organizing processes that maximize the freedom of the individual in return for voluntary self-restraint in the interests of the whole. Civic participation is driven not by the quest to increase individual advantage but rather by a desire to be a responsible contributor to the life of the community, much as the healthy cell seeks to be a responsible contributor to the healthy function of the body.

It is worth noting that in its classical meaning the term civil society referred to a type of society, a *civil* or *civilized* society, in contrast to its contemporary usage, which refers merely to the sector that is neither government nor business and led by not-for-profit institutions. To the contrary, Aristotle viewed the legitimate state not as an institution apart from the civil society but as an entity created through a union of society's members for the purpose of securing the good life—the happiness of the individual. The civil state is therefore inseparable from the union of citizens that creates it.[5] He further believed that individual happiness depends on three types of goods—"external goods, goods of the body, and goods of the soul"—and was quite explicit that good character is as central to the good life as material possessions,

> For no one would maintain that he is happy who has not in him a particle of courage or temperance or justice or practical wisdom, who is afraid of every insect which flutters past him, and will commit any crime, however great, in order to gratify his lust for meat or drink, who will sacrifice his dearest friend for the sake of half a farthing, and is as feeble and false in mind as a child or a madman.[6]

The ruthless pursuit of personal material advantage that modern economists consider normal, Aristotle would have judged pathological and destructive of both self and the civility of society.

The quality of character of the citizen was clearly of great concern to Aristotle, and he believed that this quality is shaped in part by the social circumstances of the individual. He strongly favored a middle-class society in the belief that most social evils result from extremes of wealth and poverty.

> The middle class is least likely to shrink from rule, or to be overambitious for it, both of which are injuries to the state. . . . Great then is the

good fortune of a state in which the citizens have a moderate and sufficient property.[7]

Aristotle's political philosophy stands in stark contrast to that of Thomas Hobbes, who followed him by nearly two thousand years. Each was a product of his time and historical circumstances. Aristotle was a product of the early Greek city-states, which though deeply flawed by their practice of slavery, provide some of the earliest recorded human experiments with democracy. Hobbes lived in Britain in the age of powerful absolute monarchs, empire, and mercantilism. Like Aristotle, Hobbes was concerned with defining the necessary features of a civilized society. The two philosophers, however, proceeded from wholly different assumptions about the basic nature of reality and its possibilities.

For Aristotle, life was a defining reality, a manifestation of the divine thought he believed to be the prime mover of creation. It followed in his view that humanity, as a creation of the divine, must have an inherent capacity for goodness and wisdom. Freedom and self-rule not only were possible but were essential defining principles of a civilized society. In this he was clearly in tune with the life attractor and presumed that we have the potential to achieve social coherence through self-organizing processes grounded in individual responsibility.

For Hobbes, a dead and disintegrating universe was the defining reality. Life—the accidental creation of a mindless machine—could aspire to no higher purpose than survival, reproduction, and material gratification. Only naive romanticists could be expected to restrain their pursuit of individual advantage for some illusory larger good. Thus, for Hobbes, all that stood between man and the chaos of the wild state of nature was the coerced order imposed by a strong monarch.

Liberalism's Challenge to Monarchy

By the late 1700s, Europe's expanding capitalist class was growing weary of incompetent monarchs. Successful merchants, manufacturers, and bankers were increasingly resentful of their exclusion from political privilege. They particularly resented the chartered monopolies that barred all but the crown's favored clients from entering the more lucrative areas of commerce.

These frustrations created a substantial constituency for the ideas of a number of seventeenth- and eighteenth-century European political philosophers and economists who articulated a philosophy of *economic liberalism,* which called for limiting the powers of the state and freeing the invisible hand of the market. The market, they argued, would order the self-interested behaviors of individuals toward a larger common good more efficiently than the state—and would do so without the coercive intervention of corrupt officials. These liberals did not necessarily differ with Hobbes in his basic view of the human condition, though few were so extreme—they simply pointed out the possibility of a less arbitrary and coercive approach to channeling human motivation constructively. As the Hobbesian solution appealed to the monarch, the market solution appealed to the frustrated capitalist classes.[8]

The term *liberalism,* much like the term civil society, has taken on new meanings over time, some of which vary by country. In current usage—especially in the United States—liberals are people who believe government has a necessary and consequential role in restraining market excesses and addressing social and environmental needs that markets neglect. Yet, a *neoliberal*—a term more commonly used outside the United States—is a person who, in the name of the free market, advocates downsizing and privatizing governmental functions, deregulating markets, and removing economic borders to give the forces of capitalism free reign.

For a brief time following World War II, the moderate middle ground in which big government, big business, and big labor shared power—variously known as social democracy, the mixed economy, or democratic pluralism—triumphed over the extremes of communist and capitalist ideologies to build a strong middle class in the United States and Europe. Since the late 1970s, however, the social contract underlying this power sharing has been steadily eroded as capitalism, with the support of U.S. economic and military might, has established the worldwide hegemony of big business. The broader public, which finds its freedom, democracy, and hope for a decent life slipping away, is only now awakening to the extent to which that experience is linked to this shift in power.

So who are the real liberals—the defenders of strong government or the free marketeers? The answer is that *both* are liberals in the classic sense that they share a distaste for monarchy, an avowed commitment to individual rights and freedoms, and a belief in the importance of private ownership and markets. Thus, in our postmonarchy world most everyone is a liberal of one sort or another. The real distinction is between *economic liberals,* who advocate markets as the primary mechanism for setting and implementing society's priorities, and *political liberals,* who believe that government has an important role in regulating markets and supplementing their functions with properly administered government programs and services.

Generally, political liberals focus their concern on the political rights and freedoms of the individual living person and advocate the egalitarian and populist principle of one person, one vote. Economic liberals, in contrast, place greater emphasis on property rights and market freedom—in effect advocating a more elitist ideal of one dollar, one vote. Political liberals tend to look to the state as the primary vehicle for expressing the public will and setting economic priorities. Economic liberals prefer to assign these functions exclusively to the market. Although political liberals believe that the public good requires that some property and services be owned in common, economic liberals favor privatizing almost all common property and public services. Viewing government as an essential civilizing institution, the political liberal's response to state power is not so much to weaken or abolish it as to put in place mechanisms intended to assure its democratic accountability. Economic liberals are more likely to distrust state power and seek to weaken the state in nearly all its roles except that of protecting property rights and enforcing contracts.

In the trade-off between maintaining equity and providing economic incentives, political liberals give substantial importance to equity as an essential mark of a healthy society, whereas economic liberals give more weight to the importance of economic incentives. Political liberals are more attuned to the market's potentials to extract unearned profits through the exploitation of people and nature; economic liberals are more likely to believe that in a market economy a person's wealth is an accurate measure of his contribution to society and therefore, whether large or small, is no more nor less than what he deserves.

Political liberals are prone to be overly trustful of government as caretaker and benefactor—while neglecting its authoritarian tendencies, its patterns of lethargy and inefficiency, and the inclination of professional politicians to use their control of state power to insulate themselves from public accountability. These propensities found extreme expression during the twentieth century in the decidedly uncivil communist state.

Economic liberals are similarly prone to be overly trustful of unregulated markets and corporations as arbiters of the public good—neglecting the market's bias toward the wealthy and its tendency to transmogrify into an antimarket capitalism in which powerful corporations suppress competition, externalize their costs, and create an alliance with the state in support of the global extension of corporate empires. These propensities found their extreme expression during the twentieth century in the decidedly uncivil fascist state.[9]

As we look to the future it is important that we be mindful of both the historic successes and failures of liberalism in its contrasting political and economic manifestations. Especially notable among its accomplishments is its historic defeat of monarchy and its contribution to awakening us to the dream of a world of freedom for all.

Political liberalism invented the institutions of representative democracy and established the principle that the state is properly responsible for the well-being of the whole. Economic liberalism's belief in the potentials of self-organizing systems that minimize the need for hierarchy remains one of the most truly revolutionary ideas of our time.

Once liberalism defeated classical monarchy, the ideological competition between political liberalism and economic liberalism came to define the major political struggles of the twentieth century. Each has claimed for itself the mantle of freedom and democracy, which each in its more extreme manifestations—communism on the left and fascism on the right—systematically denies. Liberalism, whether of the political or economic variety, has thus failed to eliminate oppressive institutional hierarchy, elite rule, majority exclusion, and suppression of the self-organizing potentials of living communities. For all its positive contributions, the stark reality is that the liberal quest has replaced monarchy with often equally oppressive and unaccountable corporations and nation-states—a consequence of the failure of both political and economic liberals to come to terms with the deep truth that there can be no freedom without individual responsibility. The capacity for civic responsibility is innate to life, and we can choose to create societies that nurture and honor it.

Freedom's Paradox

Freedom is both precious and elusive precisely because it stands in a region between order and chaos. There can be no freedom in the absence of a coherent ordered social system, and yet there is no freedom if that order is rigid and coerced. This is freedom's paradox: it exists in a region in which order and chaos come into a special kind of balance. A key idea in our growing understanding of self-organizing systems, this is referred to by systems modeler Christopher Langton as the *edge of chaos.*

> [It is a place where the system's components] never quite lock into place, and yet never quite dissolve into turbulence, either. The edge of chaos is where new ideas and innovative genotypes are forever nibbling away at the edges of the status quo, and where life has enough stability to sustain itself and enough creativity to deserve the name of life. The edge of chaos is where centuries of slavery and segregation suddenly give way to the civil rights movement of the 1950s and 1960s; where seventy years of Soviet communism suddenly give way to political turmoil and ferment; where eons of evolutionary stability suddenly give way to wholesale species transformation.[10]

Phase transitions between order and chaos are common phenomena in nature, as when an increase in heat causes water molecules in the ordered state of ice crystals to pass to the unordered state of a liquid. Some phase transitions, such as water's transition from ice to liquid, are quite abrupt. Others, such as the transition of most metals from a solid to a liquid state, are more gradual. This in-between state—neither solid nor liquid—is fundamental to the art of the blacksmith or the glass blower. In its ordered state the metal or glass is rigid. In its totally liquid form it is unable to hold a useful shape. In between it is malleable and can be worked in wonderfully useful and artistic ways. While nonliving matter may pass in and out of the region of freedom as it moves between order and chaos, living matter exists exclusively in this region.

Liberalism has generally sought to achieve human freedom within the constraints of a Hobbesian worldview, which has precluded its embrace of the ennobling Aristotelean ideal of a civil society. There is no reason for us to remain so constrained. If the most simple single-celled life forms could learn to cooperate to maintain the coherence of the whole, then surely we who consider ourselves the most highly evolved species on the planet might do at least as well. It is within our means to create a conscious civilization comprising politically and spiritually self-aware civil societies in which each citizen is called to participate actively in the definition and creation of a public good—much as the body's individual cells participate in creating a healthy whole.

Wholeness and coherence in one's own life and relationships are essential foundations of both individual freedom and the coherence of society. These are in turn a product of the loving relationships that nurture our individual and collective capacities for civility. Those who experience an abundance of love in their lives rarely seek solace in compulsive, exclusionary personal acquisition. That which is sufficient to one's needs brings a fulfilling sense of nature's abundance and compassion. A world of love thus becomes a world of material abundance, peace, and freedom. When we are spiritually whole and experience the caring support of community, thrift and concern for the well-being of the whole become natural parts of a full and disciplined life. One of our greatest challenges is to re-create caring communities that nurture our wholeness.

To the psychologically and socially mature individual, freedom is neither license to self-indulge nor permission to pursue personal advantage in disregard for the well-being of the whole. It is an opportunity to function freely and responsibly as a member of a coherent and fully functioning society.

Mindful living is a key to freeing ourselves from the imposed order of coercive institutions that constrain life's creative power. Developing our capacity for mindful living may, in fact, prove to be the most revolutionary act in human history. Everything else follows: the kind of work we do, how we balance our lives between paid and unpaid work, what we choose to consume, where we live, and how we participate in the life of the community of place.

It is freedom's paradox. To be truly free we must learn to practice a mindful self-restraint in the use of our freedom.

Mindfulness in the Marketplace

In *Being Peace,* Thich Nhat Hanh teaches that

> In Buddhism, the most important precept of all is to live in awareness, to know what is going on . . . not only here, but there. For instance, when you eat a piece of bread, you may choose to be aware that our farmers, in growing the wheat, use chemical poisons a little too much. Eating the bread, we are somehow co-responsible for the destruction of our ecology. . . . If we are aware of our lifestyle, our way of consuming, of looking

at things, we will know how to make peace right in the moment we are alive, the present moment. When we pick up the Sunday newspaper, for instance, we may be aware that it is a very heavy edition, maybe three or four pounds. To print such a paper, a whole forest may be needed. When we pick up the paper, we should be aware. If we are very aware, we can do something to change the course of things.[11]

A number of civic initiatives are bringing these and other kinds of mindfulness to the marketplace. They go by such names as voluntary simplicity, the Global Action Plan, The Natural Step, socially responsible investing, business codes of conduct, organic and community-supported agriculture, and holistic health. Together they are attracting millions of participants. Although each has its own distinctive focus, all have in common the feature that their participants become more mindful of their values, their place in the larger network of living relationships, and the difference between controlling and being controlled by their relationship to money. They become more aware of what is going on "not only here, but there" as well—and thereby are prepared to "do something to change the course of things."

Voluntary simplicity centers on reclaiming one's time and life energy by reducing expenditures to reduce dependence on paid employment. It helps us build our awareness of the real sources of our satisfaction. It helps those who once may have lived by the adage "Time is money" learn that "Time is life"—its real value is best measured by its contribution to the fullness of our living. We'll look further at the voluntary simplicity movement in Chapter 11.

The Global Action Plan (GAP) encourages the formation of sustainable-living support groups whose participants help one another monitor their own and their community's use of resources to increase the quality of their living while reducing their individual and collective burden on the planet. In addition to building awareness of the personal benefits of voluntary simplicity, GAP nurtures an awareness of the environmental impact of our personal consumption choices and the possibilities for bringing our own lives into balance with nature. GAP has active programs in fifteen countries and the participation of some 50,000 households and 125,000 people.[12]

While voluntary simplicity and the Global Action Plan focus primarily on individual and household action and well-being, The Natural

Step—founded in Sweden by Karl-Henrik Robèrt—starts with a scientific assessment of the nature and limits of the ecosystem and proceeds to mobilize not only individuals and households but also governmental bodies, business enterprises, and professional groups such as scientists, journalists, and teachers to help bring human activities into balance with these limits. The Natural Step starts from the whole and works back to the particular. In so doing, it increases consciousness of the whole of human relationships to the living planet. It also calls for the application of an uncompromising framework for learning to work and live in a way that produces no long-term negative impact on the environment. In addition to Sweden, where The Natural Step has become a household word, it now has affiliates in Australia, Canada, Japan, the United Kingdom, and the United States. In Sweden, more than seventy municipalities and sixty corporations such as IKEA, Electrolux, McDonald's, Sandic Hotels, and OK Petroleum have adopted The Natural Step's framework and are actively using it to change the way they do business.[13] Unlike most corporate-sponsored initiatives, such as ISO 14001, which merely create the appearance of a commitment to environmental responsibility, The Natural Step standards are tough and serious.

Socially responsible investing encourages people to pay attention to where their investment dollars are going and the values their investment choices serve. It openly rejects the prevailing Wall Street ethic that the only concern of the investor should be with balancing financial returns and risks. It says there is more to life than money and that it is both our right and responsibility to make sure our savings are not being used to advance activities that contradict our values—such as dictatorships or the manufacture and sale of tobacco and guns to children. In the United States the money invested in socially screened accounts and mutual funds rose from $62 billion in 1985 to $639 billion in 1995 to $1.185 trillion in 1997, nearly 10 percent of all money in managed accounts.[14]

In the one-year period ending March 31, 1998, ten socially screened mutual funds produced total returns of 50 percent or more, indicating that it is possible to make a statement with your investment funds without sacrificing returns.[15] I refer to it as "making a statement" for the simple reason that social investment generally involves screening out only the most egregiously irresponsible corporations. A truly responsible corporation would be one that produces and sells only safe and beneficial products, does not accept government subsidies or special tax breaks, provides secure jobs at a living wage, fully internalizes its environmental and social costs, and does not make political contributions or otherwise seek to advance legislation or policies contrary to the broader public interest. It is doubtful that any company could meet these standards and survive as a publicly traded corporation in the present global capitalist economy. If we were able to find one, it is unlikely that it would be producing shareholder returns anywhere near 50 percent, for the simple reason that it would be internalizing costs that others are passing on to the public.

This said, I am a proponent of socially responsible investing for two reasons. It makes us more conscious of where our money is going and it signals to both Wall Street and corporate management that growing numbers of investors are applying a nonfinancial values screen in assessing their performance—encouraging greater mindfulness on their part as well.

A related initiative involves socially responsible investor groups' pressing corporations to sign on to codes of corporate conduct, such as the CERES principles. Again, the constraints under which the corporation functions make it doubtful that this in itself will have consequential impact on corporate behavior. The codes do, however, encourage thoughtful people within the corporate sector to reflect on the sector's ethical responsibilities, which may lead to greater support for needed structural reforms that would give the economic advantage to responsible companies.

There are also many heartening developments in the agricultural sector. Farmers' markets, where local farmers sell their products directly to consumers, increase our awareness of who is growing our food, where, and with what methods. Buying locally produced foods also puts us back in contact with the seasons. The increasingly popular community-supported agriculture programs, in which a group of consumers get together to contract with a local farmer to buy his or her produce, also heighten such awareness.

Perhaps the largest of all these initiatives in terms of the numbers of participants is the holistic health movement, which draws people into the process of recognizing, understanding, and dealing with their bodies as living organisms embedded in a social, environmental, and spiritual context. The movement is an important contribution toward thinking of health as more than what you buy from an insurance company and raising consciousness of how our relationships with the larger web of life affect our well-being.

We see evidence at every turn of the heavy price we have paid for our pursuit of freedom without responsibility. Freedom and responsibility go hand in hand as an essential foundation of a civil society. To gain our freedom we must voluntarily limit its practice. Our capacity for mindful choice is our most powerful weapon against the pathology of capitalism, and our cultivation of that capacity is one of the more important actions we can take in the effort to create a sustainable, just, and compassionate future for all.

Necessary as it is to healthy market function, the cultivation of mindfulness is only one of the critical steps we must take toward healing our economic institutions. There is also a need for serious structural change to restore the conditions of healthy market function that encourage and reward the mindful practice of freedom with responsibility in economic life—the topic to which we now turn.

Chapter 8

Mindful Markets

If we are prepared to make an unequivocal distinction between the market economy and capitalism, might this offer us a way of avoiding that "all or nothing" which politicians are constantly putting to us, as if it were impossible to retain the market economy without giving the monopolies a free hand, or impossible to get rid of monopolies without nationalizing everything in sight?
—FERNAND BRAUDEL[1]

We are learning very fast that the belief that a free market is all it takes to have a functioning society—or even a functioning economy—is pure delusion.
—PETER DRUCKER[2]

MANY OF US have grown up with the idea that markets are the best way to organize economies. Yet our experience with the market's often devastating failures leads us to be skeptical. In truth, our experience is with a market economy in the terminal stages of a deadly capitalist cancer. We have been deeply misled by claims that the market is a license to forgo personal responsibility in favor of the unrestrained pursuit of individual greed and the wanton destruction of the weak by the strong.

The market is a sophisticated but somewhat fragile mechanism for organizing economic life so that each individual contributes to the whole while meeting his or her own needs with maximum freedom in the exercise of responsible choice. The healthy market thus encourages diversity, individual initiative and creativity, and productive effort. It can maintain these qualities, however, only so long as its participants honor the market's essential conditions and their ethical obligations to one another. Thus, the health of the market economy depends on the mindfulness of its participants.

Furthermore, as is the case in any civilized society, there must be provision for the public restraint of those who lack sufficient respect for the rights and needs of others to restrain voluntarily their personal impulses to excess. In the absence of an ethical culture and adequate public restraint the market becomes easily corrupted, with our present situation providing an extreme example.

I've become fascinated by the parallels between a healthy body and a healthy market. Recall that each cell in the living organism is a whole-part, embodying an apparent sense of both itself and the whole of which it is a part. It functions neither with the extreme individualism and wanton greed of capitalism nor with the hierarchical repression and austere self-denial of communism, both of which are deeply pathological. Rather it functions with an evident mindfulness of both self and whole to contribute to the function of a highly efficient system of extraordinary capacity. I suspect that the biocommunity provides a rather accurate metaphor for what Adam Smith had in mind when he gave birth to modern economics.

In this chapter we will look at the market as we have reason to believe Adam Smith actually envisioned it and set forth some of the necessary conditions for its healthful function. These are the conditions we must seek to create and maintain if the market is to be a life-serving alternative to capitalism.

The Whole Adam Smith

What, one may ask, does mindful responsibility have to do with Adam Smith, widely known as the advocate of the market's *invisible hand* (the idea that the market's competitive dynamic turns self-interested behavior into socially desirable outcomes)? A great deal, it turns out, for the ideologues of corporate capitalism have treated Smith much as they have treated market theory more generally, selectively choosing only those elements of his thinking that support their cause. Their characterization of his views on human motivation and morality is a case in point.

Adam Smith would surely have taken offense at being called the father of capitalism. For one thing, the term *capitalism* never appears in

The Wealth of Nations, which was first published in 1776, and didn't come into common usage until the early 1900s.[3] More important, the values of capitalism as we know it today were not Smith's values. To the contrary, his writing reveals both a considerable concern for the plight of smaller farmers, apprentices, and laborers, and a hostility toward monopolies and those who use their wealth and power in ways that harm others. Nor did he believe that people are motivated solely by self-interest or that the reckless pursuit of greed in economic affairs leads inexorably—through the intervention of the invisible hand—to a socially desirable outcome.

Smith actually wrote two very important works. *The Wealth of Nations,* for which he is best known, dealt with his views on economic life and the systems of commerce. *The Theory of Moral Sentiments* presented his views on human motivation and moral behavior. It was the latter work to which he regularly returned throughout his adult life, publishing six different editions, the first in 1759 and the last just before his death in 1790.

The very first sentence of *The Theory of Moral Sentiments* puts to rest any claim that Smith considered people capable only of acting on narrow self-interest:

> How selfish soever man may be supposed, there are evidently some principles in his nature, which interest him in the fortune of others, and render their happiness necessary to him, though he derives nothing from it except the pleasure of seeing it.[4]

Smith also believed that each individual has a responsibility to avoid harming others. He was equally clear that the state must restrain those who disregard this responsibility.

> Proper resentment for injustice attempted, or actually committed, is the only motive which, in the eyes of the impartial spectator, can justify our hurting or disturbing in any respect the happiness of our neighbour. To do so from any other motive is itself a violation of the laws of justice, which force ought to be employed either to restrain or to punish. The wisdom of every state or commonwealth endeavours, as well as it can, to employ the force of the society to restrain those who are subject to its authority, from hurting or disturbing the happiness of one another.[5]

Given the frequency of popular references to Adam Smith's "theory of the invisible hand," one might assume it is a central theme of *The*

Wealth of Nations. There is in fact only one passing mention of the invisible hand in the entire nine-hundred-page text. Smith says that the business owner "intends only his own gain, and he is in this, as in many other cases, led by an invisible hand to promote an end which was no part of his intention."[6] In this statement Smith is simply saying that when honest persons produce and sell honest products and services for the sake of their own livelihood they contribute to the wealth of the society, even though this was not their motive. Nowhere does he suggest that those who knowingly harm others in the pursuit of their personal gain also benefit society.

As I read his work, Smith likely assumed that those whose commerce benefits society are the same sorts of people who make good neighbors. It is doubtful my neighbor moved into the house next door for the purpose of improving my life, but having become my neighbor she takes care not to bring me harm and to be perceived as a good and thoughtful neighbor. I'm confident that the kind of healthy market economy we seek would have pleased the whole Adam Smith, the one who wrote both *The Theory of Moral Sentiment* and *The Wealth of Nations.* I thus dedicate my ten rules for mindful markets—necessary conditions for healthful function of a post-corporate market economy—to his name.

Adam Smith's Ten Rules for Mindful Markets

A healthy market economy relies on more than profit and market competition; it must operate in the context of both an ethical, life-affirming culture and a sound framework of public policy and regulation. It is ludicrous to presume it possible to have a good society with an economy in which the players are freed of all moral obligation beyond maximizing the bottom line. The open insistence by capitalist ideologues that the capitalist rightfully bears no responsibility for the consequences of his or her actions for the wider society is one of capitalism's more perverse aspects. They thus presume to give the most powerful among us an exception from our shared responsibility to maintain the foundation of trust that is a fundamental condition of a civilized society. It is a wholly irresponsible claim. A healthy society depends on a cultural norm of ethical behavior in all aspects of individual and public life. It also depends on the recognition that although a modest profit is an important facilitator of economic efficiency, profit is not the overriding goal of economic life.

It is equally irresponsible, however, to presume that we can structure the system of business so that corporate executives are accountable only to global finance, which pays them extravagant sums to ignore all but financial interests, and then expect these same executives to use their power mindfully in the interests of the whole of society. To heal the market we must both heal the culture and change the rules to create a system of business that honors and rewards mindful responsibility.

The following ten rules of a healthy market join together market theory and life's ancient wisdom. As the healthy market is an institution dedicated to the service of life, its rules appropriately embrace living-world values expressed in living-world language rather than the soulless language of an economics for which money is the only value and financial gain the only goal. We seek economies that are inclusive, attuned to our self-defined needs, vibrant with life, deeply satisfying to their participants, and nurturing of our social, spiritual, and intellectual growth. Bringing values back to economic life is an inescapable part of our search for life after capitalism.

Rules for Mindful Markets	
Rule 1.	Use life as the measure.
Rule 2.	Put costs on the decision maker.
Rule 3.	Favor human-scale firms and stakeholder ownership.
Rule 4.	Strive for equity.
Rule 5.	Favor full disclosure.
Rule 6.	Encourage the sharing of knowledge and technology.
Rule 7.	Seek diversity and self-reliance.
Rule 8.	Pay attention to your borders.
Rule 9.	Honor government's necessary role.
Rule 10.	Maintain an ethical culture.

The more deeply the values defined by these rules become embedded in the popular culture as the necessary and accepted standards of economic life, the less the need for obtrusive public enforcement. The more fully they are adhered to, the more likely the market is to serve its dual functions of providing for the material needs of all its participants and affording maximum opportunity for the practice of responsible freedom.

Bear in mind that these rules define conditions that distinguish the healthy and mindful market from a capitalist economy. So it should not be surprising if they appear to be politically infeasible in the current political reality of capitalism's overbearing power. Political realities can shift rather quickly, however, once people become clear about what they really want and recognize their right to claim it. We will deal with issues of feasibility and implementing steps in subsequent chapters. Our concern here is limited to outlining the necessary rules of efficient market function.

RULE 1: USE LIFE AS THE MEASURE

Life rather than money is the appropriate standard for evaluating economic choices and performance. Using money as a proxy measure of our well-being shifts our attention from life's priorities to money's priorities. We thus seek to maximize the returns to money rather than the returns to life. If we were to use life as our measure, it would lead us to ask which among a number of financially viable options will yield the highest anticipated contribution to improving our lives and the health of the planet. These, of course, become questions of values that cannot be reduced to simple numbers and therefore call for broadly participatory choice making.

Using life as the measure, the evaluation of economic performance would not be reduced to asking how much aggregate economic output has increased. Generally the best indicators of the health of human societies center on the condition of the most vulnerable among us. We might therefore ask how many more people enjoy secure and adequate diets this year over last. Since children are our most vulnerable members, their status is an especially sensitive indicator. Know the rates of infant mortality, childhood malnutrition, teenage crime, and out-of-wedlock pregnancies and you have a remarkably clear picture of a society's state of health. For natural systems, biodiversity and the size of fragile fish, bird, and frog populations are excellent indicators of the state of ecosystem health. Taking life as the measure requires developing new tools for making choices about how we will use our productive resources and for measuring market performance by its contribution to healthful living.

RULE 2: PUT COSTS ON THE DECISION MAKER

One of the market's greatest strengths is its capacity for self-organization. Whether the feedback the market provides to individual decision makers leads them to make the socially optimal choice depends on whether they bear the full costs of their decisions. Although no market allocates costs perfectly, the closer it comes the more accurate the feedback and the more likely that financial interests will coincide with the public good. An unregulated market dominated by powerful global corporations allocates very imperfectly, providing significant financial rewards for private decisions that create serious public burdens.

One approach to correct the distortions is to favor local ownership by those who have a significant personal stake in the long-range viability of the enterprise and the health of the community in which it is located. This creates a stewardship incentive to maintain the health of living resources, as owners share in the costs of environmental and social abuse. A second approach is to impose fees to offset any advantage a firm might otherwise gain from providing substandard wages and working conditions, producing defective products, or externalizing environmental costs. "Tax shift" proposals that call for reducing taxes on employment and consumption in favor of assessing fees on natural resource use and pollution fall in this category. A third approach is through regulation to set and enforce standards for a living wage, working conditions, and environmental protection. Of these, the stakeholder-owner approach is the least intrusive and the most consistent with the ideal of responsible freedom. The most intrusive and restrictive is the regulatory approach. The greater the extent to which absentee ownership is the norm, the greater the need for more intrusive governmental intervention.

RULE 3: FAVOR HUMAN-SCALE FIRMS AND STAKEHOLDER OWNERSHIP[7]

The traditional economic argument for an economy made up of small to medium-size firms centers on the idea that in a market composed of small buyers and sellers no firm or individual will be able to have a consequential influence on market price—thus maintaining pressure for efficiency and preventing any firm from capturing unearned monopoly profits. However, there are other important benefits to keeping organizations human scale—a size at which the participants can maintain living relationships based on mutual trust and caring. Such organizations tend not only to be highly productive and innovative but also to contribute to building and maintaining the social fabric of the community and provide a satisfying work life for their members. There is less need for hierarchy and bureaucratic control and greater possibility for real participation in decision making. Individual participants have more scope for exercising creativity and innovation, for developing enduring and caring relationships with fellow workers, and for bringing ethical values into the workplace. All these considerations, from the purely economic to the very human, argue for a strong policy bias in favor of the smaller firm in a mindful market.

Less widely noted is the fact that market theory, starting with Adam Smith, assumed that firms are locally owned by persons who work in them and live in the community in which they are located. They are thus full stakeholders in a way that absentee owners rarely are. This distinction is critical to both the mindful exercise of ownership rights and the firm's accountability to the life of community and place, as we shall elaborate in the next chapter.

RULE 4: STRIVE FOR EQUITY

One of the most important benefits claimed for the market is that it sets priorities based on the real preferences of consumers and thus achieves a democratic and socially efficient allocation of resources. Because one dollar equals one vote in a market economy, this claim carries a strong—but rarely stated—assumption that the dollars are distributed more or less equally. A global economy in which the majority of people live on less than $2 a day and Bill Gates increases his assets by $18 billion in a good year is going to be very responsive to Bill Gates's slightest whim and take no interest at all in even the most basic survival needs of those without money. As noted in Chapter 7, Aristotle observed more than two thousand years ago that a society without extremes of wealth and poverty is more likely to be a healthy society. He is still right.

Equity doesn't mean mandating that everyone must receive the same income. It does mean giving high priority to assuring everyone a means of livelihood adequate to human dignity and to avoiding extremes of wealth and poverty. It also means that economic rewards beyond the requirements of human dignity should be allocated in proportion to one's contribution to increasing the real wealth of society. Wealth, gift, inheritance, and progressive income taxes are important devices for continuously restoring an equity balance.

RULE 5: FAVOR FULL DISCLOSURE

To make mindful choices, people need full access to information on the quality, contents, technical specifications, production processes, and safety record of the products and services from among which they are choosing, as well as the policies and practices of the companies that produce them. Public policy should consistently side with the consumer's need to know, and it should require full disclosure of relevant information by sellers. Laws requiring factories to inform the public about their toxic releases into the air and water and requiring processed foods to carry labels with nutritional information are positive examples.

RULE 6: ENCOURAGE THE SHARING OF KNOWLEDGE AND TECHNOLOGY

One of the keys to the success of the lowly bacteria in terra-forming the earth was their ability and willingness to share freely new learning—new technical information. There is a legitimate case that those who produce beneficial innovations should have the opportunity to gain a reasonable livelihood from the product of their creative labor, but they should also be expected and encouraged to share that product with others. Ironically, the current system of intellectual property rights rarely benefits the actual inventor or innovators as it most often places the rights in the hands of a corporate entity from which the actual inventor may gain no benefit.

The desire to learn and to innovate is integral to life. Until some twenty to thirty years ago, the driving motivation behind most science was the desire to learn and to share. Academic prestige and rewards came through the publication of new knowledge for others to use, not its monopolization through patents. The idea that needed innovation will be forthcoming only to the extent that it is motivated by significant financial rewards elevates pathology to a social norm. In a healthy post-corporate society we can expect that creative expression and the joyful sharing of its products will once again be a way of life.

The point is not to eliminate intellectual property rights but rather to define them narrowly and for limited periods of time, following the basic principle that the public interest is best served by the free and open sharing of information and technology. The patenting of genetic or other living material must be strictly prohibited and no firm or individual can be allowed to violate basic market principles by acquiring monopoly rights to major areas of technology on which the well-being of society is dependent.

RULE 7: SEEK DIVERSITY AND SELF-RELIANCE

In nature, each biocommunity is responsible for its own care, self-sufficient in its own capture and use of solar energy, and master of the physical resources within its geographical boundaries. There are, of course, exchanges of information and migratory populations that enrich its life, but these are supplements to the ongoing processes of community life—not its defining core. From a systems perspective, these characteristics of the biocommunity contribute to the stability and resilience of the global ecosystem, as each entity is relatively insulated from shocks experienced by its neighboring communities. They also allow biocommunities to take different evolutionary paths, thus increasing the genetic and cultural diversity crucial to life's ongoing transcendent processes.

The model of a global system of diverse local biocommunities that function with a high degree of self-reliance in energy and materials has much to offer to human societies. It is a key to insulating local communities from the instability of the present global economy, because it makes them less vulnerable to events beyond their borders. A community engaged in the use of its own resources to meet its own needs is unlikely to have its economy devastated by a business's deciding to relocate a major factory or by financial speculators' suddenly deciding to take their money elsewhere. Nor is it likely to suffer a loss of its market because of some sudden shift in the global terms of trade.

The model is also a key to moving toward a sustainable relationship with the environment, as it requires that each community learn to live within its own environmental means, thus ending the persistent pattern of modern history whereby through colonization and unbalanced trade and foreign investment, one group manages to live beyond its own means by appropriating the resources of another. It would also give greater clarity to the cataclysmic implications of our encounter between population growth, consumption growth, and a finite natural-resource base as each nation and community faces the need to bring its consumption into balance with the limits of its resource base.

To move toward greater local self-reliance, most countries will need to implement policies that reduce their trade dependence and increase local ownership of their economies. To achieve that shift will require nullifying most existing trade agreements and negotiating new ones that protect the rights of people to set the rules of their own economies and to manage their economic relations with other countries.

RULE 8: PAY ATTENTION TO YOUR BORDERS

A preference for self-reliance does not mean closing one's borders, but it does mean managing them. Each community must have the ability to mediate exchanges at its borders with other communities to assure that these are consistent with the integrity and coherence of its internal living processes.

Recall from Chapter 2 that market theory is very clear that for trade to be beneficial to both trading partners it must be financially balanced and capital must be national. This requires that cross-border trade and capital flows be managed by each national entity. As we come to recognize the extent to which some nations have become addicted to living beyond their environmental means by appropriating the resources of others, we see that trade must be balanced not only financially but also environmentally.

RULE 9: HONOR GOVERNMENT'S NECESSARY ROLE

Although market efficiency depends on the self-restraint of an ethical culture, it also depends on clear and enforceable rules. Providing the mechanisms for the formulation of these rules by democratic consent and assuring their enforcement through legal due process are essential functions of government. Indeed, government is the necessary guardian of many of the conditions essential to efficient market function, such as maintaining public infrastructure, protecting the rights of living persons, limiting the growth of individual firms, assuring that costs are internalized and equity is maintained, providing incentives for full disclosure and sharing knowledge, and managing border relationships. We can no more afford to eliminate government's role in regulating the market than we can eliminate its role in enforcing traffic rules or laws relating to theft, rape, and murder.

The need to protect the rights and freedom of the individual from the abusive exercise of government's coercive powers is well recognized. Less recognized is the paradox that we grant government coercive powers *specifically because* they are essential to its role in protecting our rights and freedoms from those who would abuse them. The meaningful issues center not on whether governments should have coercive powers but rather on determining the extent and nature of these powers and the mechanisms by which those responsible for their exercise will be held accountable to the interests of the whole.

We are presently confronting the paradox that to restore democracy and economic health, we must reclaim and use the coercive powers of government to restrain the abuses of corporate power and ultimately to dismantle the corporation as an institution. As Paul Hawken observes in *The Ecology of Commerce,* it is big business that creates the need for big government—both to protect the public from the excesses of big business and to clean up the environmental and social messes it creates.[8] Once we have reclaimed control of our governments and returned business to human scale, we will have less need for government's intrusive restraining and correcting hand and may reduce it to more human scale as well.

RULE 10: MAINTAIN AN ETHICAL CULTURE

Concern with the development of an ethical culture is hardly a new issue for humanity. What makes it of special concern here is the extent to which the theorists of capitalist economics systematically deny both its possibility and its importance—elevating pathology to the status of a social good and teaching that altruistic behavior is naive and socially counterproductive. The culture of a post-corporate market economy must recognize the centrality of ethical behavior to both the efficient function of the market and the general health of the society. It is important that this idea become a centerpiece of economic theory and be revived as an essential subject of public, religious, and scientific education.

Moral self-restraint is an integral consequence of perceiving oneself to be part of a larger identity. A society that glorifies the exclusive pursuit of individual gain erodes this identity and undermines public trust. By contrast, the stronger the sense of a larger identity and the more mindful the dominant culture, the less the need for coercive institutions and the diversion of resources to unproductive oversight by auditors, security guards, inspectors, regulators, police, lawyers, and judges. Economic efficiency and the quality of life both increase accordingly.

The ten rules of a healthy market do not themselves define a policy agenda. Rather they provide a framework for the development of a policy agenda that seeks to create the conditions on which the mindful market depends. In the next two chapters we will focus on two major elements of this agenda: creating economic democracy and reclaiming for living persons the rights that the institutions of money have co-opted.

Chapter 9

Economic Democracy

If one concedes that financial markets largely rule the world, then all that is left for governments and central banks is to try to please these markets by pursuing the policies the bond traders demand: low inflation enforced through monetarist policies of high real interest rates and high unemployment, and policies of fiscal austerity. . . . In essence, this means abandoning the most basic principles of democracy.

—JOHN DILLON[1]

As Americans moved off the farm, they became a nation of employees rather than proprietors, becoming wage earners and modern-day sharecroppers rather than equity-empowered stakeowners. That must change.

—JEFF GATES[2]

OWNERSHIP RIGHTS have long played a major role in defining power relationships in both political and economic affairs. Our present situation is no exception. The central problem of global capitalism may be described in terms of institutional relationships that concentrate the power of ownership in the hands of an economic aristocracy that is delinked from community interests and has no accountability.

By contrast, the institutions of the mindful market must be built on a strong commitment to an economic democracy that seeks broad participation in the ownership of productive assets and the strong linkage of those ownership rights to people who live in the communities in which the assets are located. Such an arrangement is intended to accomplish two things: to protect the right of each individual to a secure and adequate means of livelihood and to encourage mindfulness in the use of economic resources by linking decision-making power to decision consequences. It thus works to secure our freedom, fulfill our material and spiritual needs, and encourage our responsibility, which is exactly what any proper system of ownership rights should do.

The point is illustrated in part by the sharply contrasting cases of two companies—Wal-Mart and Malden Mills—one exemplary of the excesses of absentee ownership and the other exemplary of the virtues of local, community-centered ownership.

Wal-Mart Versus Malden Mills

Sam Walton, who created Wal-Mart and turned it into the most powerful retail marketing organization in the United States, died in 1992 the richest man in America. His survivors now share the second-largest family fortune in the world at $48 billion, just behind Bill Gates at $51 billion. Having become the dominant force in retailing in much of the United States, Wal-Mart is now aggressively expanding its operations abroad.

Bill Quinn's book *How Wal-Mart Is Destroying America* is filled with stories and data on how Wal-Mart achieved its phenomenal success at the expense of small towns across America.[3] The retailer's basic strategy is to blanket an area with large, freestanding "box" stores at the outskirts of small towns to pull customers away from the downtown merchants. Initially, Wal-Mart gets customers and the support of the local press by advertising heavily in the area's newspapers. There is a strong emphasis on promotions that target the business of local retailers by aggressively undercutting their prices.

On average a hundred local stores will go out of business for each Wal-Mart opened, most of them family businesses that have served their communities for decades, sometimes generations. According to *Forbes* magazine, Wal-Mart's concept is clear and simple: "Discount stores in small towns and rural areas, each big enough to freeze out competition."[4] A *Fortune* magazine reporter who spent a week traveling with Sam Walton for a cover story gave this assessment, "And finally, there is the ruthless, predatory Sam, who stalks competitors—in any size, shape, or form—and finds sport in blasting them from the sky like so many quail."[5]

Although Wal-Mart claims to bring new jobs to a community, Quinn observes that because a Wal-Mart forces so many small retailers out of business, it eliminates 1.5 jobs for every job it creates. Furthermore, Wal-Mart wages are rock bottom. While it keeps the exact numbers confidential, it makes substantial use of part-time jobs to avoid paying benefits. The slightest downturn in store sales triggers layoffs. Indeed, to cut costs managers are instructed to send hourly employees home early if business is slow on a given day.

According to Quinn, once the competition is driven out and local residents have nowhere else to buy their daily necessities, Wal-Mart withdraws nearly all its local advertising and raises its prices. Some towns receive a further devastating blow when Wal-Mart later decides to open a new supercenter servicing an area formerly served by two or more of the earlier, smaller Wal-Marts. The smaller stores are closed, and the town that has already lost most of its business district then loses the Wal-Mart employment and taxes as well. Furthermore, with the local stores shuttered, people are left with no choice but to drive thirty miles or more to where the new store is located.

Now let's turn to the sharply contrasting case of Malden Mills and its owner and CEO, Aaron Feuerstein. On December 11, 1995, there was a devastating fire at the Malden Mills factory in Lawrence, Massachusetts. At the time, most textile mills in the northeastern United States had already moved to lower-cost southern states or overseas. All across the country, even highly profitable companies were laying off workers to improve their bottom lines.[6] So when Feuerstein called his workers to a meeting at the Lawrence High School gym, they expected the worst. What Feuerstein actually did that night made him a hero in Lawrence and one of the most highly respected businesspeople in America.

Feuerstein announced that he would rebuild the plant, continue to pay all employees for the next ninety days, and allow all workers to remain with the company, either getting back their old jobs once the plant was reopened or being retrained for new jobs. Furthermore, in addition to their December paycheck, each would receive a $275 Christmas bonus. He kept his promises to his workers on their pay and jobs, the plant was rebuilt to the highest standards with greater capacity than before, and it is once again doing a thriving business.

Feuerstein's humanity cost him some $15 million in wages paid to idled workers while the plant was being rebuilt. As he later told a writer for *Life* magazine, he was thinking that night, "The workers are depending upon me. The community is depending upon me. My customers are depending upon me. And my family." It was, he said, a simple decision. As *Life* summarized, "If his community, his employees, and most of all his family were watching his actions, then he had no option but to behave correctly."

Peter Jennings named him Person of the Week. Tom Brokaw called him "a saint for the '90s." President Clinton recognized him in his State of the Union Address. At every hand, the press and politicians put him forward as an example of how business could be a humane institution. The *Los Angeles Times* made him the centerpiece of a story with the header, "A New Breed of Corporation Is Emerging Whose Leaders Place Principles Before Profits."

Yes, the case demonstrates that business can be a humane institution, but the *L.A. Times* had it entirely wrong about a "new" breed of corporation. To the contrary, Malden Mills is a very *old* breed of family firm with old-fashioned community values that chose to defy the more trendy practice of putting profits before people and principle. Indeed, the *New Hampshire Business Review* noted that nearly a hundred years earlier Malden's facilities had been similarly destroyed by a devastating fire and "before the embers were cool, the mill owners called in the bricklayers, and reconstruction began. No one gave it a second thought—the mill would continue to operate and local residents would continue to be employed." In its ethical commitment, Malden Mills is most accurately characterized not as the cutting edge of global capitalism, but rather as a memory of what was simply considered the proper way to do business in a nearly forgotten past.

Most of those who embraced Feuerstein's action as a symbol of hope for a more ethical approach to business overlooked a key fact. Malden Mills is a private company, owned and managed by a family with deep roots in the community in which it is located. Furthermore, as both owner and chief executive, Feuerstein had the undisputed right to bring his personal values and loyalties to play in putting principles before profit— which he did in a major way. Such a course of action is rarely open to the CEO of a publicly traded corporation. Rather than being a hero, such a

CEO would be widely criticized for "giving away" shareholder money. Irate shareholders and fund managers would likely demand his expulsion for failing to protect shareholder interests.

Of course, combining ownership and management does not guarantee that the owner-manager will do the decent thing—as the largely family-owned and controlled Wal-Mart demonstrates. The combination, however, at least opens the possibility.

In the Wal-Mart case the problem is in part a function of the personality of an owner-manager obsessed with the bottom line. But it is also a function of size and the fact that it is an absentee owner almost everywhere it operates, with the exception of Bentonville, Arkansas. The more typical global corporation combines these features with a wide gap between owners and managers joined only by their respective financial interests. Indeed, because they hold their shares in managed investment accounts, most individual owners have no idea what companies they "own," let alone what they are doing in any given community. The only feedback on performance is financial, so that is the only thing that can be considered.

In 1993, *The Economist* estimated that the largest three hundred global corporations owned some 25 percent of the world's productive assets. This means that at least 25 percent of the assets on which the world's people and communities depend for their living are held under the most extreme form of absentee ownership delinked from concern or responsibility for their well-being. If we include the assets held by other major global corporations and take into account the rapid growth in foreign investment since 1993, the actual figure is by now probably well over 50 percent, not counting additional assets mortgaged to international banks.

In a world of want and environmental stress, this growing separation of ownership from human sensibility and accountability is not an appropriate arrangement. To have a functioning society, we must work from a living-world logic that leads us to preferences nearly the opposite of those espoused by the logic of global capitalism. A living-world logic leads us to keep size human-scale, to root ownership in the community in which real assets are located, to distribute ownership among many stakeholders, and to create strong links between the interests of owners, managers, and workers. The result is a dynamic that joins a possibility for responsibility with a high probability that it will be used.[7]

Securing the Right to Live

English philosopher John Locke is well-known for the moral defense of private property rights he articulated in *The Second Treatise of Government*, published in 1689. The defense centers on the argument that property rights secure the right of persons to a means of living created by their own labor.

Locke's argument was built on three premises. First, "God gave the world to men in common."[8] Second, "Men, being once born, have a right to their preservation, and consequently to meat and drink, and such other things as nature affords for their subsistence."[9] And third, "Every man has a property in his own person. This nobody has any right to but himself. The labour of his body, and the work of his hands, we may say, are properly his."[10]

> Everyone has the right to a standard of living adequate for the health and well-being of himself and of his family, including food, clothing, housing, and medical care and necessary social services, and the right to security in the event of unemployment, sickness, disability, widowhood, old age, or other lack of livelihood in circumstances beyond his control.
>
> —Article 25, *Universal Declaration of Human Rights of the United Nations*

Building from these three premises, Locke concluded that "As much land as a man tills, plants, improves, cultivates, and can use the product of, so much is his property. He by his labour does, as it were, enclose it from the common."[11]

Anticipating the criticism that one man's appropriation of a property might thereby deprive another of a means of living, Locke offered the following counterargument:

> Nor was this appropriation of any parcel of land, by improving it, any prejudice to any other man, since there was still enough—and as good— left; and more than the yet unprovided could use. So that, in effect, there was never the less left for others because of this enclosure for himself. For he that leaves as much as another can make use of, does as good as take nothing at all.[12]

By this logic, the right to private property is derived from the right to a means of living. The amount of the property to which one person may rightfully claim exclusive rights is limited to the amount required to produce a basic livelihood by his or her own hand and by the amount of like property available to others.

Locke then moved from the situation of pure agrarian subsistence to that of a society in which monetized exchange and industrial production had become commonplace and there was need to provide for an accumulation of capital, especially in the form of factories and equipment, beyond subsistence needs. Here he sought to rationalize the concentration of property ownership by the assumption that property rights in a monetized economy are most likely to be accumulated by clever and industrious persons who seek to realize the full productive potential of their assets. Such accumulation therefore maximizes the total wealth of society without harm to anyone and improves the well-being of all.[13] It seems, on the face of it, a sensible argument—at least until we see how it plays out in our present setting to become a defense of inequality and exclusion.

Present-day economists of the capitalist persuasion use an argument nearly identical to that of Locke to defend virtually unlimited capital concentration and inequality. In the contemporary version, the wealthy provide the investment capital that fuels economic growth to increase the total wealth of society to the benefit of all and with harm to no one. Note that the validity of the argument rests on three critical assumptions:

- The accumulated capital of the wealthy is invested in productive activity that increases useful output and thereby the total wealth of the society.

- Natural capital remains abundant relative to need so that one person's increased use of land and other resources does not deprive another of like opportunity.

- The benefits of increased useful output are widely shared.

Unfortunately, as we have seen in previous chapters, none of these assumptions currently hold up. The capital being accumulated by the rich is primarily financial and it is used to finance speculative and extractive investments that destroy living capital and future productive capacity. Natural wealth has become scarce relative to need, and its monopolization by the wealthy is actively displacing the poor and depriving them of a means of living. Finally, the benefits of economic growth are going primarily to the top 1 percent of the world population, while 80 percent suffer stagnation or absolute decline.

Property rights now support three dynamics that ultimately deprive the economically weak of any means of living whatever. They are used to exclude the poor from the land on which they might grow their own subsistence by corporations and wealthy individuals who claim land far beyond their own need for their exclusive use. They are used to eliminate and downgrade as many jobs as possible in a global economy of constantly shifting fortunes and high unemployment. They are used to justify sharp reductions in public services and safety nets on the grounds that taxing the capital-owning classes to provide services and safety nets for the poor amounts to a confiscation of their property to maintain the indolent.

Property rights continue to have an appropriate moral legitimacy when used to secure the right of all individuals as stakeholders in the assets on which they depend to produce a reasonable living for themselves and their families. They lack moral legitimacy, however, when used by those who have more than they need to exclude others from access to a basic means of living or to absolve themselves of responsibility for equitably sharing and stewarding the resources that are the common heritage of all who were born to life on this planet.

Life after capitalism depends on a fundamental rethinking and restructuring of ownership rights to move toward stakeholder ownership and human-scale enterprises.

Stakeholder Ownership

It is within the community of place that the whole range of living-world interests come together most clearly. It is also within our community of place that we experience most directly our relationship to and dependence on the living planet—the vitality of our forests and our economy, the healthfulness of our food, the quality of our air and water, and the consequences of social bonding or breakdown. It is here where we find ourselves compelled to relate to neighbors we have not chosen in search of common ground on which to balance the interests of all. It is here that the rights and powers of ownership are properly rooted.

Stakeholder ownership involves placing the rights and powers of ownership of productive assets in the hands of actual people who have more than solely a financial interest or stake in their long-term viability. Such stakeholders include workers, managers, suppliers, customers, and members of the community in which the firm's facilities are located. The basic act of transferring the rights and powers of ownership from shareholders to stakeholders changes the very nature of the enterprise from an instrument of money to an instrument of life and community.

It isn't simple. Formerly powerless stakeholders must develop the skills and the mind-set to act as responsible owners, and conflicting interests will need to be addressed. Workers will want higher wages, while customers will want lower prices. But developing new skills and self-concepts and dealing with conflicting interests, difficult as they may be, are unavoidable costs of making the institutions of any real community work. Ignoring all interests other than the financial interests of absentee owners may simplify decision making, but it is likely to leave a great many other needs unmet.

Stakeholder ownership is not a new idea. We have long experience with farmer cooperatives, credit co-ops, consumer co-ops, and worker-owned firms. Many have gained significant international recognition, as for example the Seikatsu consumer cooperatives of Japan and the Mondragon cooperatives in the Basque region of Spain. When Ben & Jerry's, the well-known, socially responsible ice cream maker in Vermont, decided to expand its capital base, the company initially limited the sale of its shares to residents of the state of Vermont, who were also its major suppliers and customers. The National Center for Employee Ownership estimates that fifteen thousand U.S. companies have some form of employee ownership plan.

Still, stakeholder ownership is no panacea and many experiments have met with significant difficulties, including that many are structured by management in such a way that the employee-owned shares are placed in a special fund controlled by management-appointed trustees who routinely vote the shares in favor of management. It is a stretch to call these employee ownership plans because the "owners" have few of the rights and powers—or for that matter the responsibilities—that ownership normally implies. They are more in the nature of company-controlled employee retirement plans limited to investing in the parent company and are likely to exacerbate the absentee mentality of management. Table 9.1 contrasts the values and relationships that tend to be associated with absentee and stakeholder ownership.

Making stakeholder ownership work requires serious commitment to the development of an active, responsible ownership culture. Although such investment is likely to have financial benefits, the more important

Table 9.1. Contrasting Forms of Ownership		
	Absentee	Stakeholder
Values	Money-centered	Life-centered
Guiding interest	Maximum profit	Secure and fulfilling livelihoods
Locus of power	Global financial markets	People and communities
Time frame	Short-term	Long-term
Accountability	Weak and distant	Strong and local
Orientation to life	Extractive	Nurturing

outcomes are not financial as much as social and spiritual—a firm that is a good place to work, is a good citizen in its community, and has economic staying power in a changing world.

The concept of stakeholder ownership set forth here is entirely different from what is commonly called *stakeholder capitalism,* which is sometimes proposed as an alternative to *shareholder capitalism.* Stakeholder capitalism embodies the idea that the responsibility of corporate management, essentially the corporate CEO, extends beyond the interests of shareholders to include the interests of workers, customers, suppliers, and members of the communities in which its facilities are located. Sometimes it includes proposals to add board members representing other stakeholder interests.

Although the concept of stakeholder capitalism enjoys considerable popular appeal, especially in Europe, it falls far short of a solution to the problems of absentee ownership, because with the present corporate structure, only the shareholder stakeholders have the legal power actually to enforce their claims on management. The gunslinging Wall Street investment houses have been using this power with a vengeance in the United States and currently have their sights set on bringing their brand of vigilante shareholder discipline to Europe and Japan. The moral authority of a few stakeholder board members carries little weight against the kind of financial power these investment brokers can bring to bear in the name of ownership rights.

There are other problems with asking a corporate CEO to be respon-sible for the often poorly articulated and conflicting interests of a broader set of stakeholders. Even if laws were rewritten to grant corporate management this kind of discretion, we have no way to hold a CEO accountable for such interests, nor do we have reason to assume that he or she would use the additional license wisely to the benefit of the whole of society. Could one really expect Wal-Mart to come into a town as a good neighbor to the small retailers who have served the community for generations? As normally defined, the idea of stakeholder capitalism has no more merit than the idea that the problems of monarchy can be solved by admonishing kings to be wise and benevolent. The solution is not to be found in the recruitment of better kings. It resides in creating a system that democratizes power and eliminates the role of the king.

Consider how dramatically different our situation would be if the assets now controlled by the world's global megacorporations were owned by human-scale enterprises owned by their workers and other significant nonfinancial stakeholders and rooted in the communities in which they operate. Those affected by the activities of these enterprises would have a clear right and opportunity to bring their interests and moral sensibilities to bear in assessing trade-offs between financial and nonfinancial goals.

It would certainly be a refreshing contrast to the present system in which the power of ownership goes to those who make virtually no contribution to the success of the firm, whereas workers who contribute their skills, muscle, and intelligence, the communities that provide infrastructure and educate the workforce, the suppliers who provide inputs and services, and the customers who provide the market have virtually no say in the decisions that affect them. It is truly bizarre that among all the many people who have a real long-term stake in the firm, we should give all the rights and privileges to those who have no more commitment to it than the gambler has to the dealer's deck of cards.

Small, Human, and Innovative

Scale is also an important issue. Meaningful participation in the exercise of ownership rights and responsibilities is easier, more effective, and leads to more satisfying work relationships in smaller, more human-scale organizations.

A 1997 survey by *Inc.* magazine and the Gallup organization found that 44 percent of persons working in small firms were "extremely satisfied" with their jobs, compared with 31 percent for medium-size and only 28 percent for large-size companies. Those who worked in small businesses were also more likely to feel that their jobs were secure and their abilities well utilized, that they had a chance to learn, and that they were fairly compensated. They were also more likely to believe in the mission of their company.[14] Not all economic activities lend themselves to small-scale operations, but if our goal is to create societies with life-centered values that work for everyone, our preference should be for the small and local whenever possible.

One of the few specifics I remember from my days as a business student in the early 1960s is the overwhelming body of evidence demonstrating that workers organized as self-managed teams with flexibility to design their own work methods are substantially more creative and productive than when organizational hierarchies impose centrally determined relationships and procedures. We studied Douglas McGregor's Theory X (authoritarian management based on the assumption that people are lazy and irresponsible) and Theory Y (participatory management based on the assumption of responsibility and creativity); Rensis Likert's concept of organizations constructed of overlapping teams (which embodied much of the contemporary concept of the holon); and the communications studies of Harold Leavitt and Alex Bavelas that demonstrated the superior problem-solving ability of groups organized as open networks. All shared a call for the end of controlling hierarchies.

An important strand of the professional literature in business organization and leadership continues along the same line. For example, Gifford Pinchot has popularized the concept of *intrapreneuring*, creating groups within a larger organization that have the freedom to innovate outside of the normal restraints of hierarchy—functioning less like corporate bureaucracies and more like fabled entrepreneurs such as Bill Hewlett, David Packard, and Steve Jobs, who created new products in their garages that spawned whole new industries.

Other greats within the organizational research and consulting field—such as Warren Bennis, Tom Peters, Peter Senge, Margaret Wheatley, Peter Block, Richard Beckhardt, Harrison Owen, and Elizabeth Pinchot—all have much the same message: hierarchy is a limited and ineffi-

The Creative Power of Networking

Development of the Linux computer operating system provides both an example of the creative power of networking and a forceful challenge to the claims of corporations, such as Microsoft, that major high-tech products like computer operating systems require the investment of millions of dollars and depend on assurances that their creators will have exclusive rights to their use and sale.

According to a National Public Radio report, Linux has millions of users. It is especially popular with high-end users on limited budgets because it allows the linking together of large numbers of relatively inexpensive personal computers into a parallel processing system with the capabilities of a supercomputer costing as much as $10 million. Such Linux-based systems were used to create many of the scenes from the movie *Titanic* and provide the computer power that we tap into when we call up one of the Web search engines on our home computers. Among its interesting features is that it carries a reverse copyright by decision of its original creator, Linus Torvalds, that prevents anyone from claiming it as their own.

Linux originated when Torvalds decided in 1991, while still a graduate student, that he wanted to create a better operating system for his personal computer than Microsoft's Windows. After creating a core system able to perform such basic things as writing data to a disk drive and retrieving it again, he made it available on the Internet, along with the raw programming instructions called the source code. He invited all who were interested to copy it, use it, and add to it—asking only that they send him copies of their improvements. To his surprise, programmers in Australia, Germany, and all over the United States took up the cause and wrote large sections of program code to be added to the system. The result is what many experts now consider to be the most sophisticated operating system available for the personal computer.

Linux, which was developed without the support or intervention of any corporation, cost virtually nothing to produce and is freely available to anyone who wants to use and improve on it. It exemplifies the kind of open process of technological innovation driven solely by the human desire to create and share that must become a hallmark of the modern mindful market economy. It also demonstrates the potential for use of the Internet to facilitate open collaborative processes of technological innovation freed from the heavy hand of the corporation and its incessant drive to monopolize knowledge.

cient mode of organization. All counsel that when given the necessary freedom, people are both responsible and innovative and will come up with far more creative products and problem solutions than they could produce when restrained by authoritarian hierarchies. All advocate greater reliance on lateral networking structures that function on the basis of shared values and information feedback.

Most organizational consultants earn their living helping corporations structure their operations to put the message of the creative power of self-organizing systems into practice. When the idea is intelligently applied it works brilliantly. The irony, however, is that most of this work is done within the context of corporations that by the nature of their legal structure remain inherently authoritarian and hierarchical. The people in the self-organizing teams of a large public corporation know full well that a new CEO can decide in an instant to fire them all and, without a moment of consultation, re-create the old hierarchy.

Human Scale on a Large Scale

If we really believe in the efficiency and innovative potentials of markets and self-organizing teams, we should give them a try—without imposing the authoritarian superstructure of the corporation as we know it. It may not be so difficult as we imagine. Take the case of a corporation that is already organized around self-managing business units or cost centers— as most already are. The transition would be fairly straightforward. Create a framework that provides incentives for the employees and other noncorporate stakeholders of each business unit—customers, suppliers, and members of the community in which the unit is located—to buy it out to function as an independent, stakeholder-owned firm.

These self-owned and -directed firms would have the option of cooperating through market-based networking structures and might even jointly own common servicing facilities. For example, an automobile rental corporation might become a system of independently owned local rental agencies that jointly own an international reservations and branding system.

In sharp contrast to the present situation, the ownership and power would thus flow from the base, from real participating owners with a stake in all aspects of their firm's operation. Equally important, no single owner would be in a position to control the whole.

Dee Hock, the founder and former CEO of Visa International, has a name for such organizations. He calls them *chaordic*—a creative melding of the words chaos and order. His two leading examples are the Internet and Visa International.[15]

The Internet started as a system for networking a few hundred computers without any central control structure. It grew to include hundreds, then thousands, then hundreds of thousands, and eventually millions of computers and organizations—still without any central control structure.

Similarly, Visa International evolved into a credit card branding and clearinghouse organization owned by and accountable to its member banks. Its operations were based on two guiding principles. First, power and governance must be equitably distributed among the members. Second, the organization must be capable of constant, self-generated change without sacrificing its essential nature and guiding principles.

Visa International is now made up of twenty-three thousand member financial institutions in more than two hundred countries and territories. Legally it is incorporated as a nonstock, for-profit membership corporation. Hock describes it as a sort of inside-out holding company, meaning that the central organization is owned by its members, in contrast to the conventional holding company, in which member companies are owned by and subordinate to the central unit. Visa International itself has a staff of three thousand people providing product and systems development, advertising, and around-the-clock operation of a global information system for clearing transactions. "Yet it cannot be bought, traded, raided, or sold, since ownership is held in the form of perpetual, non-transferrable membership rights. However, that portion of the business created by each member is owned solely by them, is reflected in their stock prices, and can be sold to any entity eligible for membership—a very broad, active market."[16] Putting aside for the moment the question of whether it is desirable to encourage people to finance purchases beyond their means at usurious interest rates, Visa International is an interesting and important example of an unconventional way of organizing large-scale economic activities in a way that anchors ownership and accountability in local stakeholders.

There are many more such examples than are generally recognized. When my wife, Fran, and I bought our new home on Bainbridge Island in Washington State, we found ourselves making frequent trips to our neighborhood Ace Hardware store. I was impressed by the selection, quality, and knowledgeable and helpful staff, but preferring to support local businesses I was troubled to be shopping at what I assumed to be a large corporate chain. I was therefore delighted when I learned that Ace is a central buying and branding unit owned by and accountable to its independently owned local hardware store members. It thus brings together the strengths of independent, locally owned community-based businesses with the advantages of central buying power—another example of a chaordic organization.

Part of the boom in small- and medium-size manufacturing around the world has been spurred by the downsizing of the megacorporations. The basic strategy of the core corporation has been to trim its own operations to the minimum required to retain control of technology, markets, brand names, and finance. All other functions, including most production activities, are contracted out to smaller firms that operate as captive suppliers. By playing suppliers off against each other, the core corporation is able to force its contractors to cut their costs to the bone, commonly by paying substandard wages and cutting corners on environmental standards and working conditions. Meanwhile, the core corporation is able to pocket more profits while presenting a public face of maintaining high environmental and employment standards in its headquarters operation.[17]

The power equation is turned on its head when groups of small producers join together to create marketing cooperatives, possibly with legal structures similar to that of Visa or Ace Hardware, through which they share technology and establish brand names, marketing, and financial clout. Ownership control, however, comes from the bottom—from local owners with a direct stake in the enterprise—rather than from the hot money world of speculative global finance.

We are only beginning to tap the possibilities for organizing economic activities with a minimum of hierarchy and central control. Indeed, one of the great challenges of our time is to learn to support the self-organizing processes of small-scale enterprise on a large scale.

The flexible manufacturing networks of the Emilia-Romagna region of Italy, centered in Bologna, have become internationally famous and are inspiring similar initiatives around the world, including in several U.S. localities.[18] One of the region's particular strengths is a world-class wood furniture manufacturing and finishing industry composed of networks of small firms supported by their producers association, CAMA. CAMA offers a variety of supporting services, such as operating a member-owned warehouse that stockpiles materials from around the world and providing member firms with buying power and inventory control that would be beyond their individual means.

Network members all have their own special skills, which are aggregated through the networks to take on larger projects and produce high-quality finished products. For example, in one instance a local architectural firm custom-designs a quality line of wood executive desks. Another firm fabricates them. Another applies a high-quality lacquer finish. Yet another finishes the desks by attaching a matching, custom-tanned leather insert in the top. Similar networks in the same region center on textiles, ceramics, metalworking, machinery, and high-fashion clothing.

In Denmark the entire industrial sector has traditionally been composed of small firms. Faced with increasingly intense competition from the rest of Europe, Danish manufacturers recently began embracing the industrial-network idea with a passion. A group of apparel firms came together to hire a designer who turned their uncoordinated product lines of shirts, pants, knitwear, and dress goods into a uniformly tailored collection aimed at the German market. Members of a consortium of small furniture makers, woodworkers, and interior designers do joint bidding on the furnishing of convention centers and other large projects.[19]

There are also advantages to be gained from networking on a very local scale. Vermont Family Forests is a network that brings together small independent woodlot owners to increase their financial returns by qualifying for certification as producers of sustainably harvested wood. By mid-1998, thirty-one landowners with a total of eight thousand acres were involved. The network includes both the landowners who grow the trees and small, local, secondary processors who turn the lumber into high-quality furniture. A key intent of the network is to cut out the brokers who collect substantial commissions for simply making a few phone calls to link growers and secondary processors.

Under the scheme being pioneered by Vermont Family Forests, a representative of the secondary processor goes directly to the woodlot to specify which standing trees the processor wants and how it wants them cut. Then a small contractor with a transportable sawmill—using high-end but small-scale technology developed in Scandinavia—is brought in to saw the logs into high-quality lumber to the secondary processor's specifications. This allows the processor to make individual pieces of valuable furniture from lumber cut from the same tree with an exact match in color and grain pattern.

The timber management plans and practices are certified as environmentally sustainable by the Forest Stewardship Council, U.S., a private nonprofit consortium working to help timber producers who meet high environmental and labor standards obtain premium prices for their products. In this instance the growers are receiving as much as 50 percent more than under conventional arrangements for the sale of their trees as compensation for their stewardship, and the secondary processors have been getting substantial cost savings and a higher-quality product—a true win-win situation that greatly strengthens local producers.[20]

In our search for lessons, much may be learned from the experience of southern countries, where perhaps the classic story is that of the Anand Milk Producers' Union in India, which became the model for the programs of India's National Dairy Development Board. Owned by a union of small milk producer cooperatives, which are in turn owned by hundreds of rural women, some owning only a single producing milk cow, it operates a large, modern dairy facility that supplies a variety of quality branded dairy products to markets throughout India.[21]

Appropriate Technology International (ATI), a rare model of how to do development right, has turned the development of small-scale enterprise networks into an art form. ATI calls it "forging new chains of enterprise" and they do it on a very large scale in sixty-one countries of Africa, Asia, and Central America. A 1996 evaluation identified 192,419 direct individual beneficiaries and estimated that from 1993 to 1996 ATI interventions had produced a total of $26 million in new or added economic benefits to participants. One key to ATI's success is concentrating on specific commodities and products—such as oilseeds, coconut, fruits and vegetables, nontimber forest products, coffee, livestock, high-value animal fiber, and fuel-efficient cookstoves—that lend themselves to small-scale production on a very large scale. Through rigorous analysis of the commodity's value chain, ATI reorganizes the system of cultivation, harvest and postharvest handling, transport, processing, distribution, and sale, so that greater value is added at the source and income is shifted upstream to the small-scale producers.[22]

All these examples underscore the basic point that large-scale needs can be met through the self-coordinated efforts of individually owned small-scale firms without subordinating them to global capital. These are all approaches to engaging in large-scale economic activity in ways that maintain human-scale size, facilitate innovation, and empower living communities by securing the means of livelihood through local ownership.

Those who mistakenly believe that the only valid market relationships are purely impersonal and profit-oriented may complain that these examples often involve relationships defined as much by bonds of affiliation and affection as by the pursuit of maximum economic advantage, thereby distorting the economic relationships. The answer to these critics is simple. Better that social relationships distort economic relations than that economic relationships be allowed to distort and destroy social relationships. A healthy market is not simply about making money. It is about meeting human needs in ways that enrich the soul and build community with reasonable economic efficiency. It is the ability of market-based and community-grounded economic enterprises to put people and life ahead of money while still maintaining a necessary level of economic efficiency that is their genius.

Locke based his argument for the sanctity of property rights on the assumption of an open frontier. Whatever the reality may have been in his day, our current reality is one of life on a spaceship. The need to secure livelihood rights based on a person's productive labor remains, but the open frontier does not. A spaceship civilization cannot long survive the distortions of a system of absentee ownership that gives control of the means of living on which the survival of billions depends to a few thousand people who act as though they were cowboys living on an open frontier.[23]

To survive on a living spaceship we must create a system of economic relationships that mimics the balance and cooperative efficiency of a healthy biological community. It must distribute rights equitably and link power to the consequences of its use. In short, we must commit ourselves to establish an economic, as well as a political, democracy. A substantial body of proven experience suggests that such systems can be built around smaller enterprises functioning as self-directing members of larger networks in ways that are efficient, flexible, and innovative and thereby secure the freedom and livelihood of the individual while nurturing mindful responsibility.

Attractive as such a vision may be, it defies the reality of global capitalism, which is taking us in the opposite direction with seemingly irresistible momentum. That, of course, is exactly the point. We must break the momentum carrying us with ever greater speed to a place we really do not want to go. To set a course to a just, sustainable, and compassionate post-corporate world we must reverse the process by which the institutions of money have acquired their rogue power and reclaim the rights, freedoms, and responsibilities that are properly ours and essential to fulfilling our promise as living beings. We now turn to that task.

Chapter 10

The Rights of Living Persons

The idea that a corporation is endowed with the rights and prerogatives of a free individual is as essential to the acceptance of corporate rule in temporal affairs as was the ideal of the divine right of kings in an earlier day.

—THURMAN ARNOLD[1]

Too many organizing campaigns accept the corporation's rules, and wrangle on corporate turf. We lobby congress for limited laws. . . . We plead with corporations to be socially responsible. . . . How much more strength, time, and hope will we invest in such dead ends?

—RICHARD GROSSMAN AND FRANK ADAMS[2]

HUMAN RIGHTS SECURE OUR FREEDOM to live fully and responsibly within life's community. We are finding, however, that as corporations have become increasingly successful in claiming these same rights for themselves, they have become increasingly assertive in denying them to living people. For example, as noted in Chapter 9, they use property rights as an instrument to deny the economically weak the most fundamental of all human rights—the right to live—by denying them the right of access to a means of living. The conflict between the person's right to a means of living and the presumed right of the corporation to the security of its property and profit is perhaps the ultimate confrontation between the natural rights of living people and the rights that the institutions of capitalism have presumed for themselves, but it is only one of many.

Supported by legions of corporate lawyers and sympathetic judges, corporations have worked through the courts to acquire ever more of the rights and freedoms that living persons gained only through long and difficult political struggle. They have in turn used the rights so acquired to extend their control over the institutions of democracy and the material, communications, and knowledge resources on which people depend to secure their living. Now, with more rights and freedoms than people, the institutions of money are well on their way to declaring themselves owners of the whole of life through the systematic effort to expand the private patenting of genetic materials.

There seems to be an ironclad relationship. The stronger the rights of corporations, the weaker the rights of persons to live fully and well with freedom, responsibility, and dignity. Thus, to restore human rights and dignity we must establish clearly the principle that human rights reside solely in living persons.

From Property Rights to the Rights of Property

In the American colonies the vote was reserved for the owners of real property—a mechanism widely favored by the landed aristocracy in the early days of democracy to confine political control to the presumably more diligent landed classes. In effect, that law connected political rights to property rather than to the person, an idea that to this day carries the seed of democracy's undoing. When a person's rights are recognized only in proportion to his or her property, it is as though rights reside in the property rather than in the person.

We have since vested the vote in *personhood* rather than *property-hood* and assumed that all is right with democracy. Meantime, in other spheres of political and economic life, the rights of property and the propertied have steadily expanded at the expense of the rights of the person. Of special significance was a decision by the U.S. Supreme Court to name the corporation, which is created by government and claimed by its shareholders as property, an honorary person entitled to the rights thereof.

In the United States the natural rights of persons are enshrined in the first ten amendments to the U.S. Constitution, known as the Bill of Rights. Indeed, the individual states approved the Constitution only once assurances were given that a Bill of Rights would be added through amendment. Each provision was thoroughly contested, publicly debated, and subject to ratification by all of the state legislatures. Since the time of ratification all other U.S. laws have been subject to the test of consistency with these constitutionally guaranteed human rights. The U.S. Constitution, however, does not use the term "human" rights. It speaks rather of the rights of persons, which most people would take to be the same thing.

In 1886, however, in the case of *Santa Clara County v. Southern Pacific Railroad,* the U.S. Supreme Court decided that a private corporation is a person and entitled to the legal rights and protections the Constitution affords to any person.[3] Because the Constitution makes no mention of corporations, it is a fairly clear case of the Court's taking it upon itself to rewrite the Constitution.

Far more remarkable, however, is that the doctrine of corporate personhood, which subsequently became a cornerstone of corporate law, was introduced in this 1886 decision without argument. According to the official case record, Supreme Court Justice Morrison Remick Waite simply pronounced before the beginning of argument in the case of *Santa Clara County v. Southern Pacific Railroad* that

> The court does not wish to hear argument on the question of whether the provision in the Fourteenth Amendment to the Constitution, which forbids a State to deny to any person within its jurisdiction the equal protection of the laws, applies to these corporations. We are all of opinion that it does.[4]

The court reporter duly entered into the summary record of the Court's findings that

> The defendant Corporations are persons within the intent of the clause in section 1 of the Fourteen [sic] Amendment to the Constitution of the United States, which forbids a State to deny to any person within its jurisdiction the equal protection of the laws.

Thus it was that a two-sentence assertion by a single judge elevated corporations to the status of persons under the law, prepared the way for the rise of global corporate rule, and thereby changed the course of history.[5]

The doctrine of corporate personhood creates an interesting legal contradiction. The corporation is owned by its shareholders and is therefore their property. If it is also a legal person, then it is a person owned by others and thus exists in a condition of slavery—a status explicitly forbidden by the Thirteenth Amendment to the Constitution. So is a corporation a person illegally held in servitude by its shareholders? Or is it a person who enjoys rights of personhood that take precedence over the presumed ownership rights of its shareholders? So far as I have been able to determine, this contradiction has not been directly addressed by the courts.

Without addressing this question directly, the courts have moved persistently, however, in the direction of expanding corporate rights and increasing the autonomy of corporate management, even from intervention by the corporation's titular owners. Corporations now enjoy unlimited life; virtual freedom of movement anywhere on the globe; control of the mass media; the ability to amass legions of lawyers and public relations specialists in support of their cause; and freedom from liability for the misdeeds of wholly owned subsidiaries. They also enjoy the presumed right to amass property and financial resources without limit; engage in any legal activity; bring liability suits against private citizens or civic organizations that challenge them; make contributions to individual candidates, political parties, and political action committees and deduct those contributions from taxable income as business expenses; withhold potentially damaging information from customers; and avoid restrictions on the advertising of harmful but legal products in the name of commercial free speech. Although their owners hold the ultimate decision-making power and the corporation is obliged to manage its affairs for the sole benefit of its owners, these owners bear no accountability for corporate misdeeds or liability beyond the loss of value of their shares. Step-by-step, largely through judge-made law, corporations have become far more powerful than ever intended by the people and governments that created them.

To Restore the Rights of the Living

Those concerned with curbing the excesses of the corporation have generally focused on one of two losing strategies. The first is to appeal to the conscience of the corporation to act more responsibly. As Robert Monks reminds us, however, in *The Emperor's Nightingale,*

> Corporations are not people; they have no conscience. Although corporate acts are carried out by individuals, even individuals with high moral standards often find themselves caught up in a corporate action that is beyond their control—or even, in some cases, their knowledge.[6]

The corporation is a legal instrument and the people of conscience who work for it are legally obligated to set aside their own values in favor of the financial interests of the institution and its shareholders.

A further barrier to corporate responsibility resides in the extent to which the existence and profitability of many corporations depend on successfully promoting harmful products and encouraging behaviors damaging to one's self and society. Could the R. J. Reynolds corporation, for example, really commit itself to discouraging anyone under twenty-one years of age from smoking, knowing this would virtually eliminate its future market for tobacco products? Could the Coca-Cola corporation decide to stop encouraging children to consume large amounts of fla-vored sugar water and encourage them to substitute clean tap water and fresh fruit juices? Could the General Motors corporation become a seri-ous advocate of urban growth boundaries and improved public trans-portation to limit dependence on the automobile?

When the Monsanto corporation announced it was divesting itself of most of its industrial chemicals production to concentrate on genetic engineering, its stock price doubled in anticipation of major increases in earnings. Can the management of the Monsanto corporation now afford to hold a new genetically engineered product off the market until it is cer-tain there is no serious possibility of harmful environmental or health consequences? In each instance, making the socially responsible choice would be equivalent to corporate suicide and surely cost the CEO his job.

The second losing strategy is to oppose corporate misdeeds cor-poration by corporation and deed by deed. The victories are costly, few, and generally only temporary because they do nothing to change the nature of the corporation or reduce its staying power. A major case in point is the legendary citizen boycott of the Nestlé corporation demanding that it stop encouraging poor mothers in Third World countries to favor bottle feeding over breast feeding—a practice responsible for untold numbers of infant deaths. To end the boycott, Nestle agreed to change its practices. Meanwhile, other infant formula producers continued similar promotions, and Nestlé itself was soon back to doing the same. On the other hand, the losses are often perma-nent, as when children die, or when citizens lose the battle to keep a Wal-Mart out of their town or to stop the clear-cut of an ancient forest by a timber corporation.

> **Restoring the Rights of the Living: Agenda Items**
>
> 1. Restore political democracy.
> 2. End the legal fiction of corporate personhood.
> 3. Establish an international agreement regulating international corporations and finance.
> 4. Eliminate corporate welfare.
> 5. Restore money's role as a medium of exchange.
> 6. Advance economic democracy.

Any initiative that raises public consciousness of corporate misdeeds makes a useful contribution and we must surely oppose corporate abuses with all the means at our disposal. However, although we may win some battles, we will continue to lose the war so long as capitalism's dysfunctional structures remain in place. To restore the rights and powers of the living we must eliminate the autonomous rights and powers of money and its institutions through a sixfold agenda aimed at restoring political democracy; ending the legal fiction of corporate personhood; establishing an international agreement regulating international corporations and finance; eliminating corporate welfare; restoring money's role as a medium of exchange; and advancing economic democracy.

Each of these six agenda items defines an important goal for citizen action. Although the agenda has universal relevance and is already being advanced by citizen initiatives in a number of countries, most of the examples I will use center on the United States. Our government and our corporations have been the major architects of the global capitalist system and hold the major levers of power. We therefore bear greater responsibility than any other country for the global crisis and for taking steps to dismantle the system that has created it.

Each agenda item defines an important initiative in its own right requiring the development of specific legislative proposals, programs of direct action, and political mobilization strategies. The purpose here is only to identify the critical focal points for citizen action aimed at transforming the existing system of economic power.

AGENDA ITEM 1: RESTORE POLITICAL DEMOCRACY

To raise the money required to wage successful campaigns, politicians must spend a large portion of their time courting favor with and tending to the interests of the biggest corporations and wealthiest investors. It has become a vicious cycle. The more the politicians bend the rules to channel an ever greater share of society's real wealth to the already rich, the more money the rich can channel to politicians to gain further advantage.

There are few issues in America on which public consensus is so clear and unanimous. Eighty-six percent of Americans believe campaign contributions influence the policies supported by public officials moderately or a great deal. Seventy-nine percent favor "putting a limit on the amount of money candidates for the U.S. House and Senate can raise and spend on their political campaigns." Eighty-one percent favor "limiting the total amount of money which business and industry can contribute to U.S. House and Senate campaigns each election." Sixty-four percent believe it would be a good idea for the federal government to provide a fixed amount of money for the election campaigns of candidates for Congress and prohibit all private contributions. And 48 percent think they are more likely to see Elvis Presley in person than to see the U.S. Congress pass real campaign finance reform.[7]

Increasingly of the opinion that political bodies have become too corrupt to reform themselves, citizens in the United States are turning to state ballot measures. In November 1996, voters in the state of Maine passed a clean-money campaign-reform initiative by a 56 to 44 percent vote after the state legislature had rejected more than forty reform proposals during the previous decade. Eleven-hundred grassroots volunteers collected more than sixty-five thousand signatures on Election Day 1995 to place the measure on the ballot. The initiative, passed in 1996, did what no state or federal legislative body had ever done—offered full public financing to candidates for state office who reject special-interest contributions and agree to campaign-spending limits. Spurred to action by the Maine initiative, Vermont's state legislature passed a similar measure by a wide majority. By mid-1998, diverse grassroots coalitions and reform-minded legislators were pursuing similar measures in fourteen other states.[8] Although state-level measures change the election rules only for state-level offices, the spreading and strengthening of these efforts sends a powerful signal to national-level politicians that the voters care.

No issue is more central to restoring the rights of living people than serious campaign finance reform. If a democracy of people based on one person, one vote is to be restored, then we must have strict limits on political giving and spending and get corporations out of the political process.

Meaningful reform will necessarily include a combination of public financing of political campaigns and provision of free television and radio time to qualified candidates as a public service obligation of those licensed to use the public airwaves, and a prohibition on any effort by a corporation to influence the outcome of an election, legislation, or referendum, or the negotiation of an international agreement or treaty.

The matter of excluding corporations from political participation merits elaboration. The authority by which a government issues a corporate charter is derived from the sovereign authority of its people. It is appropriate that those who have created the corporation determine the rules under which it will exist and function and that the corporation accept those rules or relinquish its charter and operate as an unincorporated entity. Barring the corporation from politics affirms the principle that political rights and freedoms reside in the person, not in properties or artificial legal entities.

AGENDA ITEM 2: END THE LEGAL FICTION OF CORPORATE PERSONHOOD

The legal fiction that the corporation is a natural person is a major lever by which corporations have acquired the rights they now use to deny the right of living people to a means of living. Similarly, this legal fiction is used by corporations to claim free speech rights for themselves in promoting their products without public oversight and in seeking to influence public policy, while they use a combination of speech and property rights to prohibit the exercise of the right to free speech by real people. Thus union members are barred from engaging in organizing activities on company property. Citizen activists are barred from exercising their speech rights in shopping malls. The corporations that control the mass media reserve the right to decide whose voices will and will not be heard on the public airwaves.

Step-by-step, a small number of corporations are privatizing ever more of our public spaces and reserving them solely for the exercise of their own speech rights to the exclusion of the speech rights of real persons. In these and other ways the doctrine of corporate personhood actively endangers the rights of people and presents a barrier to citizen efforts to hold corporations accountable to a larger public interest.

The time has come to launch a serious challenge against the legal fiction of corporate personhood on the principle that the natural rights of persons belong only to living persons. Although the longer-term goal is to eliminate the for-profit, publicly traded corporation as we know it, the interim objective is to restore the doctrine that a corporation enjoys only those privileges specified in its charter to facilitate the conduct of a business in the public interest and that these privileges are subject to periodic public review and withdrawal. Furthermore, the privileges extended are exclusive to the jurisdiction of the governmental entity that issued the charter and do not extend to any other jurisdiction except by the explicit action of the appropriate governmental authorities in that jurisdiction. This doctrine would place strict limits on corporate privileges, without in any way restraining or limiting the recognition and exercise of the universal rights of living persons.

There are few actions we might contemplate with comparably far-reaching positive consequences than the elimination of corporate personhood. Progress on this issue in any country would be a positive step, but it is especially important that we engage the cause in the United States, for it is here that the doctrine originated.

AGENDA ITEM 3: ESTABLISH AN INTERNATIONAL AGREE-MENT REGULATING INTERNATIONAL CORPORATIONS AND FINANCE

International trade and investment agreements such as GATT, NAFTA, APEC, and the others have become the favored venues for further extending corporate rights at the expense of democracy and the right of people to govern their own economic affairs. Created largely outside any democratic process, these agreements override democratically enacted laws protecting human and environmental interests. So deeply have our governments aligned with the interests of global capitalism that, following the Uruguay Round of the GATT negotiations that established the World Trade Organization, there was a flurry of initiatives led by the United States to put in place agreements on international investment and finance, including a Multilateral Agreement on Investment (MAI) that would preclude virtually any governmental regulation of the free international flow of speculative money and require governments to guarantee foreign investors against any losses they might incur from the subsequent introduction of environmental or health and safety regulations.[9]

A number of trade disputes between the United States and Europe brought to or resolved by the World Trade Organization (WTO) show how these agreements and institutions are used to thwart the ability of democratic governments to respond to the wishes of their citizens for responsible laws on social goals, food security, and food safety. Consider two cases in which the WTO ruled in favor of the United States and against the European Union. One was a U.S. complaint against Europeans for giving preference to bananas produced in the Caribbean over those grown in Latin America. The bananas from the Caribbean were being produced largely on small family farms and were one of the only foreign exchange earners of several small Caribbean island economies. The bananas from Latin America were being grown by U.S. agribusiness corporations—Chiquita, Dole, and Del Monte, which together control almost two-thirds of the world's banana market—on large plantations that have displaced hundreds of small farmers from their lands. The United States thus used the WTO to force Europe to end its preference for the small producers and open its markets to unrestricted access by global megacorporations. Government and company representatives maintain that political donations of $1.1 million to the Democratic Party and $1.4 million to the Republican Party by the Chiquita corporation and its chairman had no influence on the U.S. government's interest in the case.[10]

The second case involved a U.S. complaint against a European ban on the import of beef from cows treated with hormones. As the use of hormone supplements is routine in U.S. beef production, the United States complained that the ban discriminated against U.S. producers. The WTO agreed with the United States, ignoring the widespread concern in Europe that the hormones may involve health risks and a strong consumer preference to avoid eating meat from hormone-treated cows.[11] The U.S. corporations involved in the production and use of the hormones argue that such concerns are groundless and unsupported by scientific data and therefore should be disregarded—claims similar to those long made by cigarette companies regarding concerns about the dangers of tobacco smoke.

On a third issue, Europe yielded voluntarily to U.S. pressure to relax restrictions on the import of furs from the United States obtained by use of leg-hold traps, restrictions many feel were fully justified on humanitarian grounds.[12] Unresolved was a U.S. threat to bring a WTO action against France for blocking imports of genetically engineered corn on the grounds that it was simply a measure to protect French corn farmers. Here again many European consumers are concerned about the implications of genetically altered food in relation to health, ethics, and the environment, but such concerns are likely to carry little weight with the WTO unless backed by conclusive scientific findings. Even if there were no health issue, from a human interest perspective there is a strong case to be made that national governments have an obligation to both their own and the world's people to maintain food production capacity and national food security in a world likely to be threatened by severe food shortages in the near future. But there is no sympathy for such concerns in the WTO if they lead to the restriction of trade.

Managed borders are essential to the very existence of life—a principle that applies to economies as well as to cells and organisms. To create mindful markets people must be able to protect the coherence and integrity of their domestic and local economies, which is virtually impossible if their borders are wide open to foreign corporations and financial institutions they are forbidden to control. If we are to take economic democracy seriously, decisions regarding economic policies and choices must be firmly in the hands of a country's citizens.

Citizen groups have become increasingly active in opposing trade agreements that undermine the democratic rights of people. It is important that these resistance efforts continue. We must block further efforts to use trade agreements to circumvent democracy. The time has come, however, for a citizen-led initiative to demand that our governments put in place an entirely different kind of international agreement aimed at holding global corporations and finance accountable to the human interest.

This may logically begin with an international alliance of citizen groups joining to draft a prototype international agreement affirming the rights of people to set their own health, safety, employment, and environmental standards and to establish standards and mechanisms for regulating international corporations and financial flows. The document should establish mechanisms to discourage financial speculation, break up international concentrations of corporate power, and phase out the World Trade Organization, the World Bank, the International Monetary Fund, and other international agencies whose primary mission is to advance the interests of transnational capital. It should also recognize and secure the right of each individual country to set its own economic priorities and standards and determine the terms under which it will trade with others and invite others to invest in its economy. The process of drafting such an agreement should be designed to engage the broadest citizen participation and build a significant citizen political constituency demanding that our governments sign and enact the agreement as a replacement for existing corporate-sponsored trade and investment agreements.

AGENDA ITEM 4: ELIMINATE CORPORATE WELFARE

Corporate welfare is not limited to direct public subsidies and tax breaks. It includes a much wider range of externalized costs relating to such things as substandard wages and working conditions, worker health and safety, environmental damage, and dangerous and defective products. Chapter 2 noted the estimate by Ralph Estes that in the United States alone corporations annually externalize more than $2.6 trillion in costs per year, roughly five times the amount of corporate profits. The global figure may be on the order of $10.7 trillion. There is a strong case to be made that corporations provide handsome returns to their top managers and shareholders only at an extraordinary cost to the rest of society. Many would surely go out of business if required to pay their own way as market principles dictate.

An obvious starting point toward the elimination of corporate welfare is to eliminate direct public subsidies and tax breaks for corporations, because these are direct financial transfers from taxpayers to corporate managers and shareholders. The next step is to charge environmental use fees for the full public costs of natural-resource extraction and the release of pollutants into the environment. Such action would align with current tax-shift proposals that call for reducing or eliminating taxes on employment, basic incomes, and essential consumption and making up the lost income through fees for resource extraction and pollution. Such a shift from employment and consumption taxes to environmental fees would encourage employment, eliminate the most regressive sales taxes, reduce pollution and resource extraction, and encourage recycling—all highly beneficial outcomes. If the environmental fees reflect actual costs to society, it would also be a significant step toward eliminating market-distorting public subsidies.

A third step would be to establish procedures for estimating the amount of other indirect subsidies enjoyed by individual corporations and assessing a public facilities fee in that amount. The fee would recover the costs to society of corporations that fail to provide a living wage adequate to support a family, health insurance, pension contributions, and safe working conditions for their workers on the grounds that these costs are thus borne by the larger society. Similarly, it would recover the public costs of harmful and defective products such as cigarettes and unsafe automobiles. For example, cost-recovery fees would be assessed on the basis of actuarial experience with the health costs of smoking-related diseases in the case of cigarettes and accident rates and consequences in the case of automobiles.

Ideally, all countries would choose to move toward the elimination of corporate subsidies in unison. Given, however, that there is almost no prospect of this happening, it is important to establish the principle that each nation has the right to protect its own producers from predatory competition from subsidized producers by imposing compensating tariffs.

AGENDA ITEM 5: RESTORE MONEY'S ROLE AS A MEDIUM OF EXCHANGE

Money serves a useful social function as a medium of exchange. In the hands of speculators, however, it becomes an anti-democratic, anti-market instrument of instability and unjust extraction. A central goal of economic policy should be to eliminate financial speculation and restore money's primary role as a medium of exchange.

Nearly $2 trillion now changes hands in the world's currency exchange markets each day. Roughly 1 percent of that money is related to trade in real goods and services. The rest, which is largely pursuing speculative profits, creates massive international financial instability while serving little if any public purpose. The following are reforms that merit consideration.

Prohibit banks from financing speculators. As we saw in Chapter 2, the financial speculation that destabilized the Asian economies in 1997 was fueled by reckless bank lending that financed the creation of large stock and real estate bubbles. The 1998 collapse in the United States of a single highly leveraged hedge fund, Long-Term Capital Management, that made bad bets on the Russian ruble posed such a threat to the U.S. banking system that the Federal Reserve stepped in to arrange a private bailout. Long-Term Capital's gambling habit was financed with $25 in bank loans for every dollar of equity. There are an estimated 4,000 hedge funds in the world. Some have as much as $100 in loan financing for every dollar in equity. Bear in mind these bank loans represent money that banks created out of nothing and you begin to see how the enormous speculative overhang in the global money system is being created. This lending is a key source of speculative bubbles and the related financial instability that has been rocking the world.

Gambling with borrowed money is a bad idea under any circumstances. When it is done on a scale that threatens the integrity of national financial systems, there is a compelling rationale for strong public measures to eliminate it. Appropriate measures include prohibiting banks from accepting financial assets as loan collateral and from lending to hedge funds and other financial institutions for the purpose of leveraging the purchase or sale of financial securities or derivatives. Buying stocks on margin should be similarly prohibited.

Tax short-term capital gains at rates substantially higher than earned income. Giving a tax advantage to those who live from speculative gains over those who do productive work for a living is unjust and bad policy. It is appropriate to tax away virtually all gains from capital assets held less than a month as they are almost certainly speculative in nature. It is appropriate that gains from assets held for longer periods of time enjoy more favorable treatment, but in general gains from an asset held less than five years should not enjoy a tax advantage over earned income. This should be true for corporations as well as for individuals.

Encourage the use of local currencies. Money's value is based solely on a social contract—an agreement among a group of people that they will accept a particular tender in the payment of debts. A common currency not only facilitates exchange but also defines a community with a mutual interest in productive exchange among its members. The community thereby affirms its own existence and creates a natural preference for its own products. Bernard Lietaer estimates that fifteen hundred communities around the world have issued their own local currencies to facilitate local commerce.[13] The idea is not to eliminate national currencies but rather to supplement them with local currencies that necessarily stay in the community that issues them so that local workers and assets need never stand idle for a simple lack of the money to facilitate exchange.

Make the creation of national currencies a public function. A nation's money supply is created by either government's spending new money into existence or a bank's loaning it into existence. The former approach allows a government to pay for public services beyond the amount of its tax revenues. The latter generates large profits for private bankers. Though it's not generally recognized by the public, virtually all money is now loaned into existence by private banks, which means a nation's money supply and the stability of its money system depend on continuously expanding debt to create enough money to repay the old debts and avoid bankruptcy—a primary reason why capitalist economies are prone to collapse if they do not grow exponentially. Placing a 100 percent reserve requirement on demand deposits in the banking system and returning the function of creating national currencies to government would largely eliminate the federal government's need to borrow, reduce the power of the banking system, and eliminate an important source of the money world's growth imperative.[14]

Place a demurrage charge on money. Holding virtually any real asset involves a cost to the holder. Forests, factories, farmland, and buildings must be protected and maintained. Personal skills and technologies must be updated. Even holding gold involves costs for secure storage. Only those who hold money as a future claim against the wealth that others are creating and maintaining expect a secure, cost-free interest return with no effort on their part. This feature of money encourages the conversion of real wealth to money to be held in inflating financial assets, though the interests of society are best served by encouraging the creation, stewardship, and augmentation of real wealth. Money expert Bernard Lietaer suggests that the resulting distortions be corrected by charging a small demurrage fee for holding financial assets—say a quarter of a percent a month or 3 percent a year.[15] This might, for example, make it more profitable to invest in growing trees than to hold money in a bank account. Banks would continue to pay interest on savings accounts and charge interest on loans as they do now. The government, however, would levy the demurrage fee against any outstanding financial balances.

Restore the concept of community banking. At one time the United States had what is known as a *unitary banking system,* which means that each bank was individually owned and functioned as a community institution. Local savings were deposited and the money was loaned back to the community for local housing and business investment. It is appropriate to restore this concept by using antitrust rules to break up banking conglomerates and limiting federal deposit insurance to funds deposited with community banks that lend locally.

Prohibit the use of financial assets as collateral for borrowing. This would prohibit the buying of stocks and other financial instruments on margin or otherwise using financial securities as collateral for new borrowing. It would thus greatly reduce the use of borrowed money to fuel the inflation of financial bubbles.

Restrict the conversion of national and local currencies for purposes other than tourism and trade in real goods and services. Governments have not only the right but the obligation to regulate financial flows across their borders to protect national interests against speculators and other financial predators.

AGENDA ITEM 6. ADVANCE ECONOMIC DEMOCRACY

The previous elements of the agenda focus on constraining the power of global corporations and finance in order to open economic spaces within which people can create the institutions of economic democracy and a true market economy. In addition to such defensive measures, there is room for public policy to be proactive in promoting human-scale, stakeholder-owned enterprises to displace the subsidized megacorporations whose hold the earlier measures are intended to weaken.

Many such enterprises already exist in the form of family businesses, cooperatives, community-owned businesses, worker-owned enterprises, and others.[16] New ones are being formed each day. Here the need is to acknowledge the central role of these enterprises as the foundation of the new economy and expand the spaces in which they can flourish as the corporate superstructure is cleared away.

We can also salvage much from existing corporate structures by breaking down megacorporations into human-scale, stakeholder-owned firms. The measures already suggested, such as getting corporations out of politics, restoring the integrity of national economic borders, and eliminating corporate welfare, will likely make most megacorporations unprofitable and thereby increase the receptivity of their managers and shareholders to selling off their component businesses to stakeholders at appropriately depreciated prices.

Measures to support stakeholder ownership might include requiring that before a major corporation is allowed to close a plant or undertake a sale or merger of significant assets, the affected workers and community must be given first option to buy out the assets on preferential terms. There might be preferential tax treatment for shareholders who sell their shares to stakeholders under an organized stakeholder buyout program. Similarly, relief on estate taxes might be used to encourage the conversion of larger family-owned corporations to stakeholder ownership on the death of their founders. Procedures could be established for converting worker pension funds into meaningful worker ownership programs. Banks might be given incentives to provide loans on preferential terms to finance stakeholder buyouts. Financing might also be mobilized by what Jeff Gates calls a user fee on personal financial accumulations in excess of $10 million "for the privilege of utilizing the nation's private property tradition as a vehicle for accumulating assets totally disproportionate to any conceivable notion of need."[17] This would be a wealth redistribution initiative addressed directly to the need to redistribute asset ownership.

Efforts to move toward stakeholder ownership must take into account the history of worker ownership schemes that have not led to meaningful worker participation and empowerment. As noted in Chapter 9, many employee stock ownership plans (ESOPs) in the United States place the control of employee shares in the hands of management. The result is a perversion of the concept of stakeholder ownership that gives the titular stakeholder owner less power and say in management than an ordinary absentee owner. Our goal should be exactly the opposite—a much larger and more meaningful role in management by stakeholder owners than by absentee owners.

There is need to reform the legal framework and mechanisms of ESOPs to enable and encourage ESOP owners to engage in real ownership participation. Consideration might also be given to expanding existing employee ownership plans to facilitate broader participation by other nonfinancial stakeholders. Significant investment will be needed in educational programs designed to prepare workers and other stakeholders for meaningful and responsible participation. An imaginative and reinvigorated labor union movement could take the lead in advancing stakeholder ownership and providing educational support as part of an agenda to secure the rights of working people and create people-friendly working environments.

It will be appropriate to supplement these initiatives in support of stakeholder ownership with the rigorous application of antitrust legislation revamped to establish the presumption that smaller is better until proven otherwise. Thus, mergers and acquisitions would be approved only in those rare instances in which their proponents make a compelling case that the combination would significantly advance the public interest. Any firm with more than a 10 percent share in a major market might be required every five years to make a compelling case in a public regulatory hearing as to why it would not be in the public interest to break it up into more human-scale stakeholder-owned firms.

The proposed sixfold agenda attacks the foundation of unaccountable financial and corporate power and opens the way to a radical redistribution of economic wealth and power by returning human rights to living persons. Although the agenda is based on solid, conservative principles of individual responsibility and local control, it does require a frontal assault on the institutional and intellectual underpinnings of our present system of elite privilege. One might for that reason expect a massive backlash against such ideas from within the establishment. But although such a backlash must be expected, the unanimity of the present power holders should not be assumed. There is evidence of deep and growing concern among thoughtful corporate leaders, bankers, and even economists, that they may be sitting atop an increasingly unstable system on the brink of collapse.

Cracks in the Elite Consensus

For a time it seemed the world's financial and industrial elites had forged a near-seamless consensus affirming the righteousness of greed and the unregulated global market. The egregious consequences, however, have become so evident that alarms are being sounded even by some of the system's biggest winners and most dedicated defenders. Two prime examples from among the class of capitalist billionaires are Sir James Goldsmith and George Soros. Before his death, Goldsmith, a corporate raider who specialized in the buyout of timber companies and the pillage of their forest assets, began funding environmental groups and published a book called *The Trap,* which became a best-seller in Europe, on the environmental and social devastation wrought by the global economy.[18]

George Soros, the world's most famous financial speculator, startled the world with his article entitled "The Capitalist Threat" in the January 1997 issue of *The Atlantic Monthly* in which he denounced the self-destructive ideological rigidity of capitalism and labeled it a threat to the open society. Soros has since drawn attention to the inherent instability of global financial markets and the need for their effective regulation.

Another unlikely critique appeared as an op-ed article in the February 1, 1996, *International Herald Tribune* titled "Start Taking the Backlash Against Globalization Seriously." It was authored by Klaus Schwab and Claude Smadja, founder-president and managing director, respectively, of the World Economic Forum, an association of the world's one thousand largest transnational corporations. It made the following points:

- Globalization is causing severe economic dislocation and social instability.

- Although conventional wisdom says that technological change and increases in productivity translate into more jobs and higher wages, in the last few years technology has eliminated more jobs than it has created.

- Globalization leads to "winner-take-all situations; those who come out on top win big, and the losers lose even bigger."

- "Globalization tends to delink the fate of the corporation from the fate of its employees." Higher profits no longer mean more job security and better wages.

Schwab and Smadja went on to warn that "unless serious corrective action is taken soon, the backlash could turn into open political revolt that could destabilize the Western democracies."[19] Their recommendations— which centered on increasing public subsidies to the corporate sector in the form of education, training, telecommunications, and physical infrastructure—unfortunately fell far short of their analysis, but it is difficult to fault their statement of the problem.

Even more pointed in its critique and far less circumspect in its recommendations was the 150-page report released in the fall of 1996 by the Centre des Jeunes Dirigeants d'Entreprise, a twenty-three-hundred member French association of young company directors and executives. In the words of the report, "We are convinced that nonregulated capitalism will explode as communism exploded, unless we seize the opportunity to put man at the heart of our society. . . . The greatest misery in our society is social and spiritual rather than material. . . . What is needed is a fundamental rethinking about the way work and society are organized."[20]

The French report sets forth an unequivocally revolutionary agenda based on the premise that companies should be held accountable for their contribution to the well-being of society and for the workers they employ. Firms that harm society should be closed. Companies should raise their capital locally rather than going to stock markets and national or international banks. All income should be taxed and the proceeds used to provide a basic survival income to every citizen as a recognition of the fact that every human existence is beneficial to society. And there should be a maximum as well as a minimum wage.[21]

In March 1998, the Bellerive Foundation and GLOBE International—an international alliance of parliamentarians—hosted a conference in Geneva on "Policing the Global Economy." This unprecedented conference brought together for the first time a number of the global economy's leading power holders with a number of its leading critics for an equal and public three-day exchange. Although it neither resolved any of the critical issues nor changed the opinions of key protagonists, it substantially deepened understanding of the issues among the many influential intellectuals and politicians who attended.[22]

By late 1998, as the financial turmoil deepened and spread to the United States, the inherent instability of unregulated global financial markets was becoming so evident that even the most ardent defenders of laissez-faire capitalism were beginning to acknowledge the need for regulation by governments. As *Business Week* noted in an October 12, 1998, editorial, "Expanding government oversight is critical, too. The idea that free markets exist in a vacuum has been shattered. Without rules and regulations, they create anarchy."[23]

Even so, most of the establishment voices calling for the restructuring and regulation of global financial markets were focused primarily on priming the pump to get the speculation rolling again. They were a long way from acknowledging that most of the money movements being referred to as *international investment flows* are by nature extractive and disruptive and must be purged from the system if economic health is to be achieved.

We should have no illusions that the needed leadership to create economic democracy and a true market economy is going to come from within capitalism's economic and political establishment. It is a popular agenda that by its nature requires widespread citizen leadership to succeed. We may find, however, that there is more sympathy among the more thoughtful power holders than we might expect.

Seeds of a New Citizen-Led Politics

As we look to the formidable task ahead, we should remember that slavery was once legal in the United States, as was discrimination based on race. There was once a Roman Empire, later a Soviet Empire, a Berlin Wall, and until recently, apartheid in South Africa. Corrupt and unjust regimes have a way of falling once ordinary people decide their time has come.

In *Silent Coup: Confronting the Big Business Takeover of Canada,* Tony Clarke, a leader of Canada's growing citizen movement against corporate rule, points to the need to build a political movement that sets the end of corporate rule as one of its top priorities. Corporate rule is the megaton gorilla in the middle of the room that most discussions of political and economic failure have too long avoided mentioning. Acknowledging the gorilla is an essential step toward action.

The depth and seriousness of the massive dysfunctions of global corporations and the contemporary capitalist economy have only recently gained prominence in the public mind. Already, new initiatives are emerging that draw attention to the need for serious structural mechanisms to hold corporations accountable to the public interest. Indeed, the seeds of a new popular movement toward serious reform are emerging from across the political spectrum. A few of those centered in the United States are mentioned in the following paragraphs. They merit broad and enthusiastic public support from those who are seeking ways to participate in the creation of a post-corporate world.

The New Party, a grassroots citizen-led political party working under the banner of "A Fair Economy. A Real Democracy. A New Party," is systematically building a citizen-led politics around an agenda that centers on strengthening the rights and capacities of people to self-organize democratically in both political and economic affairs. It is racially diverse; works in alliance with labor, community, environmental, feminist, student, gay, and lesbian groups; and is built around values rather than personalities. Its strategy is to build political strength by winning local elections while concentrating on problems that can be addressed at the local level. It is taking a serious and systematic approach to building what it hopes may one day become a new majority party. As of 1997, 152 of the 231 candidates it had supported in election contests had won their races. Roughly half of New Party candidates are women and more than a third are people of color.[24]

A former corporate executive and staunch Republican who held a number of high-level appointments in the Reagan and Bush administrations, Robert Monks has for some years been organizing retirement and other investment funds to exercise their shareholder voting rights to oust and replace complacent managers who take more interest in increasing their personal compensation and entitlements than producing returns for shareholders. Now he is taking on the larger issue of the corporation's social performance. Monks believes that pension funds are the key to increasing corporate responsibility, because they serve a broad clientele with a long-term interest in the health of society as well as the health of the corporations in which their money is invested. He is thus organizing pension funds to take the lead in advancing shareholder resolutions holding corporate executives accountable to shareholders for (1) obeying the law; (2) fully disclosing in their financial reporting what they know or strongly suspect regarding the costs imposed by their firms on the function of society; and (3) minimizing their involvement in political processes.[25] These ideas are radical only in the extent to which they depart from current practice. Ideally, his proposals will become a centerpiece of the socially-responsible-investing movement.

The Politics of Meaning is a grassroots nonparty political movement with chapters in ten major U.S. cities promoting a value-oriented politics based on ideas articulated by Michael Lerner, editor and publisher of *Tikkun* magazine, and lawyer and educator Peter Gabel. It has announced two major initiatives to increase the integrity of economic life.[26] The first is a model resolution for adoption by city, county, and state governments committing them to take into account the history of social responsibility of corporations, as measured by an "Ethical Impact Report," in awarding public contracts. Its second initiative is a proposed "Social Responsibility Amendment" to the U.S. Constitution. It would require every corporation with annual revenues of $20 million or more to apply for renewal of its charter every twenty years. To secure its charter renewal, the corporation would be required to "prove that it serves the common good, gives its workers substantial power to shape their own conditions of work, and has a history of social responsibility to the communities in which it operates, sells goods, and/or advertises." Each five years the corporation would have to prepare and make public an Ethical Impact Report with one section prepared by management, another by its employees, and another representing community stakeholders.

The Alliance for Democracy is a progressive populist movement with forty-nine local chapters around the United States.[27] Following in the footsteps of the populist movement of the late 1800s, it aims to provide a vehicle for citizen action to end government-corporate collusion against the public interest and expose the antidemocratic nature of rule by global capital. The Alliance is carrying out long-term citizen education on issues of corporate governance and campaigning for legislative action to increase corporate accountability. It is considering a campaign in support of an amendment to the U.S. Constitution to establish that corporations are not persons and not entitled to the rights thereof. Related efforts center on redefining the processes and requirements for corporate chartering and charter revocation. The Alliance is also drafting a model international treaty on the responsibilities of international investors as an alternative to corporate-sponsored agreements aimed at freeing global investors from regulatory restraint.

The international NGO Taskforce on Business and Industry, under the leadership of Jeff Barber of the Integrative Strategies Forum, is a citizens' alliance that functions within the framework of the United Nations Commission on Sustainable Development.[28] It is working to counter initiatives from the corporate sector aimed at keeping issues of corporate accountability off the U.N. agenda. The Taskforce is also helping make visible within the U.N. system the consistent failure of voluntary codes of corporate conduct.

The Program on Corporations, Law, and Democracy (POCLAD), a national alliance of individuals concerned with corporate rights codirected by Richard Grossman and Ward Morehouse, is spearheading a campaign to restore the concept that corporate charters are limited and revokable and to pursue a wide range of legal initiatives intended to restrict corporate rights and increase corporate accountability.[29]

These and related initiatives too numerous to list are still new and small. Each, however, is growing in size and momentum, carried forward by the concern and commitment of citizens who are fed up with political corruption and the abuse of corporate power. The most prominent barrier to turning the widespread disgust into a powerful political movement is the lack of credible and well-articulated alternatives and of an awakening to the belief that change is possible.

Those to whom a living-world politics offers potential appeal come from all classes and segments of society: working people concerned with job security, respect, and honest pay for honest work; religious groups seeking to bring moral values back into everyday life; members of the women's movement concerned with equity and the balancing of work with family and community life; minority group members who advocate a political and economic agenda that meets the needs of all; members of environmental groups working to restore and protect the health of living systems; peace and human rights groups concerned with equity and the possibility of replacing global competition with global cooperation.

Other constituents for change include small business owners and managers struggling to survive as the backbone of community economies; the growing ranks of ecological economists who are providing intellectual leadership in challenging the hegemony of neoliberal economists; heads of business seeking to make business more responsible and humane; socially responsible investors, community bankers, community development foundation leaders; and the members of groups such as the Social Ventures Network, Business for Social Responsibility, and the World Business Academy.[30]

Then there are the downsized whom capitalism has discarded and the disaffected who remain within the corporate establishment while longing for alternatives. There are the retired executives who know the system from the inside and are deeply concerned for the future they leave their children. There are the youth who are rightly concerned about their own futures. There are the journalists concerned that the integrity of their profession suffers from concentrated corporate control of the media. There are the teachers concerned about the integrity of the educational process as corporate advertising and propaganda infiltrate the classroom. There are the farming households that are committed to stewardship of the earth and the production of healthful foods.

The goals of stakeholder ownership and individual responsibility affirm the values of conservatives. The emphasis on one person, one vote democracy and the recognition of government's clear and necessary role affirm the values of political liberals. It all adds up to a substantial and potentially unstoppable constituency behind the politics of a post-corporate world.

There is no more powerful expression of a society's values than its economic institutions. In our case, we have created an economy that values money over all else, embraces inequality as if it were a virtue, and is ruthlessly destructive of life. The tragedy is that for most of us the values of global capitalism are not our values. It is hardly surprising, therefore, that we find ourselves in psychological and social distress. We have fallen captive to stories that deny us meaning and institutions that demand we behave in ways at odds with our deepest psychological and spiritual predispositions.

We can change the institutions as well as the stories. We can become more mindful in our own living and thereby contribute to the creation of a culture of mindfulness and responsibility that is the foundation of freedom. We can join in efforts to apply the ten rules of mindful markets to create the conditions for healthy market function. We can participate in the places where we work in efforts to transform existing patterns of absentee ownership into a system of economic democracy grounded in stakeholder ownership. And we can join in political movements working to change the rules of commerce to favor the mindful market and to reclaim from the institutions of money the rights they have co-opted from living persons. Those inclined to dismiss such a hopeful vision as a futile attempt to stem the tide of history miss the point that the unfolding vision enjoys the potential support of a substantial though as yet largely latent political constituency.

Furthermore, as we shall see in Part IV, the vision is a composite of the goals and ideas that already motivate a multitude of citizen initiatives large and small around the world. Each of these initiatives makes its own contribution to telling a new story for the third millennium and gives expression to the values of millions of people who are at the leading edge of a global culture shift. Together they point toward a shift in human consciousness and its melding with the wisdom and creative power of the planet's living systems to open the way to new levels of experience and creative function beyond our present imagination. Herein lies the source of our hope for the future, and the theme of the final chapters in our search for life after capitalism.

Part IV

Coming Home to Life

Chapter 11

Culture Shift

Imagine yourself a historian looking back from some time in the next century. What do you judge the most important thing that happened for the world in the twentieth century? . . . My guess is it will be something . . . as quiet as a change of mind, a change of mind that is bubbling up out of the unconscious depths, spreading around the world, changing everything.
—WILLIS HARMAN[1]

We are now at the beginning of . . . a fundamental change of world-view in science and society, a change of paradigms as radical as the Copernican revolution.
—FRITJOF CAPRA[2]

PARTICIPATING IN THE 1992 EARTH SUMMIT in Rio de Janeiro was one of the most profound experiences of my life—an encounter on a magnificent scale with the awakening of a global civil society. It was a celebration of life opening to new possibilities and it gave me hope that together, we, the world's people, might yet reverse the trends of social and environmental breakdown that threaten our collective future.

The significance of this event, formally known as the United Nations Conference on Environment and Development (UNCED), was not found in the official meetings held in the grand and heavily guarded Rio Centro convention center. There the representatives of the world's governments and corporations were engaged in predictable maneuvering for positions of temporary advantage in the race to exploit what remains of the world's

211

resources under a banner of environmental concern. I spent little time there.

My excitement was generated by the meetings held on the other side of town in the NGO Global Forum. Here some eighteen thousand private citizens of every race, religion, social class, and nationality that share this small planet gathered in tents on a steamy stretch of beachfront to discuss deeply felt concerns relating to such matters as exclusion, inequality, cultural homogenization, loss of community, and destruction of the natural environment—and to craft agendas for change. They tackled head-on the issues of consumerism, planetary limits, abuses of corporate power, and the destructive consequences of an unregulated global marketplace, all issues the official delegations studiously avoided.

The people of the world played out the new story in many ways in Rio, including in their shared celebrations. Elisabet Sahtouris provides a poignant account:

> The image of humanity reorganizing itself from a chaotic mass to a new order was especially vivid from the sound stage of the huge concert held on Flamengo Beach under a brilliant eclipsing moon on our final night in Rio. Looking out over the vast crowd on the beach, I watched circles form spontaneously in dance, then dissolve as others formed. Lines of people appeared and wove their way through the mass; great roars of approval greeted every proposal for a better world that was broadcast from the nuclear sound stage.
>
> A giant cell was forming itself symbolically on that sandy beach, human protoplasm in motion, making order out of chaos beneath the ever-changing watchful eye of the eclipsing full moon. Beams of laser light patterned their way from nucleus to the boundaries of the great cell lying between the glittering sea and the dark trees of Flamengo Park, lighting the participants in rich patterns of color and sound.[3]

As we shared our visions of a world of diverse cultures, self-governing societies, and prosperous local economies grounded in values of simplicity, love, peace, and reverence for life, we came to realize the commonality of our aspirations. Even more striking for me was the extent to which we shared in the conclusion that we were ill-advised to look to either governments or corporations to lead us out of our collective crisis. There was an extraordinary consensus that the solutions to which these institutions are wedded are in fact the problem. We came away with a shared realization that we enter the new millennium facing the challenge of reinventing almost everything many of us have taken for granted. It is a task that will require millions of leaders from every nation, religion, class, race, and ethnic group.

There is scant mention of them in the corporate-controlled press or from politicians beholden to big money, yet these leaders are emerging at every hand. They are building new political parties and movements, deepening their spiritual practice, embracing voluntary simplicity, building networks of locally rooted businesses, certifying socially and environmentally responsible products, restoring forests and watersheds, promoting public transportation and defining urban growth boundaries, sponsoring youth programs, developing holistic health centers, directing their investments to socially responsible businesses, inoculating children against manipulation by advertisers and mass media, organizing recycling campaigns, demanding that trade agreements protect the rights of people and the environment—and engaging in countless other life-affirming acts.

They are present in every country, indeed every community, and every race, class, religion, and ethnic group. They include landless and illiterate peasants, retired executives, ranchers, teachers, artists, housewives, itinerant farm workers, small-business owners, farmers, janitors, physicians, researchers, corporate dropouts, local government officials, inner-city kids, loggers, wealthy intellectuals with fancy academic credentials, and gang leaders with criminal records. Together, worldwide, they— we—number in the hundreds of millions. Fed up with the failures of elitist leadership and distant bureaucracies, we are demonstrating the powerful potentials of truly democratic forms of leadership through which people take direct responsibility for their communities and their futures. Together we are creating the narrative of an epic saga, a story of humanity's reawakening to life. By its telling and retelling, that story becomes a part of our cultural heritage, reshapes our collective consciousness to redefine our image of who we are and what we can be, and strengthens the social movements to which it is giving life.[4]

Although the culture of materialism has been created by history's most sophisticated and highly paid propagandists, it is at its core a falsified, manufactured, and nonconsensual culture. If material acquisition were truly the dominant value of the human species, then surely capitalism would find it unnecessary to spend $450 billion a year to propagate it throughout the world. Nor would so many of the advertising messages and images that promote these desires be designed to appeal to our longing for acceptance, love, and contact with nature. Successful as capitalism has been in creating a mass consumer culture, the fact remains that its values are largely alien to our basic nature.

Our longing for life is finding new expression in a deep worldwide culture shift unprecedented in human history in its speed, magnitude, and implications. Part of this shift finds expression in the heroic deeds of the new storytellers who are acting to bring a life-centered future into being. We will visit a number of them in the next chapter. First, however, let's put their efforts in a larger context by looking at data from several important values surveys that provide our most compelling evidence that, contrary to outward appearances, the modernist culture that underpins the spread of global capitalism is actually in deep trouble.

A New Culture in the Making

Let's begin with the work of Paul Ray, a values researcher based in California who has been a leading figure in compiling and popularizing survey data gathered in the United States that reveal the growing momentum behind a shift to a new integral culture that affirms life in all its dimensions. Ray's ideas draw from the work of such visionary thinkers as sociologist Pitirim A. Sorokin, Hindu philosopher Sri Aurobindo, and cultural historian Jean Gebser.

Ray identifies three major cultural groupings in the United States: the *Modernists,* who embrace dominant mainstream materialist values; the *Heartlanders,* who reject modernism in favor of more traditional values of premodernism; and the transmodern *Cultural Creatives,* who have rejected modernism in favor of the values of an integral culture.[5] The Modernists actively prize materialism and the drive to acquire money and property. They tend to spend beyond their means, take a cynical view of idealism and caring relations, and value winners.

Heartlanders are distinguished by their desire to return to traditional ways of life and traditional gender roles. They tend toward religious conservatism and fundamentalism. They believe in helping others, volun-

teering, creating and maintaining caring relationships, and working to create a better society.

Cultural Creatives have a
strong commitment to family, community, the environment, interna-
tionalism, and feminism. They have
a well-developed social consciousness and are optimistic. They are
interested in alternative health-care
practices, personal growth and spiritual development, and they are care-
ful, thoughtful consumers. They
share with Modernists a receptivity
to change and with Heartlanders a
concern for human relationships,
volunteerism, and making a contribution to society. However, they
"reject the hedonism, materialism,
and cynicism of modern media, consumer and business culture, the sur-
vivor/scarcity/fear orientation of the
working class, the antisustainability
orientation of ultraconservatives,
and the intolerance of the Religious Right."[6] Two-thirds of them are
women.

> ### An Integral Culture
> An integral culture and
> consciousness involves a new
> way of looking at the world. It
> seeks to integrate all the parts of
> our lives: inner and outer,
> masculine and feminine, personal
> and global, intuitive and rational,
> and many more. The hallmark of
> the integral culture is an
> intention to integrate—to
> consciously bridge differences,
> connect people, celebrate
> diversity, harmonize efforts, and
> discover higher common ground.
> With its inclusive and reconciling
> nature, an integral culture takes
> a whole-systems approach and
> offers hope in a world facing
> deep ecological, social, and
> spiritual crises.
>
> *Duane Elgin and Coleen LeDrew,
> "Global Paradigm Report: Tracking the
> Shift Under Way,"* YES! A Journal of
> Positive Futures, *Winter 1997, p. 19.*

Ray's surveys estimate that among the adult U.S. population 47 percent or eighty-eight million people are Modernists, 29 percent or fifty-six
million are Heartlanders, and 24 percent or forty-four million are Cultural Creatives. Although the Cultural Creatives are a minority compared
with the Modernists, they are far greater in numbers than even they themselves realize. Because neither the media nor the political system takes
note of their existence, they tend to be invisible even to themselves. Even
so, their numbers are growing rapidly. As recently as the 1970s, they were
so few that pollsters didn't recognize their existence. Now they are a major
and growing cultural response to the accelerating failures of modernism.

Ray sees a subgroup among the Cultural Creatives, those he calls the "core Cultural Creatives," as the leading edge of cultural change in the United States. The core CCs (10.6 percent, or twenty million adults) are forming a deep connection to life at both the inner spiritual and the more outward social and environmental levels—thus most fully exemplifying the life-centered expression of an integral culture. They have a serious concern for psychology, spiritual life, self-actualization, and self-expression. They find cultural and ethnic diversity deeply attractive, enjoy mastering new ideas, are socially concerned, and are strong advocates of environmental sustainability and women's issues. They are engaged with the world, tend to be leading-edge thinkers and creators, and are deeply aware of modernism's failings.

The Cultural Creatives are crafting a new ecological and spiritual worldview, a new literature of social concerns, and a new problem agenda for humanity while pioneering psychological development techniques, restoring the centrality of spiritual practice to daily living, and elevating the importance of the feminine.

Ray observes that people create their cultures to solve perceived problems. Those cultural attributes that are perceived to be effective in problem solving survive. Those that do not, pass away. Whether or not the integral culture becomes dominant will depend on the extent to which it is seen to offer solutions to the problems that most concern the majority of people.

The power of the integral culture resides in its authenticity. It has emerged out of the inner awakening of millions of people to a crisis and a need for change without encouragement from mainstream media and institutions. Indeed, they remain largely unaware of its presence. It is clear therefore that its attraction is not based on expectations of economic or political rewards. To the contrary, most Cultural Creatives feel alone and isolated in their embrace of beliefs they mistakenly perceive to be exclusive to themselves. Ray's estimates of our numbers are an empowering revelation to most Cultural Creatives, an affirmation that not only are we not alone, but as modernism exhausts itself as a viable cultural system, we have the opportunity and potential to define the new mainstream of global culture. As awareness of the nature and extent of this culture shift builds, it provides important affirmation for those who already embrace its values and will assure others who may find the values of an integral culture attractive that there is social support for those who embrace them.

Modernism in Trouble

The fact that Ray places eighty-eight million adult Americans in the modernist culture implies that modernism has a greater hold on the American psyche than in fact may be the case. In his more refined analysis Ray identifies twenty-nine million of the Modernists as "alienated Modernists" who may play the modernist game, but basically reject all the values and worldviews examined in his study—including those of modernism. They are distinguished by their propensity to believe in nothing at all—perhaps the ultimate victims of modernism's alienation.

Another twenty-six million of those Ray classifies as Modernists might more accurately be called "titular Modernists." They play by modernism's rules and strive for success by modernism's definition, yet they also yearn for spiritual and psychological meaning and for the security of traditional religious beliefs. They are potential recruits to either the Heartlander or the Cultural Creative cultures. This leaves only thirty-three million solid Modernists—a number eclipsed by both the fifty-six million Heartlanders and forty-four million Cultural Creatives. If not for its stranglehold on our dominant institutions, modernism would be little more than a minority faith.

Ray's surveys provide additional evidence that modernism is in trouble. Consider the percentages of adult Americans who respond "yes" to the following decidedly nonmodernist statements: We need to treat the planet as a living system (86.97 percent). We need to rebuild our neighborhoods and small communities (83.40 percent). Humans are meant to be stewards over nature and preserve it (82.05 percent). Humans are part of nature, not its ruler (75.39 percent). I want us to return to a simpler way of life with less emphasis on consumption and wealth (67.66 percent). Government should shut down industries that keep polluting the air (62.55 percent).[7]

Other surveys corroborate the idea of a strong and growing reaction against modernism's materialistic values. For example, a national public opinion survey conducted by The Harwood Group, a public issues research firm, for the Merck Family Fund, a private foundation concerned with environmental issues, concluded that

Americans believe our priorities are out of whack. People of all backgrounds share certain fundamental concerns about the values they see driving our society. They believe materialism, greed, and selfishness increasingly dominate American life, crowding out a more meaningful set of values centered on family, responsibility, and community. People express a strong desire for a greater sense of balance in their lives—not to repudiate material gain, but to bring it more into proportion with the nonmaterial rewards of life.[8]

Perhaps The Harwood Group's most revealing finding is the significant gap between what people report as being their own values and guiding principles and those they perceive to be the prevailing norm of American society. Respondents consistently reported that most Americans are more strongly motivated by values of wealth and prosperity than they are themselves. The gap may reflect a gap between our values and our behavior. More likely, however, it reveals a difference between the values most Americans hold and the values of the modernist culture the mainstream media tell us we do or should hold. Consistent with the findings of Paul Ray's studies, The Harwood Group found that 86 percent of Americans were concerned about the quality of the environment. Ninety-three percent agreed that an underlying cause of our environmental problems is that our lifestyles create too much waste. Fifty-eight percent saw a need to teach our children to be less materialistic. Those few who were actively antienvironmental constituted a small but vocal, mostly male, minority.

The Harwood study also found that when people were asked to rate the things that would make them more satisfied with their lives, 66 percent put spending more time with family and friends as their top choice, 56 percent chose "If there was less stress in my life," and 47 percent said "If I felt like I was doing more to make a difference in my community." Only 21 percent felt a nicer car would bring them happiness. Only 19 percent felt a bigger house or apartment would do it. Sixty-two percent agreed that they would like to simplify their lives. Fifty-two percent supported the idea of limiting the amount of advertising allowed on prime time television.[9]

Such international survey data as we have available suggest that the reaction against modernism's materialistic values is widespread. In 1993 Gallup International conducted a Health of the Planet survey covering twelve industrialized and twelve developing nations. It found that a majority of people in both industrial and developing nations are concerned about the environment. Indeed, overall environmental concerns were even stronger in the developing than in the industrialized nations—a finding wholly contrary to the conventional wisdom that people in poor countries are too overwhelmed with the challenges of survival to be concerned about the environment. Furthermore, majorities in both industrialized and developing nations responded that protecting the environment is more important than economic growth.[10]

Using data from the 1990–1991 World Values Survey, drawn from forty-three nations representing 70 percent of the world's population, Ronald Inglehart identified clear evidence of a shift toward the values of an integral culture in a number of societies, including Sweden, the Netherlands, Denmark, Finland, Norway, Iceland, Switzerland, Britain, Canada, and the United States. People in these countries are losing confidence in hierarchical institutions, including government, business, and religion. As their trust in the ability of science and technology to solve problems is declining, their trust in the authority of their inner sense of the appropriate is increasing. Their interest in striving for economic gain is decreasing, while their desire for more meaningful work and the quality of the working experience is increasing. Their interest in discovering personal meaning and purpose in life is also growing. Their concern for economic growth is declining and their concern for environmental sustainability is increasing. They express higher tolerance for ethnic, sexual, and political differences and growing acceptance for new roles for women that allow them greater opportunities for self-realization. Inglehart concludes that these patterns are part of a generalized global trend toward postmodern values.[11]

The real test of a values shift is the behavior change that accompanies it. One expression of such change is found in the choices of the millions of people who are voluntarily choosing to limit their consumption in favor of simpler lifestyles. The Trends Research Institute, a respected forecasting organization, named this shift toward voluntary simplicity one of the ten top trends in America for 1997[12] and estimates that from 12 to 15 percent of Americans are now practicing participants.[13] The fact that 28 percent of respondents in the Harwood survey reported they had voluntarily reduced their incomes over the previous five years as part of a change in personal priorities suggests that the Trends Research Institute estimate is actually conservative.[14] A brief look at what these people are doing and the volition behind it gives additional texture and meaning to the survey data.[15]

Getting a Life

In 1992, Joe Dominguez and Vicki Robin launched a book titled *Your Money or Your Life: Transforming Your Relationship with Money and Achieving Financial Independence*. By mid-1998, it had sold 750,000 copies in English, had been on *Business Week*'s best-seller list for two and a half years, and was selling well in five other languages. The authors' message is at once simple and profound. We have a choice to give our lives over to making money to buy "stuff" we neither want nor need. Or we can get clear on what brings us real happiness, take control of our spending, and get a life.

Dominguez and Robin point out that the advertisers who promote and shape our consumer culture seek to condition us to the idea that by trading our life energy for the money needed to buy their products, we will fulfill our hopes for "power, happiness, security, acceptance, success, fulfillment, achievement, and personal worth."[16] But those of us who buy into the advertisers' message find our time so consumed by jobs we dislike to obtain money to buy products that give us little real satisfaction that we have no time left for living—to enjoy family and friends, participate in the life of the community and its many forms of cultural expression, and nurture our intellectual and spiritual development. In the end, we forsake the only real path to the fulfillment of our hopes and find ourselves slipping ever deeper into the alienation and spiritual emptiness from which the advertisers promise their products will rescue us.

A choice for voluntary simplicity means spending less time working for money, leading lives less cluttered by stuff, and spending more time living. It is not a call to sacrifice. It is a call to a better, more meaningful, and more satisfying way to live. It is a choice for life at a very personal level. The response of growing millions of people suggests that it is an idea whose time has come.

It is significant that the message of *Your Money or Your Life* seems to hold a special appeal to middle-class professionals who have lived the American Dream, awakened to the fact that it is a pointless rat race with no finish line, and chosen to give the race back to the rats in favor of a higher quality of living. *Boston Globe* columnist Ellen Goodman quite simply sums up the insanity of the normal life of the upwardly mobile modernist:

> "Normal" is getting dressed in clothes that you buy for work, driving through traffic in a car that you are still paying for, in order to get to the job that you need so you can pay for the clothes, car, and the house that you leave empty all day in order to afford to live in it.[17]

Jacqueline Blix and David Heitmiller, who wrote *Getting a Life: Real Lives Transformed by Your Money or Your Life* in order to share their experience, are examples of two upwardly mobile Modernists turned Cultural Creatives.[18] When they met at a New Year's Eve party, Blix and Heitmiller were both on the fast track of professional middle-class upward mobility. Having discovered one another, they decided to chase the "good life" together. In addition to a combined income of nearly $100,000, they had lots of credit cards—and used them all. However, to pay the bills and gain conventional stature they became increasingly absorbed in the pressures of their corporate careers. The more they earned, the more they spent, and the harder they had to work to pay the bills for expensive cars, a big house, fancy jewelry, and exotic vacations. Their work seemed meaningless and left them feeling both dissatisfied and financially insecure. Blix came to realize the only thing she could relate to in her job was the money.

Their transformation took them six years. At the end of that time, by gradually eliminating unnecessary expenses and investing prudently in government bonds, they had a sufficient nest egg to generate the interest needed to cover their reduced expenses without paid employment. Though their lives now move at a slower pace, they are active and full. They are writing and publishing books and articles on things they care about, like the joys of voluntary simplicity. They have deepened their friendships. They are more engaged in the life of family and community. They have time to read and reflect on ideas and to explore the wonders of nature right in their own neighborhood. They now find themselves living more consciously and purposefully.

At one level their experience seems consummately elitist—living a life of ease supported by the interest from government bonds—which can never work for more than a small minority of the population. At another level, they have made a choice that is at once life-affirming and deeply subversive. Just imagine the blow it would strike to global capitalism if the majority of the world's middle-class professionals began living consciously, getting clear on their priorities, consuming only what they need, spurning meaningless jobs, and giving of themselves to rebuild their families and communities as strong, inclusive, life-centered institutions.

The choice to live consciously with clear priorities and to make one's consumption decisions based on one's real needs and values is not limited to the financially advantaged. People from all socioeconomic levels, including from low-income neighborhoods and countries, are also learning to recognize and immunize themselves against the corrupting influences of advertising and incessant media messages and thus to make more intelligent use of their time and their incomes, no matter how abundant or meager.

Robin and Dominguez identify five things that are drawing people to the voluntary simplicity movement:

- The financial insecurity being keenly felt even by the survivors of corporate downsizing;
- The time famine experienced by people working long hours just to make ends meet;
- A desire to be ecologically responsible and reduce one's burden on the earth;
- A realization that maintaining an extravagant lifestyle is time-consuming and often hard work; and
- A recognition that simplicity is spiritually uplifting and consistent with an ethical commitment to live simply so that others may simply live.

The beauty of it is that whatever the motive that draws people to a choice for life over money, they eventually come to recognize the collateral benefits. It is in every respect a freer and better way to live.

These are all encouraging signs that materialism is losing its grip on the popular psyche and that we are witness to the awakening of a sleeping giant—life reasserting itself in the form of an emerging shift in our cultural consciousness. As people awaken to the limitations of modernism's values, they become more aware of the values that give their lives meaning and bring them real satisfaction. In so doing, they begin building the foundations of a new culture. Though the extent and implications of the shift remain largely hidden even from those of us who are a part of it, the work of people like Paul Ray, Vicki Robin, Duane Elgin, and Ronald Inglehart is helping us recognize the significance of what is happening and the potentials for change that it opens.

It is not only in people's personal lives that the emergence of the integral culture is finding expression. It is as well being expressed in countless initiatives by ordinary people doing extraordinary things to create livable communities and a just, sustainable, and compassionate world. They are also tellers of the new story. Their tales speak to the future it is ours to create.

Chapter 12

The New Storytellers

Women and men everywhere are behaving in an unprecedented way: audaciously taking responsibility for the whole human family and the future of life on the planet.
—HAZEL HENDERSON[1]

Small actions and choices can have major, although unpredictable, effects in determining what comes next. Among the possibilities is that the thousands of experiments and millions of choices to live more consciously will coalesce into a new civilization that fosters community, provides possibilities for meaning, and sustains life for the planet.
—SARAH VANGELDER[2]

IN THE NEW STORY ordinary people are taking charge, assuming responsibility for themselves and their communities, and withholding their power from the institutions that have abandoned life for money. Each story involves its own heroes putting their modest means, and sometimes even their lives, on the line in service to the well-being of the whole.

What sets the more interesting of these stories apart from conventional stories of civic responsibility and acts of charity is the extent to which they involve people working together as communities to make conscious choices and take a stand against powerful establishment forces in order to create a future that places life ahead of money. Each story contributes to building a new consciousness of neglected possibilities that may extend far beyond the place of its origin.

Usually the story starts with a modest initiative by persons with none of the evident attributes we associate with heroic figures. Most fail. Nearly all are soon forgotten. Yet when we choose to look, we can see that the number of those who are winning victories both large and small is growing, growing to the tens of thousands. We see as well the formation of alliances, at first tentative, always shifting, creating new patterns, occupying new spaces, adding new strength, becoming more coherent. They become like dancers engaged in a grand and joyful dance in which the creative improvisation of each one adds energy and vitality to the evolving, renewing coherence of the whole.

The individual stories are many and varied. They come from around the world. In this chapter I simply want to share a few of my favorites to add reality and substance to larger brush strokes of the rest of the book. I start with a simple story from Seattle, Washington, about two fellows of modest means who scored a political victory over the establishment with their sense of humor, determination, and a plywood sign.

Ordinary Heroes

In 1997, Dick Falkenbury, a cab driver, and Grant Cogswell, a part-time poet, put forward a ballot measure that promised to relieve Seattle's traffic congestion with a billion-dollar extension of the popular, but short, monorail system that was built for the Seattle World's Fair in 1962. Their campaign, which cost an estimated $2,000, consisted largely of walking around Seattle with a plywood billboard showing a map of their proposed enlargement of the monorail system. Critics dismissed them as silly, naive, and irrelevant. The Seattle chamber of commerce called on voters to "send these dreamers and con artists back to the drawing board." Instead, Seattle's citizens gave the ballot measure, which mandates that Seattle city council members will lose their salaries if they don't put the measure into effect, a 53 percent victory.[3] Thus, two people of modest means inspired the people of Seattle to speak their mind about their dream of a more livable city in a ballot measure that broke all the rules of big-money politics.

The minorities who live in the urban ghettos of the United States have a long history of acquiescing to decisions made by authorities in which they have no say. Now they too are starting to say, "No more." The Mothers of East L.A. (MELASI), an environmental-justice group organized by the women of a predominantly Hispanic-American section of

Los Angeles, is an example. It was founded in 1984 when a group of mothers decided to put an end to the persistent pattern of corporations and governments targeting their community as a preferred site for hazardous and disruptive projects. They have since successfully blocked an impressive list of such projects planned by others for their neighborhood, including a state prison, three waste incinerators, an oil pipeline, a chemical treatment plant, and a dump site, among others.

Having honed their organizing skills on blocking projects they did not want, they have broadened the definition of *environment* to include the whole range of conditions that affect the quality of life in their community—including crime, unemployment, failing schools, dangerous working conditions, and pesticide-filled food, and turned to creating the kind of community they do want. They found strong allies among the community's youth and are now carrying out a variety of constructive activities including graffiti and litter cleanup in the business district, a community youth garden, a tobacco prevention program, and a water conservation program. MELASI is now an active member of an international network of similar communities fighting for environmental justice and a new way of living.[4] It is an example of a continuously repeating progression from passivity to protest, to proaction, to the formation of national and international alliances.

A surprisingly similar story of community heroics comes from Japan, where the people of Kito village decided they were not willing to sacrifice themselves to a new dam project that would inundate their village. Accustomed to localities buckling under its decisions, the central government had announced its plan for the dam in customary fashion—without consultation. In decidedly uncustomary fashion, the people of Kito said, "No!" They refused even to sit with the central government to negotiate.

The struggle, which went on for twenty-five years, gained national attention and helped open a national dialogue on the failures of previous dam projects, the costs of relentless economic development, and the need for greater local democracy. In June 1997, the government announced that construction of the dam had been canceled.

Some credit the people of Kito with stimulating a new national consciousness that rivers are "living natural entities, organically linking mountains and sea and their adjacent communities." According to Japanese-history professor Gavan McCormack, it is difficult to identify in over a hundred years of Japanese history any precedent for such a triumph by a local community against the combined forces of the national and prefectural political bureaucracies. In their victory, Kito's people, according to McCormack, have helped to craft a new national story that highlights the values of "political devolution, local empowerment, fiscal responsibility, and environmental sensitivity."[5]

Many important contributions to the new story give currency to themes that trace back decades, even centuries, to rediscover ties to life that money-world institutions have disrupted. In India, physicist, philosopher, and feminist Vandana Shiva has been working with farmers to revive earth- and community-friendly farming practices that modern agriculture methods threatened to displace. She believes that sound farming practice is also sound environmental practice. In her words,

> Some environmentalists believe that to protect biodiversity you must exclude people. In their view you either have production or you have protection. I have seen farms as beautiful as a native forest. I feel it important to bring ecology and biodiversity into the heart of production rather than keeping it outside. . . . It has in fact taken the corporate sector many years and millions of dollars of propaganda to make people dependent on the unsustainable agricultural practices that generate enormous profits for global agribusiness. . . . [If] you create the right conditions, people will come to see the whole economic system in a different light and will choose the sustainability option.[6]

Through bitter experience, Indian farmers are learning that the technologies aggressively promoted by transnational agribusiness corporations leave them at risk because they now depend on buying large inputs of chemicals, nonreproducing hybrid or genetically engineered seeds, and other inputs on credit from distant companies. The corporations capture handsome profits, genetic diversity is lost, the environment suffers, and farmers bear the costs when soil fertility declines and crops fail.

To free themselves of this dependence, the farmers are mobilizing to restore traditional methods of cooperative preservation, selection, and sharing of traditional seeds so everyone in the community can plant the best available seeds and optimize the overall village food supply. They are rediscovering that when mono-cropping is replaced by diversified agroforestry farming systems, there is no reduction in the total production of usable plant material. In some areas whole generations of farmers who have known nothing but chemical agriculture are discovering that by returning to good traditional practice, their incomes increase, they enjoy a better diet, their soils improve, soil erosion is reduced, moisture is better retained—and they break their dependence on the global economy. A new pride in local cultural and biological diversity follows.[7]

Some of the more interesting stories involve dramatic transformations of the storytellers themselves. Among the most gripping of these is one from America's inner cities—the case of Antonio "King Tone" Fernandez, leader of the Latin Kings, a street gang in Queens, New York, best known for violent thuggery, gun trafficking, drug dealing, and murder—even of its own members. King Tone is himself a former crack addict with a police record. He straps on a bulletproof vest each morning before venturing out, weaponless, on some very tough streets to carry forward his message of a twelve-step self-help program against violence, crime, and drugs.

Fernandez is making jobs a top priority. While handing out job application forms at a Latin Kings gathering to which many participants had brought their children, he explained to a *New York Times* reporter, "I already got the Kings to stop killing each other. And if I'm telling the drug dealers to stop, too, then I've got to replace that money with a job where they can make a living." Reverend Gordon Duggins, an Episcopal priest, is helping King Tone incorporate the gang as the Almighty Latin King/Queen Nation, Inc., to spearhead investment in locally owned, employment-creating businesses.

The Latin Kings are regularly harassed by unsympathetic police and city officials who seem threatened by the idea of reformed gang leaders exercising responsible community leadership. Father Duggins strongly defends Tone as "smart and painfully honest and committed to doing the right thing" and refers to him as a "prophet" among his people.[8] King Tone quite literally lays his life on the line each day to tell both his people and the world a powerful and uplifting story of the possibilities for transforming a Hobbesian jungle of exclusion and violence into a living community.

Award programs such as the Right Livelihoods Award (known as the alternative Nobel Prize), the Goldman Prize for environmental leadership, and the Ashoka Fellows Program of support and recognition for social entrepreneurs are especially rich guides to the new storytellers. The following is a sampling of tales about changing relationships to the living earth and transforming political cultures from the experiences of more than a thousand Ashoka Fellows from around the world.[9]

In Slovakia, Michal Kravčk is demonstrating that using many small, locally managed catchments to store water is a more cost-effective and environmentally sound approach to managing water resources than large dams and diversions. In rural South Africa, Elna Kotze is creating local citizen-led land-use forums organized around watersheds to advance sustainable land use practices and provide a new and more democratic model for land-use planning.

In Ecuador, Jaime Idrovo Uiguen is working with farmers on the high plain to reclaim drought-stricken and impoverished soils by resurrecting precolonial agricultural methods and combining them with postmodern organic farming methods. The farmers with whom he works have established working models of traditional terraces, consolidated and repaired ancient irrigation systems, and recovered soils using organic composting and varied cultivation methods. In addition to the economic and environmental benefits, the effort is renewing the people's pride in their culture and traditions.

In Mexico, Luz Rosales is spearheading a movement to create a new political culture based on ethical principles such as respect for diversity and the role of the citizen in dealing with social issues. In 1991 she cofounded the Citizen Movement for Democracy, which fielded electoral observers to eliminate fraud at elections and increase voter turnout. In India, Ashraf Patel has created and introduced into the schools and colleges a multifaceted curriculum to sensitize Indian urban youth to important social issues and provide them with the intellectual framework and opportunities to exercise strong and socially responsible leadership.

Each of the hundreds of thousands of such efforts, spearheaded by individuals and groups motivated by a commitment to improve the life of the whole, brings new depth and texture to the story of people reclaiming power and responsibility to create a better future for all. Each demonstrates the potential and desire deep within each of us to express and enhance our own being through service to the whole.

"A Woman's Place"

The deadly tale and the money-world culture and institutions that it inspired were almost without exception male creations and embodied an unbalanced expression of male energies. The awakening is in part about female energies coming to the fore toward the creation of more balanced and integrated societies. This is reflected by the importance of female leadership in two critical areas—the environmental movement and new business formation. The women pioneers in these and other areas are telling stories that give a whole new meaning to the phrase, "A woman's place. . . ."

Mary Joy Breton's book *Women Pioneers for the Environment* makes no special claim for women as the leaders of the environmental movement. She simply tells story after story of women who have heroically put their own lives on the line in defense of the life of the planet and leaves it to the reader to realize that the strength of the environmental movement is in substantial part a result of women's courage and leadership. The following is only a brief sampling drawn from Breton's collection on the tellers of the new story of humanity's obligation to care for the natural environment.[10]

Breton begins with the historical account of Amrita Devi, an Indian woman who some three hundred years ago defied the axe men of the Maharajah of Jodhpur who had come to cut the sacred trees of her village. Breton sets the context:

> For centuries Indian women managed the forests of the steep Himalayan foothills as a communal resource. The trees in this important Asian watershed held soil in place, put oxygen in the air, and stored and purified the monsoonal rains, slowly releasing water into catchments during the dry season. The forest also provided the region's inhabitants with fuel wood, leaves for animal fodder, shelter materials, medicinal herbs, mushrooms, fruit, honey, and nuts, as well as raw materials for local crafts. To villagers, the hillside forests were a matter of life and death.

Wrapping her arms around the first tree marked for cutting, Devi cried, "A chopped head is cheaper than a felled tree." As the axe came down and she crumpled to the ground, her three daughters each in turn took her place and each in turn was killed. By the end of the day more than 350 women and men had been slaughtered before the Maharajah yielded to their cause and promised to spare the trees. Amrita's story was the inspiration of the famous Chipko, or tree huggers, movement around which thousands of women mobilized to put their lives on the line in non-violent defiance of official power to protect the trees they recognized as givers of life. Their victories of the 1970s and 1980s won logging bans on what remained of the Himalayan forests.

Following in this tradition, women continue to be at the forefront of protecting forests all around the world. One of the more famous is Wangari Maathi, who founded and leads Kenya's Green Belt Movement, an organization with a membership of more than sixty thousand women who have planted over seventeen million trees. Another is Colleen McCrory, who supported herself and her family at the edge of destitution as she forged a coalition of four hundred citizen groups representing a million people in campaign after successful campaign to protect the most spectacular of western Canada's old-growth forests in the face of a vicious smear campaign financed by logging interests. Judi Bari endured harassment and trumped-up charges from FBI agents, and was nearly killed by the blast from a bomb planted in her car during her struggle to save the California redwoods. Very much in the tradition of the Chipko movement, she continued as a leader of nonviolent direct action initiatives until her death from cancer in 1997, her commitment and courage never wavering.

Many people trace the origins of environmental politics in the West as a serious political force to Rachel Carson's *Silent Spring*, which first appeared as a *New Yorker* series in 1962. *Silent Spring* drew attention to the massive destruction of life caused by the misuse of chemical pesticides.

Carson was threatened with lawsuits and her work was disparaged not only by the industry trade journals and industry-funded publicity but also by the generally respected *Science* magazine, and by *Time, Newsweek,* and *Reader's Digest.* Throughout the rest of her life she endured vitriolic attacks on her science and her character. The public, however, saw through the vicious industry-sponsored campaigns. Less than three months after the publication of *Silent Spring* some forty bills had been introduced in various state legislatures to regulate pesticide use. The environmental movement as a political force was born.

About twenty-four years after the publication of *Silent Spring*, Theo Colborn, Dianne Dumanoski, and John Peterson Myers wrote *Our*

Stolen Future, examining the link between synthetic chemicals that mimic endocrine hormones in our bodies and deformities and reproductive malfunctions in fish, birds, other animals, and humans.[11] The initial reaction of the chemical companies was reminiscent of their response to the release of *Silent Spring.* They launched a counteroffensive refuting its conclusions. Hostile editorials and op-ed pieces appeared in *The New York Times,* the *Washington Post,* and *The Wall Street Journal*—some by scientists who later revealed they had never read the book. Perhaps it is a sign of the changing times that industry has since come to take the message seriously and embarked on a search for substitutes for the fifty-one chemicals that have been identified as acting like hormones in living bodies, the problem has received sympathetic press coverage, and Colborn was invited to give a major address at the opening plenary session of the second annual State of the World Forum in San Francisco in October 1996.

During the 1990s, women were critical in bringing a life-affirming citizen perspective to the agreements produced by the series of U.N. conferences on the environment, population, social development, human rights, women, and human settlements. Bella Abzug, founder of the Women's Environment and Development Organization (WEDO), was a leading figure. Under her leadership, WEDO organized the women's caucus at each of these conferences, which invariably turned out to be the best organized, the most fully informed, and the most effective in influencing the official proceedings. As a male participant in three of the U.N. conferences, I learned that the best route to meaningful influence was to work with and through the women's caucus and follow their lead.

Restoring human values and relationships to a more central role in economic life, women may also emerge as the force that transforms the system of business. On April 20, 1998, National Public Radio's *All Things Considered* series aired a program that confirmed what I had been hearing for several years from friends working in the corporate sector: a great many women are leaving corporate life to start new businesses, and many among them are motivated to create a business that is both profitable and aligned with their values. Although they are not necessarily going into business to change the world, their efforts may prove to be the most important economic news of our time.

This story includes some startling facts. According to the U.S. government, by the late 1990s women owned about 40 percent of all small businesses in America and were starting new businesses at about twice the rate of men. The rate for minority women was three times the national rate. Similar trends in female entrepreneurship are being reported from around the world.

Surveys conducted by the National Foundation for Women Business Owners reveal that women entrepreneurs are driven by a number of motives—some by an idea for a product or service, others by the desire to be their own boss and escape the frustrations of corporate life, including rigidity, the glass ceiling, and a feeling their contributions are not recognized or appreciated. Most women entrepreneurs have previous experience in professional or management positions and 58 percent say nothing could attract them back to the corporate world.

Women entrepreneurs perceive their management styles to differ from those of men. They see themselves as being more informal, more respectful of employees, allowing greater autonomy, and providing greater flexibility for employees to meet family and personal needs. These perceptions are supported by actual differences in personnel policies, with women entrepreneurs being more likely than their male counterparts to offer flextime, job sharing, and tuition reimbursement. They are also more likely to offer profit sharing while their firms are still small.

Women entrepreneurs are also more likely than men to be involved as volunteers in community life. In the United States, 78 percent of the women business owners surveyed spend time in volunteer work outside of business, compared with 48 percent of all adults and 56 percent of all business owners. Most also encourage their employees to volunteer in community activities.

The pattern that emerges suggests that women business owners are particularly sensitive to the needs of the whole person and they desire to help people balance and integrate home, work, and community life. Women as much as men find their options as business owners limited, however, by the realities of a global marketplace in which competitors with different values are nipping at the heels of their business. If present trends continue, women will soon be the majority among small-business owners and it seems likely in due course that they may become a major force for changing the rules of the marketplace.[12]

Responsible Wealth

Some of the new storytellers are appearing in unlikely places. In January 1997, a small group of wealthy Americans who take exception to the policy agendas of the greedy rich banded together to form an organization named Responsible Wealth. With a membership limited to individuals in the top 5 percent of the U.S. population in household income (those having $125,000 or more in annual income) or assets ($500,000 or more net worth), Responsible Wealth is an elite organization with a difference. Its mission is to change the economic rules that are tilted in favor of people like themselves at the expense of others less fortunate. The group educates policy makers and the public about the devastating consequences of growing inequality and supports measures intended to close the wage gap, limit the influence of big money in politics, and increase the share of the total tax burden carried by corporations and the wealthy. Many of its members have pledged to act on their commitments by donating their gains from the 1997 capital gains tax cut to organizations working for equity and against tax breaks for the wealthy. By June 1998, 125 members had pledged more than $1 million to such public interest causes.[13]

A similar commitment to placing the public good ahead of private profits lies behind the formation of Business Leaders for Sensible Priorities. Led by Ben Cohen of Ben & Jerry's Homemade, Inc., ice cream company, the group brings together business leaders who believe government has a responsibility to serve the needs of society rather than the bottom lines of corporations. Its primary focus is on reorienting the U.S. federal budget from military to social and local economic development priorities. Its members spearheaded a successful attack against new funding for the B-2 bomber and are publicizing the fact that 54 percent of the U.S. government's discretionary funding goes to military spending. The group's members believe this money would be better spent on such decidedly noncorporate agendas as creating living-wage, community-based jobs, providing health care for America's five million uninsured children, paying U.S. arrears to the United Nations, protecting the environment, ending world hunger, funding the National Endowment for the Arts, and advancing any number of other positive agendas.[14]

Responsible Wealth and Business Leaders for Sensible Priorities involve people of wealth and connection acting in their personal—in contrast to their institutional—capacities. They thus have a freedom to bring their conscience and moral sensibilities into play in ways that persons acting in institutional roles often do not. They are telling, through their actions, yet another piece of the new story—that equality and business accountability are essential to the well-being of society and that those who enjoy the benefits of wealth and privilege have a special obligation to use these resources to create a better world for all.

Positive Localism

At the end of 1997, President Clinton, the Republican congressional leadership, the editorial pages of every major U.S. newspaper, and America's largest corporations threw their full weight behind "fast track" legislation that would give the president authority to negotiate international trade agreements subject only to a yes or no vote by Congress with no amendments and limited debate. At the last minute Clinton withdrew the bill to avoid its certain defeat. What happened? The press attributed it to Clinton's bungling and the political clout of labor. The truth lay elsewhere in a new story the press either could not see or chose to ignore—the awakening of the public to the reality that international trade and investment agreements are being used to increase corporate freedom at the expense of human freedom.

Certainly labor was a major player in the fast track defeat, but it was joined by a broad and committed coalition of religious, human rights, minority, environmental, family farm, and small-business groups representing a broad cross section of America—some of whom had previously taken little interest in trade issues. Those environmental organizations that had earlier supported the North American Free Trade Agreement (NAFTA), in the belief that side agreements honoring environmental and labor standards would prove beneficial, realized they had been duped and joined with their anti-NAFTA colleagues in a solid stand against fast track. Following citizen defeats on NAFTA and the General Agreement on Tariffs and Trade (GATT) at the hands of powerful, well-funded corporate lobbies, the failure of fast track was seen by many in the movement as a turning point. Although many struggles against the corporate trade agenda remain, this was the first demonstration in a long while at the national level that the political will of awakened citizens can prevail against the amassed power of the world's largest and most politically powerful corporations.[15]

The citizen victory over fast track brought another element to the new story—the idea that localism can be a positive ideal. There has long been a tendency within intellectual circles to consider globalism progressive and localism provincial and antiprogress. Those who style themselves as progressives have rejoiced in cultural diversity and taken pride in their cosmopolitan vision of one world united in peace and prosperity. Localism, by contrast, has commonly been associated with racism, fundamentalist provincialism, and a failure of creative imagination.

So when the Sirens of the money world issued their call for a world without economic borders, most progressives saw no cause for alarm and a potential for much good. Few of us took any real interest in global trade agreements. In my own case, it was only in 1991 that I began to recognize the significance of these agreements as decidedly unprogressive instruments for serving money at the expense of life. Gradually, over the last decade, there has been a popular awakening to what is really at stake.

Along with that awareness is coming a realization that place and borders are essential to healthy life, community, and human well-being. That realization, in turn, is creating a new *positive localism* that seeks to protect the integrity of the local while at the same time celebrating diversity and supporting international cooperation in the service of people and the planet.

The international dimension of this new story is unfolding with particular clarity from the meetings and conferences of the International Forum on Globalization (IFG), of which I have the privilege of being a founding member. The IFG is a global alliance of citizen activists and organizations that first convened in San Francisco in January 1994 to oppose the forces of economic globalization. Yet it is impossible to label it as isolationist. Each and every one of its members shares a dedication to the ideals of cultural diversity, racial equality, democracy, environmental sustainability, and international cooperation. For me, one of the most exciting and fulfilling aspects of belonging to this group has been the ongoing search for a common vision of the kind of world we *do* want. Although we come from widely diverse backgrounds and cultures and differ on a number of other issues, we share a belief that fair and equitable international cooperation and exchange starts with strong, local communities and economies, rooted capital, and a balanced relationship with the environment.[16]

Life-Centered Nations

Local stories begin to take on new meaning when countless numbers of them begin to meld into holistic movements aimed at redefining national goals and transforming national institutions. The growing number of such national stories is a key source of my own hope for the human future.

In Chile, a national network of 145 local environmental organizations known as the Chilean Ecological Action Network (RENACE) is engaged in such a movement. Most of RENACE's individual members are small organizations with few resources, but working together they may hold the key to changing a nation. Their goal is to rebuild Chile's civil society, devastated by the long years of terrorism of the Pinochet dictatorship that finally ended in 1989, and enlist the Chilean people in transforming that country into a national model of a just and sustainable society. The process centers on regional consultations organized by RENACE members in cooperation with other membership groups such as unions, indigenous peoples, social groups, and farmers organizations. These consultations engage a cross section of the population in creating a vision and agenda for the kind of country the people of Chile truly want. According to Sara Larrain, coordinator of RENACE and one of the movement's key leaders, "Sustainable Chile will give civil society groups in Chile a concrete agenda of the things we want to accomplish. Our work will have more focus and we will be able to take the initiative in national debates rather than simply coming out against harmful initiatives."[17]

A related process is well along in the Philippines, which may have the densest fabric of networked civil society organizations of any country in the world. Tens of thousands of nongovernmental organizations and people's organizations specialize in issues such as the environment, sustainable agriculture, health, agrarian reform, religious affairs, rights of urban squatter communities, peace, cooperatives, women's rights, and many others. These are joined in numerous sectoral networks that are in turn joined in multisectoral provincial and national networks. Together these structures form the foundation upon which a new consensus is being built regarding appropriate directions for Philippine national development.

Mainstream Philippine nongovernmental organizations (NGOs) have long shared a vision of a society embodying the values of economic justice, community, and environmental sustainability. They rarely, however, engaged in national policy dialogues about the kinds of trade and economic policies required to support their vision. The participation of Philippine NGOs in the 1992 United Nations Conference on Environment and Development (UNCED) in Rio de Janeiro was a turning point.

Junie Kalaw, a leader of the Philippine environmental movement, played a central role in organizing the meetings of civil society organizations there. After Rio, he took the lead in encouraging the Philippine government to organize the Philippine Council on Sustainable Development (PCSD) to create a national Agenda 21 outlining how the Philippines would fulfill its UNCED commitments. A grouping of some three hundred NGOs elected their representatives to the PCSD, which was chaired by the head of the National Economic Development Authority—the national economic planning body.

The original draft of the Philippine Agenda 21, prepared with little NGO involvement, presented a doctrinaire neoliberal perspective on economic growth and relations. The draft was rejected by the NGOs, which then set about writing their own version of the document. The final consensus document, signed by President Fidel Ramos on September 26, 1996, was based largely on the NGO version. It outlined a national agenda centered on developing the full human potential of the country's people and grounded in principles of social and economic justice, self-determination, cultural, moral and spiritual sensitivity, ecological sustainability, and global cooperation.

Nicky Perlas, who as an NGO representative to the PCSD helped shape the NGO input to the final Agenda 21 document, recognized that getting the government to agree on principles was only the beginning. If the principles were to be more than nice words, they would have to be translated into policy actions at odds with the country's existing neoliberal policies and the government's commitment to open the Philippine economy to foreign corporations and investors. Change would require active and broadly based citizen support.

So while still negotiating with the government on the principles that would be the foundation of the Philippine Agenda 21, Perlas traveled around the country holding workshops with civil society groups on the implications of pending commitments being finalized under the GATT. His objective was to help members of these groups see how the proposed agreement would undermine the work of virtually every civil society sectoral grouping in the Philippines: the church, women, co-ops, fisherfolk, farmers, labor, and others.

These regional workshops prepared the way for a national conference in Manila cosponsored by six major NGO networks representing some five thousand individual member organizations. At the conference, facilitated by Corazon Soliman, another NGO representative to the PCSD, and held shortly before the official release of the Philippine Agenda 21, the NGO representatives for the first time affirmed a shared economic analysis naming neoliberal economic policies and economic globalization as important causes of the problems besetting the Filipino people and put forth a framework to address the underlying economic and trade issues.

In commenting on the significance of the meeting, Perlas said, "For some time, we had strong network structures, but the substantive content of their communications was limited to specific issues. Now we have the frameworks and the content, a coherent critique, and vision to match the structures." Although still far from their ultimate goal, leaders of the coalition have been working with the highest levels of government to integrate the Agenda 21 vision into the government's planning documents and positions in international organizations and treaty negotiations.[18]

In North America, Canadians are similarly engaged in creating their own new story. Fed up with a conservative government that consistently placed the rights of global corporations ahead of the rights of Canadian people and communities, they rallied in their October 1993 national election to vote all but two members of the ruling Tory party out of parliament. It was one of the most sweeping repudiations of a democratically elected government in history. However, once seated, the new Liberal party government went on to carry out essentially the same policies as the government that preceded it. This led many Canadians to believe that global economic interests had usurped control over their government and the Canadian economy. A citizen organization, the Council of Canadians, was formed to develop and advance a "Citizens' Agenda for Canada." By late 1998, Council membership had reached 100,000.

Grassroots consultations were held throughout the country to define the kind of society that Canadians want for themselves and their children. The Canadian agenda asserts the right of every person in this world to productive and fulfilling employment, food, shelter, education, pensions, unemployment insurance, health care, universally accessible public services, a safe and clean environment, protected wilderness spaces, cultural integrity, and freedom of communication. According to Maude Barlow, founder and national chairperson of the Council,

> To rebuild democracy we must start back at the roots—in our communities. The only way to fight is together. Across sectors; across countries; across race, gender, and age lines; employed and unemployed; city and rural, we must find one another and realize that the movement we are creating is the only thing that comes between us and the global feudalism of the new economy. We must not accept the prevailing propaganda that globalization and corporate rule are inevitable. To say we have no choice is intellectual terrorism. Fair trade, full employment, cooperation, cultural diversity, democratic control, fair taxation, environmental stewardship, community, public accountability, equality, social justice: these are the touchstones of our vision and it is within our means—it is our right—to choose them.[19]

In the years since UNCED the forces of a quiet revolution have steadily grown stronger and more coherent as more people join in the dialogue through countless meetings and initiatives at local, national, and global levels. The phrase "we the people" is taking on new meaning as we awaken to the reality that our collective future depends on people everywhere taking back the power and responsibility we have yielded to increasingly alien institutions and crafting a new story of a possible human future. It is a future created by ordinary people literally living it into existence as they discover new possibilities in themselves and translate them into new realities. Again and again we see the pattern. From passivity to protest, from protest to proaction, from local proaction to national and international alliance building.

We are in the midst of a fundamentally new phenomenon in the modern human experience, the creation of a new civilization from the bottom up. The creative leadership comes not from conventional power holders, or even from intellectuals and artists. It comes rather from ordinary people who are doing extraordinary things to build functioning local communities and ecosystems. Most are driven more by a simple desire to create viable living spaces in the midst of a troubled world than by grand visions of planetary change. Yet as they link together in ever expanding and strengthening alliances, they are as well reclaiming expanding physical, social, and economic spaces for life. Day by day, they are creating a new planetary reality through processes that mimic the self-organizing dynamics of healthy ecosystems.

From their collective efforts and aspirations a grand vision is emerging, a new story of the meaning of the human experience and its possibilities—a story not of conquest or new material wonders but rather of life and humanity's place in its continued unfolding. The story embodies an idea so powerful, so deeply resonant with the voice of our inner spirit as to defy containment. We are living beings and our time has come to reintegrate our way of being with the being of the planet, to become one with life with a new understanding of our place and role within the whole. Let's now look at some of the larger themes of this grand story.

Chapter 13

Life Choices

Life and livelihood ought not to be separated but to flow from the same source, which is Spirit. . . . Spirit means life, and both life and livelihood are about living in depth, living with meaning, purpose, joy, and a sense of contributing to the greater community.
—MATTHEW FOX[1]

To you the earth yields her fruit, and you shall not want if you but know how to fill your hands. It is in exchanging the gifts of the earth that you shall find abundance and be satisfied. Yet unless the exchange be in love and kindly justice, it will but lead some to greed and others to hunger.
—KAHLIL GIBRAN[2]

WE STAND AT A CRITICAL POINT of choice between two stories—two paths to contrasting futures. One is the story of a universe that begins and ends in death. The other is the story of a universe that begins in life and unfolds as an expression of life's creative force.

Envisioning the path of life requires that we know what we truly value, that which in our more reflective moments we identify as the essential elements of good living. Alisa Gravitz, the executive director of Co-op America, a membership organization focused on positive use of economic power, observes that people most everywhere, when asked about those essential elements, come up with much the same list:

- A secure means of livelihood that provides for our basic material needs while earning us a place of respect in our community;

- A strong, nurturing family, friends, and a supportive, peaceful, and secure community that allows us to explore and develop our capacity for loving relationships;

- The opportunity to learn and to give expression to our awareness and understanding of ourselves and the world around us both intellectually and artistically;

- Good physical health and the opportunity to engage in athletics, dance, and other forms of physical expression that make our bodies tingle with life's energy;

- A sense of belonging to place, community, and life, yet with the freedom to make personal choices—and sometimes to wander and explore without the obligations of place;

- A clean and healthy environment vibrant with the diversity of life; and

- An assurance that our children will have an opportunity for the same.

Having lived much of my life in places as different as the United States, Ethiopia, Nicaragua, the Philippines, and Indonesia, and visited many others equally diverse, I find myself in agreement with Gravitz. Though people's modes of expression and relating may differ due to the influences of culture, religion, language, and class, underneath there is a longing for the same essentials of a good and healthy life. For me this unity in diversity affirms that we are all born of a single spirit striving to know its many possibilities.

The items on Gravitz's list are well within the material and technical means of each and every society to provide for all its people. Perhaps the solution to our present collective predicament remains illusive for the very reason that it is so obvious and familiar. We are not being called to step off the edge of some cliff into a dark and vast unknown. Our experience of what lies ahead may prove more like returning home after a long journey that has opened our eyes to new possibilities in the deeply familiar. That which in our more mindful moments we really want, we can have, if we but muster the will to make healthful choices for ourselves and our societies that bond us with life's creative regenerative processes. In this chapter we will review some of those important choices.

Being Whole Persons

The field of health care is one of the many places where we can see with stark clarity a choice between two quite different paths based on different assumptions about the nature of our own being and the purposes our economic institutions are to serve. One is the direction of corporate medicine driven by the profit imperatives of insurance and health maintenance corporations. The other is the path of holistic health practice driven by the preferences of health-conscious individuals and health-care professionals. We see strong trends in both directions.

In its increasingly familiar manifestation, corporate medicine treats the body as a collection of discrete physical parts and biochemical processes to be fixed by surgical or chemical interventions administered by standardized and interchangeable health-care professionals. In a typical clinic visit, which may be days or weeks after an appointment is requested, the patient must quickly describe his or her problem to a physician who makes a diagnosis and prescribes treatment or makes a specialist referral in an encounter that may take all of five to ten minutes. The patient is then out the door with no necessary expectation the two will ever meet again. If the prescribed treatment or referral involves unusual expense, it must be reviewed against company protocols and approved or denied by a clerical employee without medical training who never sees the patient.

In its more advanced manifestations, holistic health practice is, by contrast, unhurried and involves a continuing professional, yet caring, relationship between the individual and a team of practitioners from a variety of traditions and disciplines, including fully qualified physicians, who work together in a mutually supportive fashion to activate, strengthen, and work with the natural healing processes of both mind and body. Although its practice includes chemical and surgical interventions, it deals with the whole person within his or her social and environmental context and gives preference to the least intrusive intervention appropriate to the condition. The basics of its practice include a diet of nutritious, fresh, whole, organically produced foods, plenty of fresh air and clean water, exercise, healthy human relationships, regular intellectual stimulation, and a spiritual practice that reduces stress and centers the mind and body. As John Robbins observes in *Reclaiming Our Health,*

Taken together, factors such as the food we eat, whether and how we exercise, the way we give voice to our feelings, the attitudes we hold, and the quality of the environment in which we live are far more important to the quality of health we experience than even the most sophisticated medical technologies. It has been liberating to see that health comes from learning to live in vibrant harmony with ourselves, with the nature world, and with one another.[3]

If we choose the path of holistic health, the health-care model of our future may look something like anthroposophical cancer hospitals in Germany and Switzerland that "combine an efficient and effective use of conventional medicine for cancer with intensive use of naturopath, homeopathic, and anthroposophical remedies."[4] Robbins reports on his visit to the Lukas Klinik, an anthroposophical facility in Arlesheim, Switzerland:

Art, music, and movement are part of the daily activities, along with herbs and a vegetarian diet based on organic fresh fruits, vegetables, and whole grains. The underlying belief is that when patients express their passions, talents, and gifts they activate their innate forces of self-healing.[5]

Here is an example of the choice in cancer treatment between treating the whole person rather than assuming that the cure rests solely in the hands of the doctor through the administration of surgery, radiation, and toxic chemicals.

We can individually choose which approach to health we will embrace in our own lives and which of the competing choices we will support in the evolution of our health-care systems. There appears to be a strong and growing interest in more holistic approaches among both users and health-care providers. Indeed, survey data indicate that in 1997, 42 percent of adult Americans made use of some form of alternative care not taught in medical school—including herbal therapy, chiropractic, acupuncture, and massage therapy.[6]

There are many reasons for this trend. Partly it is economic. Holistic providers generally charge lower fees and have less overhead. There is also a natural human preference for the more personal and attentive care and relationships that most alternative practitioners offer. Even corporate health programs are beginning to offer a range of alternative care options, for purely economic reasons. Behind it all, however, is a sense of changing values and a growing sense of the living self. There is also an increasing awareness that many of the relevant choices are collective as well as individual—and they are not confined to questions of how we will organize to fund and deliver health-care services.

Holistic health is easiest and most natural to practice when we live in a place where farmers are growing healthy food, public policy assures high standards of environmental quality, the dominant culture values cooperative work relations and economic security, and life's creative processes are integral to the prevailing worldview. Healthful living becomes difficult, even heroic, when we live in a place where the only available foods are products of chemical-intensive industrial agriculture, the air and water are contaminated, unemployment is high, few of the available jobs pay a living wage, and the prevailing worldview holds materialism to be the highest value. Our collective task is to create a world in which good health is the natural path in every aspect of our lives, including in our relationship to the earth and the food it yields to us, in the uses to which we allocate our precious physical spaces, and in the values we honor by our choice of the indicators by which we assess the state of our well-being.

Eating Well

As living beings we replace some 90 percent of the molecules in our bodies each year in a continuing exchange of energy and material with our environment. Our total existence depends on consuming the once-living cells of plants and other animals and converting their flesh and energy reserves into our flesh and energy reserves. It is an act of communion, an affirmation of the intimacy of our connection to the web of life.

In the days not so long ago when the substantial majority of us grew our own food, the nature of our relationship to the living earth was clear and immediate. Our lives were organized around the demands of the land and the rhythm of the seasons. Our diets centered on whole foods eaten fresh or preserved by home methods. There was rarely an intermediary between producer and consumer.

Much about today's agricultural system is a great blessing. Few miss the arduous toil and uncertainty that remain a part of living directly from the land. But we have now gone to the far extreme of a food system that delinks us not only from the land but also from place, seasons, and even from fresh, whole foods.

We have come to take for granted the remarkable variety of "fresh" and processed foods available in our supermarkets throughout the year, unmindful that we are filling our bodies with foods that are rarely fresh, have commonly traveled thousands of miles, and are likely to be contaminated with toxic chemicals, antibiotic residues, artificial hormones, synthetic additives, engineered genetic materials, and disease-causing bacteria. The resemblance to the natural foods for which evolution designed our bodies is largely cosmetic.

I had the pleasure of meeting Annemarie Colbin one evening when she graciously hosted a gathering in her New York apartment at which I was invited to speak to the Friends of the Institute of Noetic Sciences. Annemarie Colbin is a best-selling author on the relationship between the health of our minds and bodies and the foods we eat. After the guests had left she shared with me some of her insights. I was fascinated by the clarity with which her theories point to a symbiotic relationship between healthful eating and healthful stewardship of the living earth.[7]

Colbin suggests that just as life is more than the chemical composition of its cells, so too food is more than the sum of its nutritional elements. She believes that when we eat, we ingest into our own bodies not just nutrients but also the residual life energy of the animal and vegetable materials we are consuming. Thus, the fresher the food, the more of the residual life energy that remains intact and the greater its contribution to the vitality of our own minds and bodies. This would explain why we often feel stronger and more alert when we eat fresh, whole, organically grown foods. Speculative though her thesis may be from a scientific perspective, it fits with what we are learning of life's complex energy transfer processes.

Colbin also believes that nutritional needs vary from person to person by individual makeup, lifestyles, seasonal changes in weather and temperature, and the adaptations made by our ancestors to particular diets. Thus, unlike many nutritionists, Colbin does not advocate specific dietary prescriptions based on formulas and lists of the nutrient contents of various foods. Rather she suggests that whenever possible, we choose foods that are:

Whole. In general, the closer the food is to the way that nature provides it, the greater and more balanced its nutritional and energy content.

Fresh, natural, and organically grown. "Not canned, not frozen, certainly not irradiated or genetically engineered; free of chemical additives, colorings, preservatives."

In season. There is an interesting fit between the foods that are locally available during a given season and the seasonal needs of our bodies. Thus we eat salads and fruits during the summer and soups and stews in the winter.

Local. Local foods are picked riper, do not lose nutrients in travel, and are more likely to be in sync with the seasonal needs of our bodies.

In harmony with tradition. Paying attention to what our ancestors ate gives us important clues to the particular foods to which our own genetic makeup is likely to be attuned.

Balanced. Variety, including variety in flavors, colors, and textures, helps lead us to a balanced diet.

Delicious. What tastes good to us, at least when we are eating whole, natural foods, is a useful guide to what our bodies do and do not need.

A dietary practice based on these principles brings us back into contact with the living, natural productive systems of our own localities and creates a demand for the socially and environmentally sound human-scale organic production of healthful foods. Thus we see further evidence of life's deep coherence, for what is best for the health and vitality of our bodies is also best for the land and for the creation of more sustainable, just, and compassionate economies.

Harvesting the Earth's Bounty

The choices that lie on the agricultural side of this equation are beautifully presented by Donella Meadows in two contrasting case studies from Europe.[8] The first of her cases comes from a modern chemical- and energy-intensive factory farm called Babolna in Hungary. Largely indistinguishable from many similar agricultural operations in the United States, Babolna specializes in the mass production of animals in tight confinement. Originally a state farm, it has since been reorganized as a joint stock company. It turns out sixty million chickens a year, bred to be ready for slaughter in forty-nine days. Beyond providing McDonald's with a supply of McNuggets for Eastern Europe, its output is shipped by jet airplanes to Russia, Saudi Arabia, and South America. In its hog-raising operations, it rushes piglets delivered by cesarean section to nursery facilities as their mothers are being turned into sausage.

One and a half million acres, 13 percent of Hungary's arable land, is devoted to producing corn for the company's feedlots. The farmers who own and work this land are under contract to Babolna, from which they are required to buy their seeds, chemicals, and equipment, and to which they must sell their crops for its feed mills. All production methods and prices are dictated by the company. Chicken production is licensed out in the same way. Such contracting arrangements are increasingly popular with large agribusiness corporations around the world because they allow the company to maintain tight control while assuring its own profits and transferring to the farmer the risks of crop and animal failure inherent in any agricultural enterprise.

Meadows's second case is from the Hermannsdorf farm near Munich, which was created by Karl Ludwig Schweisfurth to demonstrate his vision of "food from the region for the region." The farm's few hundred acres of wheat, rye, barley, maize, and hay, and twelve acres of fruits and vegetables, are all grown organically—including what is raised for animal feed. Pigs and cattle are raised in small groups in facilities that allow them to move freely between their sheds and the outdoors. Manure is processed by a biodigester to provide some 20 percent of the operation's heat and electricity and all the fertilizer for its fields. A huge Bavarian barn has been retrofitted to house a bakery with wood ovens that produce sourdough breads from fresh-ground whole grains, a microbrewery that turns out beer from organic barley and hops purchased from thirty neighboring farmers, and a cheese production facility that makes Parmesan, Camembert, Emmentaler, cream cheese, and buttermilk. The cheese maker buys its milk from local organic dairy farmers and processes it without pasteurization, because Schweisfurth believes high temperatures take the life out of milk. A slaughterhouse turns twenty hogs, three beef cattle, eight calves, and ten sheep a week into fresh meat, smoked hams, and sausage.

All the food produced is sold at the peak of freshness through a local restaurant and nine nearby stores. Schweisfurth considers the present size of the farm, which produces enough food for about ten thousand people, to be about the ideal size. He believes that a larger operation would not be able to maintain the same quality and freshness. He dreams of a network of independently owned and operated Hermannsdorfs that would each buy and process organic produce from neighboring farmers to supply fresh meat, cheese, beer, and bread to outlets within twenty miles of each farm's location.

Here we have two distinct views of the future of agriculture—both modern, sophisticated, and financially viable yet starkly different in their methods of production, the nature and quality of their products, and their relationship to the lives of people and place. In many respects they mirror the contrast between the industrial and holistic approaches to health care.

In the Babolna future, chemicals, mechanization, nonrenewable fossil fuels, and rigid confinement overwhelm the natural processes of life to generate profits for absentee owners by producing frozen meats for corporate-owned fast food chains selling standardized food items of questionable nutritional value in distant markets to people enticed by sophisticated advertising to devalue their traditional food cultures. In the Hermannsdorf future, medium-size, independently owned organic farms work with nature's processes within a framework of community values and obligations to produce fresh, high-quality, locally processed foods primarily for home preparation and consumption by local consumers who honor the food traditions of their culture. The Hermannsdorf farm puts into practice Annemarie Colbin's principles on the food production side and provides a metaphor for many of the life choices we now face.

It bears mention here that in this as in most of the other life choices we face, we are repeatedly told by corporate interests that there are no acceptable alternatives to the status quo. For example, we are warned that moving from chemical-intensive to organic agriculture on a major scale will result in a drop in yields that will impose hunger and starvation on hundreds of millions of people. Ironically, our existing system of industrial agriculture is doing just that—imposing hunger and starvation on hundreds of millions of people.

Those of us who are among the world's fortunate 20 percent tend to think of the modern food system as highly productive and secure. After all, our supermarkets are stocked to overflowing. Rarely mentioned is the fact that our abundance is obtained in part by colonizing the land and water needed to provide basic diets for the other 80 percent of the world, including the more than a billion people for whom hunger and deprivation are a daily experience. Even in the United States nearly 35 million people experience chronic food insecurity or hunger.[9]

Furthermore, the systems of industrial agriculture are efficient only in the sense that they employ little labor—a questionable benefit in a labor-surplus world. In terms of energy from petroleum, a nonrenewable resource, they are highly inefficient. Studies done in the 1970s found that our industrial food system requires some ten calories of carbon fuel subsidy to put a single food calorie on our table. Roughly a third of the subsidy goes to producing the food, another third to processing and transportation, and the final third to retail marketing, household refrigeration, and cooking.[10] Subsequent studies have reached similar conclusions.[11]

By contrast, in her study *The Violence of the Green Revolution*, Vandana Shiva found that even the least productive preindustrial systems of rice cultivation for which data are available average an energy output of 8.3 calories for each calorie of input. The most energy-efficient preindustrial rice production systems average more than 20 calories output to each calorie of input.[12]

Robert Netting, in his classic study *Smallholders, Householders*, reports that studies of actual farming experience consistently find "productivity per unit of land is inversely related to farm size." Although big landowners find it profitable to produce lower yields of a single crop using energy-intensive technology, it is to the "small holder's advantage to produce in a more diversified, continuous, skilled labor–demanding manner in order to make fullest use of more restricted resources." It is also a consistent finding that the methods used by small holders are more likely to prevent environmental degradation.[13]

We are presently feeding the high-consuming portion of the world's population by using methods that draw down the earth's stores of ancient sunlight (fossil fuels), result in rapid soil erosion, deplete the fertility of the soils that remain, and deprive the poorest among us of even a minimally adequate diet. These are serious matters in a world facing increasing food insecurity from the depletion of natural capital, rapid growth of the human population, and a growing demand for ever more exotic diets by the financially advantaged.

To this disquieting picture we add the fact that factory methods of meat production are extremely cruel and pose increasingly serious threats to our own health. As John Robbins notes, "The conditions in which these creatures are housed, and the diets they are fed are so unnatural, cruel, and disease-producing that a steady supply of [antibiotic] drugs is needed to keep the animals alive. This use has contaminated the food chain with drug residues, and contributed enormously to the development of antibiotic-resistant bacteria."[14]

Choice of the life-affirming option in agriculture can at once engage more people in doing useful work, reduce hunger, allow us all to eat fresher, healthier, whole foods, and help us regain a lost sense of connection to the natural processes on which the regeneration of our bodies depends. That seems quite a good bargain.

Places for Living

Another set of critical choices has to do with the use of our increasingly scarce physical spaces. Nearly everywhere in the world we now see trends toward a Los Angeles–style urban sprawl that is turning land once devoted to farmlands and forests into sprawling strip malls and parking lots. Sprawl is driven by the understandable impulse to get away from the noise, pollution, crime, high taxes, and concentrations of poverty that have become characteristic of many cities. Its consequence, however, is to destroy more of what we really value.

From 1970 to 1990, more than thirty thousand square miles of land in the United States—nearly four times the size of the state of Massachusetts—were reclassified from rural to urban by the U.S. Census Bureau. During that same period the urban population density of the United States decreased by 23 percent, whereas total population increased by 22.5 percent and the number of vehicle miles traveled by that population increased by 98.4 percent.[15]

With sprawl comes an increased dependence on the automobile and a decrease in human interaction because people no longer encounter one another going about their daily routines on sidewalks and in local shops and parks. The costs of providing essential services such as electricity, water, sewage, and transportation escalate as a result of declining density. The interests of the affluent who can afford to move from the inner city are delinked from the interests of those who cannot—speeding urban deterioration and deepening the class and often the racial divide. As suburbs are taken over by automobiles and strip malls, the greenery and relative tranquillity that originally attracted people to the suburbs is lost, creating incentives to extend even further the colonization of open spaces by cars and concrete in search of the constantly receding vision of suburban tranquillity.

Although sprawl is the dominant trend, we see evidence of a countertrend that defines another critical life choice. Terry Moore has been part of a citizen-led effort to turn Portland, Oregon, a city only fifty miles from the hometown of my childhood, into one of the nation's most livable cities. Her activism led to her winning a seat on the Council of the Metropolitan Service District, a role in which she spends a lot of time in public workshops that bring together businesspeople, government officials, and ordinary citizens to discuss the city's future. She commonly asks the participants to make up individual lists of what they would like their communities to have and be in fifty years.

> When people put down everything they want, they get a city that's many times more dense than we could ever imagine based on projected population growth. They want to have a movie theater. They want to have their shops, and restaurants, and coffeehouses. They want to be able to walk. And they want to have a community center. And they want to have apartments. And they want to have jobs in their communities.[16]

We are learning, with a degree of tragic irony, that the key to creating livable human habitats is not to reduce the density of human habitation by creating sprawling suburbs. Quite the opposite. It is to organize our living spaces in ways that increase residential density and mix residential and commercial use, while sharply reducing or even eliminating the use of cars. Such steps increase human interaction and bonding and free up space for walkways, bicycles, grass, trees, and flowers.

Portland has become an inspiring example of this process.[17] It all began when environmentalists teamed up with Oregon's Republican governor, Tom McCall, to push through a law signed in 1973 requiring every city and county in the state to write land-use plans defining urban growth boundaries to limit sprawl and protect farms, forests, and open spaces. The idea was not simply to force developmental energies back toward the urban core. It was also to obtain the population density that makes public transport viable and revitalizes the economic, social, and cultural life of the city. The issue of controlling Portland's sprawl came to a political head in 1975 when community groups in working-class southeast Portland lodged a successful campaign to persuade Mayor Neil Goldschmidt to cancel plans for a freeway that would have devastated their communities to accommodate suburban commuters.

Thirty years ago Portland's downtown was written off as dead. Today it boasts coffeehouses, parks, restaurants, lively storefronts, office towers, and rehabilitated warehouses housing interesting small shops. The number of downtown shops has doubled since 1971, with no increase in parking spaces—a light rail system and an efficient bus service (free within the downtown area) have made them unnecessary. The people of Portland now enjoy one of the most livable downtown city areas in the United States, demonstrating what can be accomplished when public-spirited politicians work together with politically savvy citizens who care about life as much as they care about their pocketbooks to make their community work for everyone.

When Fran and I visited Portland in the summer of 1997, we joined the many local people strolling along the Willamette River on the beautiful green expanse of Tom McCall Park and enjoyed dinner in a charming floating restaurant while watching the wild ducks swim by. At the time we didn't even realize that not long before, this had been the location of an unsightly freeway that blocked human access to the river.

The story of the livable city seems to be spreading. In 1996, voters in the California county of Sonoma approved measures to establish growth boundaries around four cities, the first such action in California.[18] The state of Maryland has also passed a "Smart Growth" law that allows the state to withhold or limit subsidies for schools, sewers, or roads outside of defined Smart Growth areas.[19]

What we are learning here is that we have been trading living space for driving and parking spaces. A choice for sprawl is a choice favoring the profits of oil, automobile, and construction companies. A choice for growth boundaries and public transportation is a choice for a higher quality of living.

Measuring Progress

As children, many of us delighted in tracing our own growth, perhaps by marking a permanent record of our height on a wall or door frame. Becoming bigger was our goal. Then with maturity we reached a point at which growth no longer added to our stature but merely to our girth, and we turned our attention to other measures of accomplishment.

Though we have been slow to realize it, that shift must occur for societies as well. Up to a point, increasing the quantity of consumption can indeed contribute to the quality of our living. The point invariably comes, however, when further growth means adding not stature but rather bulk that diminishes the quality of our living. We must then embrace new measures of our collective progress.

During World War II a system of national income accounts was developed to assess the productive capacity available to support the war effort. That war ended long ago, but growth in the gross domestic product has subsequently become the leading indicator against which policy makers assess national well-being and progress. For high-income countries that measure makes no more sense than taking the growth of one's girth as an indicator of improving personal health. More recently, stock price indices like the Dow Jones Industrial Average and the Standard & Poor's index of five hundred stocks have nearly eclipsed GDP as the more closely watched measures, with many TV and radio stations issuing hourly reports on every market fluctuation. Using such indices as measures of a society's well-being makes even less sense than GDP, because what an index of the inflation in financial assets really reveals is the rate at which the very wealthy are increasing their financial claims on a declining pool of real wealth at the expense of everyone else.[20]

So long as we rely on indicators of money-world health and performance as the measures of our well-being rather than on indicators of living-world health and performance, we will surely continue to give preference to policies beneficial to money over those beneficial to life. This defines another of our critical life choices.

During the 1990s, citizens and local governments in a number of communities around the world began defining and tracking indicators of community health. Many have been inspired by the work of a group of more than a hundred concerned citizens of Jacksonville, Florida, who initiated such an indicators project in 1985. The Jacksonville group now tracks seventy-five indicators relating to education, economy, public safety, natural environment, health, social environment, government and politics, culture and recreation, and mobility on an annual basis. According to Redefining Progress, a policy think tank in San Francisco that is following these efforts, there are now nearly 150 such initiatives in the United States alone, plus related efforts in Canada, New Zealand, and India.[21] Together their work is helping illuminate the potential of using new indicators of well-being to shift our policy focus from money to life.

In Seattle, Washington, the process began with a one-day conference in November 1990 in which community leaders from all facets of Seattle city life gathered to discuss the possibility of citizens' choosing their own measures for long-term community well-being. The conference resulted in the creation of a civic organization called Sustainable Seattle and initiated a process that engaged hundreds of Seattle citizens in selecting the indicators to be monitored. The process yielded an initial list of ninety-nine indicators, winnowed down through subsequent consultations to forty, which are shown in the following list. Together they give a whole-system picture of movement toward or away from sustainability and tell a nuanced story of the future to which many of Seattle's people aspire.[22]

Environment
- Wild salmon
- Ecological health (stream quality and vegetative cover)
- Soil erosion
- Air quality
- Pedestrian- and bicycle-friendly streets
- Open space near urban villages
- Impervious surfaces

Population and Resources
- Population
- Water consumption
- Solid waste generated and recycled
- Pollution prevention
- Local farm production
- Vehicle miles traveled and fuel consumption
- Renewable and nonrenewable energy use

Economy
- Energy use per dollar of income
- Employment concentration
- Unemployment
- Distribution of personal income
- Health care expenditures
- Work required for basic needs

- Housing affordability
- Children living in poverty
- Emergency room use for non-ER purposes
- Community reinvestment

Youth and Education
- High school graduation
- Ethnic diversity of teachers
- Arts instruction
- Volunteer involvement in schools
- Juvenile crime
- Youth involvement in community service
- Equity in justice
- Adult literacy

Health and Community
- Asthma hospitalizations for children
- Low birth weight infants
- Voter participation
- Library and community center usage
- Public participation in the arts
- Gardening activity
- Neighborliness
- Perceived quality of life

The final list of indicators is instructive for what is missing as much as for what is included. Though we find ten indicators of economic health, economic growth is nowhere among them. Indeed, for several of the indicators the desired outcome is a reduction in material consumption, as for example, vehicle miles traveled and fuel consumption, water consumption, and health-care expenditures.

When economists construct indicators, they center on money. When people construct indicators, they center on life. Similarly, although economists seek to reduce all progress to a single measure, people are more likely to accept the reality of life's complexity.

By all accounts, the indicator most participants in the Seattle exercise selected as their number one measure of the region's sustainability and quality of life was the size of the seasonal spawning run of wild salmon. The courage and determination of these extraordinary wild creatures as they return to the place of their birth has long inspired a sense of awe and spiritual meaning among the people of the Northwest. There is an almost primordial recognition that the condition of the wild salmon is a measure of the health of the watersheds on which all of the region's life depends. Toxic chemicals, loss of forest cover, disruption of stream flows, and urban sprawl all contribute to diminishing the salmon runs and the life energies that sustain those of us who live there.

Sustainable Seattle's focus on living indicators is also evident in the way they measure stream quality. Rather than using a conventional test of the presence or absence of contaminants, they use what is known as a *benthic index of biological integrity*, a measure of the diversity and density of bottom-dwelling (benthic) invertebrates. These are the mayflies, stoneflies, worms, mussels, and other groups of insects and animals without backbones on which fish, birds, amphibians, and other animals rely for their food. The cleaner the water, the more they thrive.

Indicators relating to pedestrian- and bicycle-friendly streets, open spaces near urban villages, reduction of fuel consumption and vehicle miles traveled, increased participation in gardening, library, and community center use, and neighborliness all reflect a concern with the physical and social quality of urban life. Indicators relating to local farm production, employment concentration, and community reinvestment reveal the value placed on economic diversification and local ownership. A strong equity thrust is revealed in the decision to include indicators of unemployment, personal income distribution, the amount of work required to meet basic needs, low birth weight infants, children living in poverty, adult literacy, and equity in justice (disparities in the arrest rate by race). There is also awareness of the extent to which the health and well-being of children, society's most vulnerable members, provide sensitive indicators of the health and well-being of the larger society.

Indicators influence public policy only to the extent they are taken seriously. Perhaps the most important consequence of initiatives such as Sustainable Seattle is their contribution to engaging a broad segment of the population in a serious values-assessment process. Those who participate are led to reflect deeply on what they really value and how they will know whether it has been achieved. To agree on indicators we must take responsibility for making choices about our future, itself an important step toward healthful living—as many communities around the world that have undertaken such exercises are discovering.

As we begin reordering our priorities in favor of life, an extraordinary realization comes into focus: much of the destructive and unsustainable burden that we place on the planet results from choices that deprive many of us the most basic means of living and diminish the lives of all, often for the primary purpose of increasing corporate profits. The time has come to accept and use our power of responsible freedom to create economies and societies dedicated to the service of life—our own lives included.

Chapter 14

Engaging the Future

*Suppose you had had the revolution you are talking and dreaming
about. Suppose your side had won, and you had the kind of society you wanted. How would you live, you personally, in that society?
Start living that way now! Whatever you would do then, do it now.
When you run up against obstacles, people, or things that won't let
you live that way, then begin to think about how to get over or
around or under that obstacle, or how to push it out of the way, and
your politics will be concrete and practical.*

    —PAUL GOODMAN[1]

*We encourage others to change only if we honor who they are now.
We ourselves engage in change only as we discover that we might
be more of who we are by becoming something different.*

    —MARGARET WHEATLEY AND MYRON KELLNER-ROGERS[2]

OUR TASK is no longer one of creating countercultures, engaging in political protest, and pursuing economic alternatives. To create a just, sustainable, and compassionate post-corporate world we must face up to the
need to create a new core culture, a new political center, and a new economic mainstream. Such a bold agenda requires many kinds of expertise
working at many levels of society—personal and household, community,
national, and global. It requires breaking the bonds of individual isolation
that leave us feeling marginalized when in fact we may already be part of
a new majority. There are thousands of useful tasks to be undertaken.

Because this book has focused on the economic dimension of this challenge, my emphasis here is on the economic subset of the larger change agenda. The strategy is twofold: withhold resources from the institutions of capitalism and build sustainable community-based alternatives for meeting our needs.

Starve the Cancer, Nurture Life

Cancer feeds from the energy reserves of what remains of the healthy body. It expropriates life's energy to sustain its own deadly growth.

Virtually the same is true for the capitalist cancer. Capitalism, however, is more insidious than a conventional cancer. By establishing its control over our jobs, investments, food, medical care, clothing, transportation, energy sources, and increasingly even our schools and prisons, it makes us depend on its presence and then blackmails us to yield to it ever more of our life energies as the price of our survival. If we had the means simply to remove its institutions from our midst by some equivalent of radical surgery, radiation, or chemotherapy, our economy would collapse and we would be left with no means of sustenance.

Again, we must turn to life for an analogy in our search of a more viable approach. One of the body's natural defenses against cancer involves denying the cancerous tumor access to the body's bloodstream. The cancer is thus starved to death as the body's available energy stores are devoted to rebuilding its healthy cells. This analogy holds the key to eliminating the capitalist cancer from our midst: withhold legitimacy and energy from the institutions of capitalism as we redirect our life energies to building and nurturing the institutions of a life-serving, mindful market economy. A simple phrase says it all: *Starve the cancer, nurture life.* Or more specifically: *Starve the capitalist economy, nurture the mindful market.*

The large goal is to displace the institutions of global capitalism with a global system of mindful market economies. The process involves gradually increasing the options the mindful market offers us as we reduce our dependence on those offered by the institutions of capitalism. For example, I buy my wine from the local Bainbridge Island winery, located within walking distance from my home and run by a wonderful family who add something of their love of the earth and our island community to every bottle of wine they produce. (See "From the Earth with Love.") Each time I buy a bottle of wine from my neighbor rather than one bottled by the

Gallo corporation, or purchase a head of lettuce at our Saturday morning farmer's market that is grown by another wonderful neighbor on her organic farm rather than a lettuce from our local Safeway corporation outlet that is grown thousands of miles away by the Del Monte corporation on a factory farm, I act to nurture the mindful market economy while withdrawing legitimacy and resources from the capitalist economy. And each time I forgo the purchase of something I don't really need, substitute a product made by my own hand, or engage in a cooperative exchange with my neighbor, I weaken my dependence on the money created and controlled by capitalism's institutions. And, in most instances, I also reduce my burden on the planet.

Start from Where You Are

Obviously, we are not going to bring down the institutions of capitalism just by buying a locally grown head of organic lettuce, though it is a useful start. We must work in many ways at many levels. The best that can be done here is to offer a general framework and a few illustrative suggestions that you may find helpful in defining a personal strategy to help

> ### From the Earth with Love
>
> Most things we eat or drink are anonymous. We don't know where they are grown. We lack even the identity, never mind the personal philosophy, of the person who grew them. Wine from small wineries gives us a direct link with a specific place and a specific person: the vineyard and the winemaker. Most "grocery store wine" has lost its identity, the product of absentee owners who buy grapes from whoever gives the best price. They hire and fire winemakers at will. Small wineries that grow their own grapes are islands of reality in a world where, daily, thousands of tiny compromises erode the line between what is real and what is profitable.
>
> We wish to remain at a size where we ourselves can continue to touch the earth, the vines, the wine, and you, the wine drinker. We can stay this size by selling directly to you. Your praises, criticisms, and advice are a basic part of our wine growing. We find the care of our vineyard and its fruit to be a rewarding life experience which we enjoy sharing with you.
>
> *Gerard and JoAnn Bentryn*
> *Bainbridge Winery, Bainbridge Island, Washington*

starve the cancer and nurture life. There are no universal blueprints. Indeed, the one universal response to the question, "What can I do?" is "Start from where you are." That means making use of the resources at

Connecting

For each action item suggested in this chapter, a multitude of organizations offer resources and opportunities for engagement. I've mentioned a few of them in previous chapters and provided contact information in footnotes, but the resource listings I can provide here are limited and, given the rapid development of events, will be quickly out of date. The best overall source I know for practical suggestions and contact information responding to the question, "What can I do?" is *YES! A Journal of Positive Futures,* published quarterly by the Positive Futures Network, P.O. Box 10818, Bainbridge Island, Washington 98110, phone (206) 842-0216, fax (206) 842-5208, e-mail yes@futurenet.org. For information on subscribing, see the insert at the end of this book. Also visit the Positive Futures Network Web site at www.futurenet.org.

your command, and most important, doing what allows you to become more of who you really are.

If you are a member of a church, you might organize discussion groups and events to examine the issues raised in this book and explore how individuals can act on them as an expression of their spiritual values. Or you might initiate a study group that deepens the group's sense of connection to place by gathering and sharing information on such things as the history of the locality where you live, the foods that are produced there, the source of your water, the distinctive characteristics of your native species, and how your local ecosystem has changed over time. If you found this book useful, recommend it to a friend.

If you are a parent, you might campaign to make your local schools advertising-free zones. If you are a teacher and your school requires students to watch Channel One, you might use it as a resource for teaching students to deconstruct advertising and propaganda messages to help immunize them against media manipulation. Or you might engage your students in projects that deepen their understanding and caring about their local ecosystems. If you teach in a university, especially in a school of business, organize a course on the moral defense and critique of capitalism to engage students in a critical examination of the issues relating to the design of an economic system.[3]

If you are a natural networker, you might work with others to develop a guide to local organizations and initiatives for people in your locality who are looking for ways to become positively engaged. Or you

might compile and publicize a directory of local, stakeholder-owned
businesses. Your efforts might even
lead to the formation of new alliances
among these groups to strengthen the
newly emergent whole.

If you are the CEO of a large corporation, you could establish a policy
that your corporation will not make
political contributions or otherwise
seek to influence elections or legisla-

Economic Democracy
Frank T. Adams and Gary B.
Hansen, *Putting Democracy to
Work: A Practical Guide for
Starting and Managing Worker-
Owned Businesses* (San Francisco:
Berrett-Koehler, 1992) is a
helpful resource for those
undertaking a worker ownership
initiative, whether a new startup
or a worker buyout.

tion. Better yet, organize the breakup and employee buyout of your corporation to turn it into a network of independent stakeholder-owned, community-based businesses. If you are an investment counselor or money
manager, build a specialty in socially responsible investment and the
financing of stakeholder buyouts. If you are a small-business owner, build
your identity as a values-led community-based enterprise and engage in
the formation of networks and alliances of like-minded businesses.

If you are a union member, campaign for applying a social responsibility screen to the investment of union pension funds, with special
attention to investing only in companies that hire union workers and have
good employee relations. Promote the use of pension funds to finance a
labor buyout of selected corporations to convert them into stakeholder
enterprises.

If you work with small farmers in a low-income country, encourage
them to save and use local seeds and not become dependent on the seeds
and chemicals of transnational corporations. Help them organize to resist
the takeover of their lands by corporations and development projects
such as those funded by the World Bank and other foreign development
agencies. If you are a citizen of a low-income country, join the citizen
resistance against IMF and World Bank structural adjustment programs.
If you work for the World Bank, the IMF, or the World Trade Organization, help break the veil of secrecy by getting key internal documents into
the hands of citizen groups working to hold these institutions accountable
to the public interest.

If you are a politician, consider building your campaign on a pledge
to take only small contributions and to support serious campaign reform.

Sponsor policy reforms consistent with the policy agendas set forth in Chapters 9 and 10. If you are an economist, become active in the International Society for Ecological Economics and participate in building and popularizing a market economics for a living planet.[4] If you are a lawyer, connect with one of the groups named in Chapter 10 working on issues relating to the legal status of corporations and help develop a legal strategy to overturn the doctrine of corporate personhood.

If you are a resident of a low-income neighborhood, especially a minority neighborhood, your community is likely to be a favored site for polluting industries, waste disposal, and the routing of new highway construction—and will likely be underserved by public transportation. If existing groups are working to stop harmful projects, demand the cleanup of existing facilities, and promote public transportation suited to your community's needs, consider getting involved with one of them. If an effective group does not already exist, create one.

If you have talents as a speaker, develop a presentation on the relationship of the business system to the health of the environment and make yourself available to groups interested in delving into such issues. If you are a journalist, write stories about the newly emerging culture; values-led, stakeholder-owned businesses; and the many citizen initiatives moving us toward a post-corporate world—the stories that corporate PR specialists don't want told. If the publication from which you earn your bread and butter has no taste for such stories, do them on a pro bono, freelance basis for independent publications that still believe journalism has a role beyond generating advertising dollars.

If you are inclined to political activism, you might get involved in campaigns to end corporate welfare in all its many forms, strip corporations of their rights of personhood, and get big money out of politics.

Whoever you are, you have an important role in changing the system—for change will only come from the actions of millions of people and each of us is important.

Intervene at Multiple Levels

Although the most important changes generally begin within ourselves, they must eventually be translated into changes in community, national, and global institutions. We must be mindful of the changes needed at all these levels and contribute to their realization. The basic themes, however, remain the same. Start from where you are to starve the cancer and nurture life.

Let's take the levels one at a time and explore some of the possibilities. Bear in mind this is a list of possibilities focused on changing the economic system. It is neither prescriptive nor comprehensive, but only a partial answer to the question, "What can I do?"

PERSONAL AND FAMILY

At the personal and family level our opportunities to shift the energy of the economic system center on issues of consumption, where we live, and how we obtain and use our money. The following are some specific things you might consider.

> **Make Your Money Count for Life**
>
> Co-op America offers a rich variety of practical resources relating to reducing consumption, finding socially and environmentally responsible products and businesses, and making socially responsible investments. Its Web site, which has won a number of awards, is an excellent place to start. Go to www.coopamerica.org. Or contact them directly for membership information at Co-op America, 1612 K Street, N.W., Suite 600, Washington, D.C. 20006, phone (800) 584-7336, fax (202) 331-8166.

SIMPLIFY YOUR LIFE

In a capitalist economy, cutting back on consumption is a revolutionary act. Cut back on clutter and unnecessary consumption. Sort out which expenditures are really important to you and which are not. Figure out your real take-home pay after deducting taxes and the costs of transportation, clothing, and tools used in your occupation. Then calculate what you earn per hour and translate each prospective purchase into the hours of your life energy that you must devote to your job to pay for it. Each time you make a purchase, ask whether the item is worth that many hours of life energy you might be using in other ways. For greater support, form a voluntary simplicity group to share ideas and experiences.[5]

BUY SMALL AND LOCAL

Making your purchases at small stakeholder-owned firms and buying locally produced products are also revolutionary acts against capitalism. Patronize your local farmers' market or organize a community-supported agriculture program with a local farmer. Participate in the "Thanksgiving conspiracy," which involves planning and producing your Thanksgiving dinner based exclusively on foodstuffs produced within thirty miles of your place of residence, and encourage others in your community to do the same.[6] In good market fashion, you are voting with your dollars. It may take some research to figure out what is produced locally and how you can adjust your consumption patterns to meet more of your needs through the market—rather than the capitalist—economy, but that is part of the consciousness-raising process. Again, consider forming a support group to share experience and information.

CHOOSE A LIFE-AFFIRMING JOB

Consider taking a lower-paying job doing work that has real meaning with a values-led, community-based organization or enterprise that is contributing to the life of the community and the planet.

KEEP INFORMED

Reach out beyond the mainstream media by becoming a regular reader of journals and books published by reliable alternative press groups that report on news and issues relating to corporate agendas.[7]

PUT YOUR CASH IN A COMMUNITY BANK

Do your banking with an independent bank or credit union committed to serving your community. If the banks in your community are all branches of one of the large national or international banks, ask the branch manager for the figures on how the local deposits to that branch compare with the branch's total lending in your community for local businesses and home ownership. If local deposits are substantially greater than local lending, you know that local money is not supporting the local economy. Consider banking by mail with a community bank located elsewhere. At least you will know your money is supporting someone's local market economy rather creating economic instability in the global financial casino.[8]

VOTE WITH YOUR SAVINGS

If you participate in the stock market, choose a mutual fund that screens investments for social responsibility or make use of an investment service or adviser who specializes in socially screened stocks. Use your ownership vote to support positive shareholder initiatives. Also, avoid consumer debt. Those who maintain debt balances on their credit cards mortgage their lives to capitalism.

REDUCE YOUR AUTOMOBILE DEPENDENCE

Living without a car is no small challenge in most American localities, and auto manufacturers, oil companies, and construction contractors all benefit from keeping it that way. We serve ourselves and life by reducing that dependence. When deciding where to live and where to work, try to choose the location that allows you to walk, bicycle, or take public transportation to work, shopping, and recreation. In many households, just eliminating the need for a second or third car is a positive step.

FUND CHANGE

Support nonprofit organizations that are challenging the capitalist system and working in favor of equity, environment, and community. Whatever your level of income, reserve a portion for charitable giving to these organizations.[9] You can even support groups doing work in which you believe by such a simple act as signing up with a long-distance phone service that offers discounted rates and donates a portion of your payment to groups working for systemic change.[10]

COMMUNITY

At the community level, action opportunities center on strengthening the local market economy, creating a healthy livable environment, and building a sense of community based on mutual trust and caring. Contributing at this level requires that we reach out and become a part of our community's public life. The following are a few ideas you might consider.

JOIN AN INDICATORS PROJECT

If your community has a sustainability or livability indicators project, get involved. If not, consider organizing some friends to initiate one. The more people involved in dialoguing on the nature of the community in which they want to live and in selecting the indicators by which they will know when they have it, the more likely the effort will have a meaningful impact.[11]

Create a Sustainable Community Economy

The Rocky Mountain Institute (RMI) offers a variety of technical and organizational resources for increasing community sustainability. See its Web site at www.rmi.org for current information, or contact RMI, 1739 Snowmass Creek Road, Snowmass, Colo. 81654-9199. For those interested in organizing a program to create a strong community economy based on the use of local resources to meet local needs, see Michael J. Kinsley, *Economic Renewal Guide: A Collaborative Process for Sustainable Community Development.* Available from RMI, it is an excellent practical guide and also includes an extensive directory of additional resources.

CREATE A DIRECTORY TO THE MINDFUL MARKET

A barrier to supporting the mindful market economy is figuring out which products come from values-led local firms. Perhaps you have created a support group and you are developing a serious information base. Your next step might be to publish, distribute, and publicize a community directory to your local mindful market.[12]

SUPPORT OR CREATE A COMMUNITY CURRENCY

Local currencies reduce dependence on money controlled by capitalist banking institutions, build a sense of community, strengthen the identity of local businesses and products, and make visible the distinction between money that stays in the community and money that doesn't. If your community has a local currency, give it your support. If not, consider forming a group to establish one.[13]

ENCOURAGE GROWTH BOUNDARIES, AFFORDABLE HOUSING, AND PUBLIC TRANSPORTATION

The move to establish urban growth boundaries to limit sprawl, reverse urban decay, create pedestrian-friendly neighborhoods, and increase the viability of public transportation is an idea whose time has come. If your community has a growth management plan designed to increase its livability, consider getting involved. If not, then consider organizing support to create one. Be sure affordable housing is an element of the agenda, so that people at all income levels will have access to the improved livability of your area.[14]

WORK FOR COMMUNITY ECONOMIC SELF-RELIANCE

There is a growing divide between localities that approach economic growth by providing subsidies to attract facilities from global corporations and those that are strengthening smaller local businesses. If these issues interest you, find out who is responsible for economic development policies in your community and get involved, either by seeking a seat on the relevant local commission or by organizing a watchdog and lobbying group to mobilize support for sensible economic policies.[15]

GET POLITICAL

There is no democracy without an active citizenry. The only way we are going to bring change to our corrupted political system is through greater involvement by citizens who care about their community. Run for office and bring your values into the political mainstream. Build your campaign in part on a pledge to finance your election with small contributions and avoid obligations to big-money interests. Much of the impetus for change is coming from local levels and there are important opportunities to make a difference as a local officeholder.[16] Furthermore, to reclaim national politics we must first build a local base. If you're fed up with the pandering to big money by the major political parties, consider joining a smaller party, such as the New Party, which is engaged in building its base on a platform of citizen democracy in both political and economic life.[17]

NATIONAL

At the national level, the action agenda centers on political education and changing the rules of the game to favor democracy and the market economy.

USE YOUR POLITICAL FRANCHISE

Study the issues, track the voting records of your legislators or parliamentarians, find out who finances their campaigns, and use your vote to favor the politicians who are trying to serve the public interest. Let the politicians who represent you know you are watching their records and that you favor serious campaign finance reform that gets big money out of politics, strong environmental regulation, a living wage, strong antitrust enforcement, small and medium-size local business, stakeholder ownership, strong unions, and a progressive tax policy. Let them also know that you oppose international trade and investment agreements that increase the rights and reduce the accountability of global corporations and financial institutions;

funding for the International Monetary Fund, the World Bank, and the World Trade Organization; corporate subsidies; the privatization of social security; capital gains tax cuts and other tax breaks for the wealthy; bank deregulation; patents on life; and corporate intellectual property rights monopolies—to name a few issues that bear directly on the balance of power between capitalism and democracy and the market economy.[18] If the politicians who represent you don't represent your interests, others probably feel unrepresented as well. Consider running for national office yourself.

GET ACTIVE IN POLITICAL MOVEMENTS AND ADVOCACY GROUPS

Although the major political parties may be hopelessly captive to big-money interests, there are many political movements and advocacy groups that are not. These groups are vehicles for mobilizing broad grass-roots support behind initiatives that advance the public interest on issues such as those listed in the previous paragraphs. Pick out one or two with a strong grassroots base that align with your interests, get involved, and give special attention to campaign finance reform.[19]

INTERNATIONAL

At the international level, a positive agenda centers on people-to-people exchange and dialogue that builds a globalizing civil society as a potent force for positive change.

GLOBAL NETWORKS

There are many global citizen organizations working in solidarity on issues ranging from voluntary simplicity to opposing international trade and investment treaties that are designed to strengthen corporate rights and weaken their accountability. If the issues you are working on at community and national levels have an international dimension, you may want to link your local and national efforts into a related international network or alliance.

GLOBAL INSTITUTIONS

Global institutions are an especially appropriate concern of global networks. Citizen groups have come to realize that the most powerful of our international institutions are generally those—such as the World Bank, the International Monetary Fund, and the World Trade Organization—that have been created to serve and strengthen global capitalism. Groups of concerned citizens worldwide have responded with well-organized initiatives aimed at holding these institutions accountable to the human and environmental interest. There is much to be done to weaken and ultimately close these harmful institutions as we work to replace them with institutions dedicated to protecting the economic rights of people and communities. If this agenda interests you, find a relevant network and get involved.[20]

MUNICIPAL FOREIGN POLICY

As national governments have pursued foreign policies largely alien to the values and interests of many of their citizens, a number of towns and cities have put forward their own positions on key foreign policy issues. For example, some have boycotted corporations that do business with repressive regimes, such as in Burma or apartheid South Africa. In many instances local governments around the world are reaching out to work directly with one another to prod and challenge their national governments on official positions relating to such issues as global warming, nuclear disar-

International Resources

One of the most comprehensive international Web resources for those seeking to engage in creating a post-corporate world is the Web site (www.apc.org) of the Association for Progressive Communications (APC), a global alliance of twenty-five national and regional computer networks. APC's mission is to support organizations, social movements, and individuals through the use of information and communications technologies to build strategic communities and initiatives that make meaningful contributions to human development, social justice, participatory democracies, and sustainable societies.

The APC Web site provides a variety of resources in its own right, but most important, it offers links to its member networks around the world. Each member network provides links to hundreds or thousands of member organizations, many of which maintain Web sites of their own with links that extend far beyond the APC member networks. These links will lead to activist citizen groups in most every country of the world, as well as to international networks dealing with nearly all of the issues addressed in this book. Those looking for international networks will do well to give special attention to the Web site of the Institute for Global Communications (IGC), the U.S. affiliate of the APC, at www.igc.org.

mament, and human rights. While national governments have been negotiating the Multilateral Agreement on Investment (MAI), aimed at virtually eliminating the ability of national and local governments to regulate
international investors and speculators, a number of towns and cities in
the United States, Canada, Britain, Australia, and other countries have
passed official resolutions declaring themselves MAI-free zones to underscore their protest against this attack against democracy. Those who
define values and progress in terms of money define international cooperation primarily in terms of financial relationships. As we awaken to life
as our defining value and measure of progress, we come to see that the
foundation of more meaningful international cooperation centers on
people-to-people communication and the free exchange of friendship,
information, and technology. We are learning that international relations
are too important to be left to national governments captive to corporate
interests. If your municipal government has an active foreign policy, get
involved. If not, learn what other local governments are doing and campaign to get yours involved. Give special support to initiatives aimed at
strengthening the rights of peoples to protect their economic and environmental interests against predatory global capital.[21]

Start from where you are. Do what's right for you. Give yourself permission to be the one. And together we can and shall create a positive, life-
friendly future for humanity and the planet.

Enchanted by the Sirens' song, we have yielded to the institutions of capitalism the power to decide our economic, social, and technological priorities. Intimidated by their power, we have been reluctant to see the
naked truth that they bear the Midas curse, appropriating the life energies
of whatever they touch to the end of making money. Finding our choices
narrowed to the options capitalism finds it profitable to offer us, we seek
meaning where there is none to be found and become unwitting accom-
plices in fulfilling the deadly curse.

Given the seriousness of our situation, it may seem anticlimactic to
suggest that our survival depends on something so obvious and undra-
matic as embracing the living universe story as our own and making
mindful choices for democracy, markets, and healthy lifestyles. Perhaps
we have been so busy searching the distant horizon for exotic answers to

our deepening crisis that we have failed to notice the obvious answers that are right in front of us.

Or perhaps we have been reluctant to face the troubling truth that it is our voice that sings the Sirens' song. It is we who divert our eyes from the emperor's nakedness. It is by our hand that the Midas curse turns life into money. We can sing as well life's song, find the courage to speak of the emperor's shame, and put our hands to life's service—discovering along the way more of who we truly are as we live a life-fulfilling future into being.

The gift of self-reflective intelligence gives our species a capacity for mindful choice well beyond that of any other. Yet we have avoided the responsibility that inevitably goes with freedom by assuming it is not within our means. We have further diminished ourselves by developing elegant ideological arguments to rationalize our irresponsibility.

Thus, we have approached democracy as though it were a license for each individual to do as he or she wishes when in truth it is about acting on the faith that each individual has the capacity for full and equal participation in making responsible choices mindful of the needs of all. We have approached the market as though it were a license to amass unlimited individual wealth without individual responsibility, when in truth it is about meeting basic needs through the mindful participation of everyone in the equitable and efficient allocation of society's resources. We have treated the good life as a process of material acquisition and consumption without limit, when in truth it is about living fully and well in service to life's continued unfolding.

Whatever the barriers to our taking the step to species maturity, our era of adolescent irresponsibility is ending for the very reason that we have reached the limits of the planet's tolerance for our recklessness. It is now our time to accept responsibility for our freedom or perish as a species that failed to find its place of service in the web of life.

Epilogue:
Planetary Consciousness

Awareness of an all-pervading mysterious energy articulated in the infinite variety of natural phenomena seems to be the primordial experience of human consciousness, awakening to an awesome universe filled with mysterious power.
— THOMAS BERRY[1]

Perhaps the most basic challenge humanity faces is to awaken our capacity for collective knowing and conscious action so that we can respond successfully to the immense social and ecological difficulties that now confront us.
— DUANE ELGIN[2]

THERE ARE THOSE RARE and precious moments when it seems as if a window opens onto our soul and we catch a glimpse into ways of knowing and communicating of which we had no previous knowledge. I vividly recall such an experience in the summer of 1961 when traveling by train from Jakarta to Bandung on the island of Java in Indonesia. As the train found its way up through the terraced rice fields, I felt as if I were being transported into another reality. As far as the eye could see the rice terraces reached up the hillsides, human artifacts melding with nature's contours. Out across the vast landscape several hundred people could be seen tending the fields, using the same labor-intensive, life-giving technologies developed many generations earlier by their distant ancestors.

I had heard that while people who grow up in Western cultures experience time as linear, people who grow up in Asian cultures tend to view it as circular. I had come to Indonesia wondering whether this accurately characterized the Indonesian worldview but scarcely knew how to frame the question to my Indonesian acquaintances. As the lush beauty of the rice fields flowed slowly past the train window, I found myself slipping into a deep state of consciousness that melded with the reality of my setting and seemed to become one with the consciousness of the people working in the fields. Then I knew. Change is both constant and unchanging as time passes through the repeating patterns of each day, the waxing and waning of the moon, the cycle of the seasons, and the birth and passing of each generation reliving the experiences of those that came before. The natural flow of time is one of circles, within circles, within circles. The rightness and beauty of this brought a deep sense of peace and connection to the living earth.

During moments of deep reflection, I have since experienced a similar sense of empathic connection to the collective pain and joy of all the world's living beings and the tragedy of the gap between what could be and the reality of what is. Such moments leave me with little doubt that a capacity for profound empathy is integral to our being and that we have great potential for the practice of responsible freedom that is systematically suppressed by the institutions of global capitalism.

A related experience in a very different setting occurred during my participation in the citizen forums at the United Nations Conference on Environment and Development in Rio de Janeiro, described in Chapter 11. Eighteen thousand people from every part of the world had come together to share their dreams for the planetary future. In terms of race, culture, religion, and socioeconomics, it was perhaps the most diverse gathering of its size ever held on our planet. It was a profoundly moving moment when I came to realize the extent to which we held a common vision of the world we hoped to create. It was the first visible manifestation of the emergence of a global civil society. Yet the experience suggested something even deeper—the emergence of a planetary consciousness without precedent in the human experience.

Since the Rio conference these processes have gained in strength and structure. Through countless local, national, and international forums, millions of citizens are now learning, sharing information, developing common strategies, and strengthening the human bonds that are forging the foundation of a new global civilization. Electronic communications technologies, especially the Internet, allow the participants in these many physical forums to communicate instantly at little cost over vast distances, affirming, challenging, and melding their dreams and insights into new understandings and agendas for a community of place called earth. News rarely mentioned in the mainstream press passes instantly through these electronic networks, facilitating processes of global collective action. Much as capitalism uses the power of secrecy, centralized authority, and massive financing to champion the cause of money, a globalizing civil society is using the power of openness, voluntary commitment, and the ability to self-organize everywhere at once to champion the cause of life.

To participate in these densely interconnected communication networks of people who care deeply for the places where they live and the future of all life is to experience a new way of being and relating—at once grounded in every person and every place, yet transcending both individuals and geography. The many physical and cyberspace forums in which we gather serve as learning centers to help us hone our capacities for mindful choice and participation in highly democratic processes as we reflect, think, share, and deepen our sense of the creative possibilities that lie ahead. We learn as we participate, growing in confidence in our ability to function as part of a conscious self-organizing, life-serving planetary whole. Having lived a quarter of my life in Asia, I find special meaning in what I experience as a melding of the Western emphasis on the individual and the Eastern emphasis on the collective as we rediscover life's profound wisdom: that the power of the individual depends on the health and integrity of the whole, just as the potential of the whole depends on the individual's exercise of the creative initiative that flows from mindful freedom.

I find particular inspiration in the idea that successful species find their niche within life's web at once to sustain themselves and to contribute to the whole. It is evident that our own prospects remain doubtful as long as we continue to live as though it were our birthright only to take, diminishing in the process the diversity, regenerative capacity, and evolutionary potential of the whole of life. We must now learn to live as one with the planet, taking only what we need, and discovering our place of service to life's continuing quest.

It is an inescapable reality that by the presence of our numbers and technology we are altering the course of planetary evolution. The question of whether or not it is our right to do so is of little relevance. The more meaningful question is whether we will acknowledge responsibility for the consequences—a responsibility we can escape only at the price of our self-extinction. It is our self-reflective consciousness that gives us the capacity to recognize the inevitable consequence of continuing on our present path. It is, therefore, the key to our salvation.

We have seen that the process of life's transcendent unfolding follows a persistent pattern of wholes joining to create new and greater wholes with abilities that cannot be predicted simply by a knowledge of their parts. I believe we are now on the threshold of such a melding toward the creation of an intelligent, self-aware planetary consciousness.

Indeed, the whole of human experience may easily be interpreted as a process of preparing us for such a step, beginning from the time our earliest ancestors realized they had the ability to reflect on their own awareness. The preparation continued with our early religious and philosophical reflections on our place in the universe and the foundations of moral behavior. It gained momentum with the Copernican revolution, which unleashed a flood of technological innovation, and with the early voyages of discovery that led over time to the virtual elimination of the geographical barriers that had separated us from one another. The preparation carried on through colonialism, two world wars, our ventures into space, the exponential growth of international air travel, and the creation of unified global communications facilities that now make it possible for information and ideas to span the globe in an instant.

Just as periods of disease and disability can serve as powerful moments of individual learning, the period of capitalist expansion, for all its tragedy, pain, and violence, has enriched our knowledge and awareness of the whole of the planet and its inhabitants. It has led many of us to establish bonds of friendship and affection that bridge the boundaries of culture, religion, class, and geography; helped us realize that all of humanity shares a common destiny inextricably linked to the living systems of the planet; and now leaves us poised to move to a new level of self-aware consciousness. Perhaps in this respect, global capitalism merits appreciation for its contribution to creating both the potential and the necessity to take this next step to species maturity. However, to take this step requires that we put capitalism and the institutionalized irresponsibility of our adolescence behind us and align ourselves and our technologies with life's continuing quest to know itself through the transcendent actualization of yet-unknown possibilities.

Learning to cooperate on an ever-larger scale has long been an important key to human advancement, as it has been to the evolution of life itself. As the scale of our cooperation has expanded, so too has our perception of the boundaries of the whole of which we are a part. The time has now come to expand our sphere of cooperation and identity to embrace the well-being of the planetary whole as critical to our personal well-being.

I believe that the task ahead depends even more on our spiritual awakening than on our political awakening for the simple reason that political resistance usually plays itself out through competition for the instruments of money's creation and allocation. Political victory alone merely leads to a shuffling of the power holders and a change in the rules by which money's power is distributed, but the new leaders remain largely figureheads in a world in which money—not life—is the real master. The struggle is played out on money's turf, by money's rules, to realize money's values. Only as we awaken to the understanding that what we really want is life, not money, can we begin to shed the chains of our enslavement to money's values and institutions and open ourselves to finding our place in life's unfolding.

Although our window of opportunity for making this choice may be closing, in the time scale of creation the earliest human form appeared some four million years ago, about twenty-three seconds to midnight on the creation-day clock. Science estimates that our planet has another five billion years ahead of it before the death of our sun and the recycling of its materials. If the present cosmic experiment with creating a species with the potential for planetary consciousness proves a failure, creation has ample time to try again.

That we are positioned to take this step at the precise historical moment at which it becomes imperative for our survival that we do so, is for me a source of awe and inspiration. It is as if a wise and caring intelligence beyond our knowing, having seen to it that we have the preparation necessary to our success, now leaves us to choose for ourselves whether to accept or reject the responsibilities—and to bear the consequences of our choice.

Notes

Prologue. A Story for the Third Millennium

1. Willis Harman, *Global Mind Change*, 2nd ed. (San Francisco: Berrett-Koehler, 1998), p. 185.
2. David C. Korten, *When Corporations Rule the World* (West Hartford, Conn.: Kumarian Press and San Francisco: Berrett-Koehler, 1995), p. 12.

Chapter 1. The Sirens' Song

1. Jim Hoagland, "The World's Bottom Line: Money Is Everything," *International Herald Tribune*, April 12–13, 1997, p. 6.
2. Michael Nagler, "Compassion: The Radicalism of this Age," *YES! A Journal of Positive Futures*, Fall 1998, p. 14.
3. Edward McNall Burns, *Western Civilizations: Their History and Their Culture*, 5th ed. (New York: W. W. Norton, 1958), pp. 522–523.
4. Carl Sagan, *The Dragons of Eden* (New York: Random House, 1977), p. 7.
5. As quoted by Laurence Berns, "Thomas Hobbes," in Leo Strauss and Joseph Cropsey (eds.), *History of Political Philosophy*, 3rd ed. (Chicago: University of Chicago Press, 1987), p. 397.
6. *Webster's New Collegiate Dictionary*, 1973, p. 544.
7. Burns, p. 521.
8. Richard Tarnas, *The Passion of the Western Mind: Understanding the Ideas That Have Shaped Our World View* (New York: Ballantine Books, 1991), p. 420.
9. Burns, p. 468.
10. Burns, p. 468.
11. Anna F. Lemkow, *The Wholeness Principle: Dynamics of Unity Within Science, Religion & Society* (Wheaton, Ill.: Quest Books, 1990), p. 143.
12. The story is documented by William Leach in *Land of Desire: Merchants, Power, and the Rise of a New American Culture* (New York: Pantheon Books, 1993). Or see Korten, pp. 149–158.
13. Leach, pp. 11–12.

14. Stuart Elliot, "Advertising: Healthy Economy Shows Up in a Vital Sign: Ad Spending," *The New York Times,* June 18, 1997, p. D4. Education expenditure is from United Nations Development Programme (UNDP), *Human Development Report 1996* (New York: Oxford University Press, 1996), p. 198.

15. For a detailed analysis of Channel One and the impact on its viewers see William Hoynes, "News for a Captive Audience: An Analysis of Channel One," pp. 11–17, and Mark Crispin Miller, "How to Be Stupid: The Lessons of Channel One," pp. 18–23, both in *Extra!* 10, no. 3, May/June 1997.

16. Elliot, p. D4.

17. UNDP, p. 72.

18. Duane Elgin, *Collective Consciousness and Cultural Healing, A Report to the Fetzer Institute* (San Anselmo, Calif.: Millennium Project, October 1997), p. 25.

19. Alexander W. Astin, Sarah A. Parrott, William S. Korn, and Linda J. Sax, *The American Freshman: Thirty Year Trends 1966–1996* (Los Angeles: UCLA Press, 1997).

20. Bernard Lietaer, "Beyond Greed and Scarcity," an interview by Sarah van-Gelder in *YES! A Journal of Positive Futures,* Spring 1997, pp. 34–35. For a thorough examination of the nature and consequences of debt-based money systems see Michael Rowbotham, *The Grip of Death: A Study of Modern Money, Debt Slavery, and Destructive Economics* (Charlbury, Oxfordshire, U.K.: Jon Carpenter Publishing, 1998).

Chapter 2. The Naked Emperor

1. *The Economist,* September 20, 1997, p. 17.

2. Lynn Margulis and Dorion Sagan, *What Is Life?* (New York: Simon & Schuster, 1995), p. 182.

3. George Soros, "The Crisis of Capitalism," *Atlantic Monthly,* February 1997, pp. 45–58.

4. Historian Fernand Braudel, in *Civilization & Capitalism,* Vol. 2 (Berkeley: University of California Press, 1982), pp. 232–239, gives a detailed historical account of the origins and definitions of the terms *capital, capitalist,* and *capitalism.*

5. Sarah Anderson and John Cavanagh, "The Top 200: The Rise of Global Corporate Power," report issued by the Institute for Policy Studies, Washington, D.C., September 25, 1996.

6. Leslie Wayne, "Wave of Mergers Is Recasting Face of Business in U.S.: $1 Trillion in Deals in '97," *The New York Times,* January 19, 1998, p. A13.

7. Wayne, p. A1; Peter Truell, "Buoyant Stock Market Keeps Mergers in Pipeline," *The New York Times,* January 5, 1998, p. D3; Melanie Warner, "The Year of the Very Big Deals," *Fortune,* November 24, 1997, pp. 36–37; William Wolman and Anne Colamosca, *The Judas Economy: The Triumph of Capital and the Betrayal of Work* (Reading, Mass.: Addison-Wesley, 1997), p. 69; Gene Koretz, "The Injury from Insider Trading," *Business Week,* November 24, 1997, p. 32; Stephanie Strom, "Mergers for Year Approach Record," *The New York Times,* October 31, 1997, p. A1; Charles Stein, "Another Boom Seen: Downsizing," *Boston Globe,* December 18, 1887, p. A31.

8. Steven Lipin, "Murphy's Law Doesn't Apply: The Conditions Are Perfect for Continued Growth in Mergers," *The Wall Street Journal,* January 2, 1998, p. R6.

9. Edmund L. Andrews, "High Noon in Europe: Big Wall Street Banks Gallop In, Guns Ablaze," *The New York Times,* July 13, 1997, sec. 3, p. 1.

10. Paul Lewis, "Euro to Ignite Merger Boom, Analysts Say," *The New York Times,* December 27, 1997, p. D1.

11. Andrew Pollack, "Korean Companies Are Looking Ripe to Foreign Buyers: Selling Spree Expected," *The New York Times,* December 27, 1997, p. A1.

12. Melody Petersen, "When an Auditor's Hats Clash," *The New York Times,* January 7, 1998, p. D1.

13. "Justice's Cartel Crackdown," *Business Week,* July 27, 1998, pp. 50–51.

14. Ben Lilliston and Ronnie Cummins, "Organic Vs. 'Organic': The Corruption of a Label," *The Ecologist* 28, no. 4, July/August 1998, pp. 195–200. For information on citizen groups monitoring U.S. government action on organic standards visit www.purefood.org.

15. Helena Paul, "Moral Bankruptcy: Adoption of the EU Life Patents Directive," *The Ecologist* 28, no. 4, July/August 1998, pp. 203–206.

16. Charles V. Bagli, "State and City Have a Deal to Keep the Stock Exchange," *The New York Times,* May 20, 1998, p. A20.

17. Louis Uchitelle, "Taxes Help Foot the Payrolls as States Vie for Employers," *The New York Times,* August 11, 1998, p. A1.

18. Donald L. Barlett and James B. Steele, *America: Who Stole the Dream?* (Kansas City, Mo.: Andrews and McMeel, 1996), p. 214.

19. Barlett and Steele, p. 19.

20. Robert Reich, *The Work of Nations* (New York: Alfred A. Knopf, 1991), p. 281.

21. "The End of Corporate Welfare As We Know It?" *Business Week,* February 10, 1997, pp. 36–37.

22. Greenpeace, "The Subsidy Scandal," www.greenpeace.org.

23. Based on personal communication with Paul Hawken, 1998.

24. Ralph Estes, *Tyranny of the Bottom Line: Why Corporations Make Good People Do Bad Things* (Berrett-Koehler, 1996), p. 190.

25. Robert Pear, "Audit of Medicare Finds $23 Billion in Overpayments," *The New York Times,* July 17, 1997, p. A1.

26. David Ricardo, *The Principles of Political Economy and Taxation* ([1817] London: Guernsey Press, 1973).

27. William Greider, *One World, Ready or Not: The Manic Logic of Global Capitalism* (New York: Simon & Schuster, 1997), p. 228.

28. It is actually a bit more complicated because the Federal Reserve requires the bank to maintain a small reserve against withdrawals.

29. Marjorie Kelly, "Why All the Fuss About Shareholders," *Business Ethics,* January/February 1997, p. 5. Kelly is presently writing a book elaborating on the point that the contribution of shareholders to the success or failure of a public corporation is inconsequential relative to the rewards to which they are legally entitled.

30. "Business Eyes a Financing Gap," *Business Week,* July 6, 1998, p. 20.

31. David E. Sanger, "Case No. 3: Asian Illness Threatening Vital Organs," *The New York Times,* November 22, 1997, p. D2.

32. "A World of Trouble," *Business Week,* June 15, 1998, p. 40.

33. John C. Edmunds, "Securities: The New World Wealth Machine," *Foreign Policy* 104, Fall 1996, p. 118.
34. Edmunds, p. 119.
35. Edmunds, p. 119.
36. Edmunds, p. 119.
37. Partrick McGeehan, "Wall Street Bonus Babies Strike It Rich," *Rocky Mountain News,* December 7, 1997, p. 2G; "Security Brokerages Take Lead in Industry Performance," *The Wall Street Journal Interactive Edition,* February 26, 1998; and "Shareholder Scoreboard," *The Wall Street Journal Interactive Edition,* February 26, 1998.
38. *Business Week,* March 18, 1996, p. 28.
39. Lawrence Mishel and Jared Bernstein, *The State of Working America* (Washington, D.C.: Economic Policy Institute, 1997), p. 289, as reported in *Dollars and Sense,* no. 215, January/February 1998, p. 2. Persons in defined-benefit retirement funds receive no benefit from stock appreciation.

Chapter 3. The Midas Curse

1. William Greider, *One World, Ready or Not: The Manic Logic of Global Capitalism* (New York: Simon & Schuster, 1997), p. 227.
2. Paul Hawken as interviewed by Sarah vanGelder, "The Next Reformation," *In Context,* no. 41, Summer 1995, pp. 17–22.
3. Karl-Henrik Robèrt, "Beyond the Chatter of Monkeys: Getting to Environmental Basics," *PCDForum Column* no. 26, February 25, 1992, p. 1.
4. Lester R. Brown, "The Future of Growth," in Lester R. Brown et al., *State of the World 1998* (New York: W. W. Norton, 1998), pp. 3–4.
5. Reports that the rate of population growth is declining have led some to assume mistakenly that the population problem has been solved. In fact it is far from solved. The world population growth rate is now down to 1.5 percent a year. Although this may seem low, even with current progress the latest United Nations projections anticipate a global population of 9.4 billion by 2050 and an eventual leveling off at 11 billion sometime after 2100— roughly the equivalent of adding four more Chinas to the world population. These are purely statistical calculations that take no account of the likelihood that violence, starvation, dehydration from water shortages, and epidemics resulting from the social and environmental collapse due to overcrowding will stop our growth long before such numbers are reached. I consider population growth a very serious issue. I have not chosen to give it consequential attention in this book only because I feel I have little to add at this moment to a discussion already well developed elsewhere. The relationship between a growing population and a declining resource base is examined in David C. Korten, *When Corporations Rule the World* (West Hartford, Conn.: Kumarian Press and San Francisco: Berrett-Koehler, 1995), Chapter 2, pp. 25–36.
6. This section is based on Alan Durning, *This Place on Earth: Home and the Practice of Permanence* (Seattle: Sasquatch Books, 1996), pp. 25–59.
7. For a detailed technical assessment see Herman E. Daly and John B. Cobb Jr., *For the Common Good* (Boston: Beacon Press, 1994), pp. 62–84 and 443–507. For a more popularized discussion see Clifford Cobb, Ted Hal-

stead, and Jonathan Rowe, "If the GDP Is Up, Why Is America Down?" *Atlantic Monthly,* October 1995, pp. 59–78. An excellent video documentary "Who's Counting? Marilyn Waring on Sex, Lies, and Global Economics," produced by the National Film Board of Canada, Studio B, is available from Bullfrog Films, Box 149, Oley, Penn. 19547; phone: (800) 543-3764.

8. Economists do calculate net domestic product by deducting depreciation, but it is not the figure by which they measure progress. For an extended authoritative discussion see Daly and Cobb, Chapter 3, "Misplaced Concreteness: Measuring Economic Success," pp. 62–84.

9. Pioneering work is being done on this issue in the United States by Redefining Progress, One Kearny Street, 4th Floor, San Francisco 94108; phone: (415) 543-6511; fax: (415) 543-9687; and in the United Kingdom by The New Economics Foundation, Vine Court, 1st Floor, 112-116 Whitechapel Road, London E1 1JE; phone: (441-71) 377-5696; fax: (441-71) 377-5720.

10. Richard Douthwaite, *Short Circuit: Strengthening Local Economies for Security in an Unstable World* (Dublin, Ireland: Lilliput Press, 1996), pp. 23–24. Australia data as calculated by the Australia Institute are reported in *Adbusters,* Autumn 1997, p. 59. Data for the Netherlands are reported in the New Economics Foundation, "More Isn't Always Better: A Special Briefing on Growth and Quality of Life in the U.K.," London: The New Economics Foundation, circa 1997 (undated), p. 6. For updates and additional data from Austria, Chile, Italy, and Sweden, visit www.foe.co.uk/progress.

11. Janet N. Abramovitz, "Sustaining the World's Forests," in Lester R. Brown et al., *State of the World 1998* (New York: W. W. Norton & Company, 1998), pp. 25–26.

12. Carl Riskin, "Behind the Silk Curtain," *The Nation,* November 10, 1997, p. 11.

13. Nicholas D. Kristof, "Across Asia, a Pollution Disaster Hovers," *The New York Times,* November 28, 1997, p. A1.

14. Nicholas D. Kristof, "Asian Pollution Is Widening Its Deadly Reach," *The New York Times,* November 29, 1997, p. A1.

15. Riskin, p. 11.

16. "The Wild, Wild East," *Business Week,* December 28, 1992, pp. 50–51, discusses the issue of China's widespread crime.

17. United Nations Development Programme (UNDP), *Human Development Report 1996* (New York: Oxford University Press, 1996), p. 1.

18. Greider, p. 232.

19. Robin Broad with John Cavanagh, *Plundering Paradise: The Struggle for the Environment in the Philippines* (Berkeley: University of California Press, 1993), pp. 24–30.

20. Bob Herbert, "In America: Nike's Boot Camps," *The New York Times,* March 31, 1997, p. A5.

21. "The Richest 400 People in America," *Forbes,* 1997 ed., p. 170.

22. Chris Busby, "2001: Entering the Era of Radioactive Consumerism," *The Ecologist* 27, no. 4, July/August 1997, pp. 132–133; Zac Goldsmith, "Legalized, Random Genocide," *The Ecologist* 28, no. 1, January/February 1998, pp. 2–5.

23. Ralph Ryder, "'Sustainable' Incineration and Death by Dioxin," *The Ecologist* 27, no. 4, July/August 1997, pp. 135–136.

24. Jed Greer and Kenny Bruno, *Greenwash: The Reality Behind Corporate Environmentalism* (New York: Apex Press, 1996), p. 11. Authoritative sources for the ongoing tracking of corporate crimes against the living world include *The Ecologist*, c/o Cissbury House, Furze View, Five Oaks Road, Slinfold, W. Sussex RH13 7RH, U.K.; phone/fax: (44-1403) 782-644; *Multinational Monitor*, P.O. Box 19408, Washington D.C. 20036; phone: (202) 387-8030; e-mail: monitor@essential.org; Web: www.essential.org/monitor (which claims to be "The Net's most comprehensive database on the activities of multinational corporations"); *Earth Island Journal*, 300 Broadway, Suite 28, San Francisco 94133; phone (415) 788-3666; e-mail: journal@earthisland.org; Web: www.earthisland.org; and Corporate Watch at www.corpwatch.org. *The Wall Street Journal, Business Week*, and the financial pages of most major newspapers are also good sources.

25. Greer and Bruno.

26. *PR Watch*, published quarterly by the Center for Media & Democracy, 3318 Gregory Street, Madison, Wis. 53711; phone: (608) 233-3346; fax: (608) 239-2236, specializes in public interest reporting on the public relations and public affairs industry. See also Murray Dobbin, *The Myth of the Good Corporate Citizen: Democracy Under the Rule of Big Business* (Toronto: Stoddart Publishing, 1998); and Sharon Beder, *Global Spin: The Corporate Assault on Environmentalism* (White River Junction, Vt.; Chelsea Green Publishing, 1998).

27. UNDP, *Human Development Report 1997* (New York: Oxford University Press, 1997), p. 9.

28. "The Global Power Elite," *Forbes*, July 28, 1997; "The World's Working Rich," *Forbes*, July 6, 1998, p. 190; and *The Wall Street Journal Almanac 1998* (New York: Ballantine Books, 1997).

29. "Executive Pay," *Business Week*, April 20, 1998, pp. 64–70.

30. "Executive Excess '98: CEOs Gain from Massive Downsizing," *Fifth Annual Executive Compensation Survey*, Institute for Policy Studies and United for a Fair Economy, 733 15th Street N.W. #1020, Washington, D.C. 20005, phone: (202) 387-9382.

31. David Cay Johnson, "American Style Pay Moves Abroad: Importance of Stock Options Expands in a Global Economy." *The New York Times*, September 3, 1998, pp. C1, C4.

32. Molly O'Neill, "Despite the Bad News, the Fishing Is Good: Leaving No Sea Untouched, a Global Effort Relies on Air Transport," *The New York Times*, October 22, 1997, p. F1.

Chapter 4. The Incredible Journey

1. Jacques Monod, *Change and Necessity* (1970), as cited by Edward Goldsmith, "Scientific Superstitions: The Cult of Randomness and the Taboo on Teleology," *The Ecologist* 27, no. 5, September/October 1997, p. 196.

2. Goldsmith, p. 198.

3. This is a highly abbreviated and simplified account of an incredibly rich and complex history based on Elisabet Sahtouris, *EarthDance: Living Systems in*

Evolution (Hill City, S. Dak.: Rat Haus Reality Press, 1995), available at www.ratical.com/LifeWeb/; Lynn Margulis and Dorion Sagan, *What Is Life?* (New York: Simon & Schuster, 1995); and Brian Swimme and Thomas Berry, *The Universe Story* (New York: HarperCollins, 1994)—supplemented by extended personal discussions with and detailed critical feedback from Elisabet Sahtouris. Some dates are from the IBM *World Book Multimedia Encyclopedia* on CD-ROM. The time periods involved in the early formation of the cosmos, the earth, and the emergence of life are approximations subject to change as science uncovers new evidence. Many details remain in dispute, and new findings will surely result in rewriting portions of the story in response to new data. For example, some now believe that life may have originated at heat vents in the dark depths of the ocean. See also Sidney Liebes, Elisabet Sahtouris, and Brian Swimme, *A Walk Through Time: From Star Dust to Us* (New York: John Wiley & Sons, 1998).

4. James Lovelock, *Gaia: A New Look at Life on Earth* (Oxford: Oxford University Press, 1995).
5. Margulis and Sagan, p. 73.
6. For further discussion of the unlikely occurrence of earth's atmosphere see Lovelock, *Gaia*, p. xiv.
7. Swimme and Berry, p. 94.
8. Swimme and Berry, p. 98.
9. Sahtouris, 1995, Chapter 5.
10. Margulis and Sagan, p. 90.
11. Swimme and Berry, p. 143.
12. Swimme and Berry, p. 145.
13. Swimme and Berry, p. 146.
14. John Noble Wilford, "Could Neanderthals Talk? Fossil Record Suggests a Resounding 'Yes.'" *International Herald Tribune,* May 4, 1998, p. 9.
15. Observations on the evolution of consciousness are based on Duane Elgin, *Awakening Earth;* and Swimme and Berry.
16. Raine Eisler, *The Chalice & the Blade: Our History. Our Future* (San Francisco: Harper San Francisco, 1987).
17. Sahtouris, Chapter 13; Swimme and Berry, pp. 183–184.
18. Swimme and Berry, p. 184.
19. Swimme and Berry, p. 225.
20. Swimme and Berry, p. 231.
21. Edward McNall Burns, *Western Civilizations: Their History and Their Culture,* 5th ed. (New York: W. W. Norton & Company, Inc., 1958), pp. 461–462.
22. Lee Smolin, *The Life of the Cosmos* (New York: Oxford University Press, 1997), pp. 44–45.
23. Smolin, p. 34.
24. Willis Harman and Elisabet Sahtouris, *Biology Revisioned* (Berkeley, Calif.: North Atlantic Books, 1998), Chapter 1.
25. Margulis and Sagan, p. 185.

Chapter 5. Organism as Metaphor

1. Richard Dawkins, *The Blind Watchmaker: Why the Evidence of Evolution Reveals a Universe Without Design* (New York: W. W. Norton, 1986), p. 10.

2. Lynn Margulis and Dorion Sagan, *What Is Life?* (New York: Simon & Schuster, 1995), p. 184.

3. This description of the distinction between the machine and the organism as metaphor is based on Mae-Wan Ho, "The New Age of the Organism," in *Architectural Design Profile* no. 129, "New Science = New Architecture," 1997, pp. 44–51.

4. Mae-Wan Ho, *Genetic Engineering: Dream or Nightmare? The Brave New World of Bad Science and Big Business* (Bath, U.K.: Gateway Books, 1998a), p. 223.

5. Janine M. Benyus, *Biomimicry: Innovation Inspired by Nature* (New York: William Morrow, 1997), p. 6.

6. Margulis and Sagan, p. 22.

7. Chilean biologists Humberto Maturana and Francisco Varela have given life's power to self-create the name *autopoietic,* the Greek term for self-creating. Fritjof Capra, *The Web of Life* (New York: Doubleday, 1996), pp. 96–99; and Margulis and Sagan, p. 23.

8. Robert A. Weinberg, "How Cancer Arises," in *What You Need to Know About Cancer* (New York: W. H. Freeman, 1996), p. 3.

9. Margulis and Sagan, p. 192.

10. Margulis and Sagan, p. 23.

11. Mae-Wan Ho, "On the Nature of Sustainable Economic Systems," *World Futures* 51, 1998b, pp. 199–211.

12. This section is based primarily on Mae-Wan Ho, *The Rainbow and the Worm: The Physics of Organisms* (Singapore: World Scientific, 1993); and Ho, 1998b, pp. 199–211.

13. Ho, 1997, p. 50

14. Mae-Wan Ho, "The Physics of Organisms and the Naturalistic Ethic of Organic Wholeness," *Network,* no. 54, Spring 1994, pp. 6–7.

15. Ho suggests that in addition to our "brain consciousness" we also have a "body consciousness" that works through the liquid crystalline structure of the body in tandem with but separately from the brain and central nervous system to achieve the instantaneous coordination of body functions among our cells. This fascinating, but speculative, thesis is based on the observation that the body's membrane lipids and proteins belong to a class of molecules known as *liquid crystals,* which have some of the characteristics of both crystals and liquids, as well as unique characteristics of their own. The structural alignment of liquid crystals is easily affected by electromagnetic fields, which is the basis of the liquid-crystal-display screens now commonly used in digital watches, calculators, and other electronic devices. Using a modification of the imaging technique used to examine the internal structure of mineral crystals, Ho has demonstrated it is possible to observe the coherence of the dynamic order of the body's liquid crystals, proving that the molecules in this seemingly liquid substance actually move in phase with one another—in contrast to the random movement of molecules in ordinary liquids. (This summary is based on a personal communication from Ho.)

16. Mae-Wan Ho, "The Biology of Free Will," *Journal of Consciousness Studies* 3, no. 3, 1996, p. 239.

17. Willis Harman and Elisabet Sahtouris, *Biology Revisioned* (Berkeley, Calif.: North Atlantic Press, June 1998), Chapter 1.
18. This summary is adapted from Benyus, pp. 251–277.
19. M. Mitchell Waldrop, *Complexity: The Emerging Science at the Edge of Order and Chaos* (New York: Simon & Schuster, 1992), p. 13.
20. The model was developed by Craig Reynolds. As recounted by Waldrop, pp. 241–242.
21. As quoted by Capra, p. 80.
22. Based on Capra, pp. 75–97.
23. Arthur Koestler, *The Ghost in the Machine* (New York: Random House, 1976).
24. For an exhaustive exposition of the ways in which the concept of holarchy contributes to our understand of life and consciousness see Ken Wilbur, *Sex, Ecology, Spirituality: The Spirit of Evolution* (Boston: Shambhala, 1995).
25. Dorion Sagan, "What Narcissus Saw: The Oceanic 'Eye,'" in Lynn Margulis and Dorion Sagan, *Slanted Truths: Essays on Gaia, Symbiosis, and Evolution* (New York: Springer-Verlag, 1997), p. 194.
26. Capra, p. 9.
27. Capra, pp. 9–10.
28. Wilbur, pp. 22–23.
29. This discussion of cancer is based on a collection of articles presented in a special issue of *Scientific American* titled "What You Need to Know About Cancer" and published in book form by W. H. Freeman, New York, 1996.
30. Sagan, p. 194; and Richard Dawkins, *The Selfish Gene* (Oxford: Oxford University Press, 1976).

Chapter 6. Embracing Life's Wisdom

1. As quoted by Janine M. Benyus, *Biomimicry: Innovation Inspired by Nature* (New York: William Morrow, 1997), p. 1.
2. As cited in Herman E. Daly and John B. Cobb Jr., *For the Common Good* (Boston: Beacon Press, 1989), p. 209.
3. "An Untimely Retreat by Vietnam," *The New York Times*, January 12, 1998, p. A20.
4. Benyus, p. 7.
5. John H. Holland, as reported by M. Mitchell Waldrop, *Complexity: The Emerging Science at the Edge of Order and Chaos* (New York: Simon & Schuster, 1992), p. 185.
6. Elisabet Sahtouris, "The Biology of Globalization," www.ratical.com /LifeWeb/.
7. Lynn Margulis and Dorion Sagan, *Microcosmos: Four Billion Years of Evolution from Our Microbial Ancestors* (New York: Summit Books, 1986), p. 248.
8. See Richard Dawkins, *The Selfish Gene* (Oxford: Oxford University Press, 1989).
9. Lee Smolin, *The Life of the Cosmos* (New York: Oxford University Press, 1997), p. 155.
10. Smolin, p. 155.
11. Hartmut Bossel, *20/20 Vision: Explorations of Sustainable Futures* (Kassel, Germany: Center for Environmental Systems Research, University of Kassel, 1996), pp. 2-7–2-8.

12. Design Element 9 is based on Stuart Cowen, "Reinhabiting a Wild Cosmos," *Original Blessing*, May-June 1998, p. 7.

Chapter 7. Responsible Freedom

1. As quoted by Duane Elgin and Coleen LeDrew, *Consciousness Change* (San Anselmo, Calif.: Millennium Project, 1997), p. ii.
2. Joanna Macy, *World as Lover, World as Self* (Berkeley, Calif.: Parallax Press, 1991), p. 35.
3. Thich Nhat Hanh, *The Sun My Heart* (Berkeley, Calif.: Parallax Press, 1988), p. 38.
4. Jean L. Cohen and Andrew Arato, *Civil Society and Political Theory* (Cambridge, Mass.: MIT Press, 1992), p. 84.
5. Aristotle, *Politics Book I*, Part 2, in Stephen Everson (ed.), *Aristotle: The Politics and the Constitution of Athens* (New York: Cambridge University Press, 1996) p. 13.
6. Aristotle, *Politics Book VII*, Part 1 (Everson), p. 166.
7. Aristotle, *Politics Book IV*, Part 11 (Everson), pp. 107–108.
8. Scott R. Bowman, *The Modern Corporation and American Political Thought: Law, Power, and Ideology* (University Park: Pennsylvania State University, 1996), p. 6.
9. Bertram Gross, *Friendly Fascism: The New Face of Power in America* (Boston: South End Press, 1980).
10. M. Mitchell Waldrop, *Complexity: The Emerging Science at the Edge of Order and Chaos* (New York: Simon & Schuster, 1992), p. 12.
11. Thich Nhat Hanh, *Being Peace* (Berkeley, Calif.: Parallax Press, 1987), pp. 65–66.
12. For information on GAP, contact Global Action Plan for the Earth, Post Office Box 428, Woodstock, N.Y. 12498; phone: (914) 679-4830; fax: (914) 679-4834; e-mail: info@globalactionplan.org; Web:www.globalctionplan.org/.
13. For addresses of national offices of The Natural Step see www.naturalstep.org/. Or contact The Natural Step, U.S., P.O. Box 29372, San Francisco 94129-0372, phone: (415) 561-3344; fax: (415) 561-3345; e-mail: tns@naturalstep.org.
14. Cliff Feigenbaum, "Responsible Investing," *YES! A Journal of Positive Futures*, Spring 1998, p. 10.
15. "Top Ten SRI Mutual Funds," *The Greenmoney Journal* 7, no. 1, Summer/Fall 1998, p. 5. This is one of several excellent periodicals on socially responsible investing. *The Greenmoney Journal*, West 608 Glass Avenue, Spokane, Wash. 99205; phone: (509) 328-1741 or (800) 318-5725; Web: www.greenmoney.com. $35 per year.

Chapter 8. Mindful Markets

1. Fernand Braudel, *Civilization & Capitalism 15th–18th Centuries. Vol. III. The Perspective of the World* (in French, 1979; Berkeley: University of California Press, 1992), p. 632.
2. Peter Drucker, "The Relentless Contrarian," *Wired*, August 1996.

3. Fernand Braudel, *Civilization & Capitalism 15th–18th Centuries. Vol. II. The Wheels of Commerce* (Berkeley: University of California Press, 1982), p. 237. Braudel indicates that the term was also unknown to Karl Marx when he wrote *Capital* (vol. I of the three-volume *Capital* published originally 1867).

4. Adam Smith, *The Theory of Moral Sentiments*, D. D. Raphael and A. L. Macfie (eds.) ([1759] Indianapolis, Ind.: Liberty Fund, 1984), p. 9.

5. Smith, 1984, p. 218.

6. Adam Smith, *An Inquiry into the Nature and Causes of the Wealth of Nations* ([1776] New York: Modern Library, 1937), p. 423.

7. Human-scale, stakeholder-owned enterprises are a centerpiece of the economic model advocated by E. F. Schumacher in *Small Is Beautiful: Economics as if People Mattered* (New York: HarperCollins, 1973).

8. Paul Hawken, *The Ecology of Commerce: A Declaration of Sustainability* (New York: Harper Business, 1993), p. 163.

Chapter 9. Economic Democracy

1. John Dillon, *Turning the Tide: Confronting the Money Traders* (Toronto: Ecumenical Coalition for Economic Justice, 1997), p. 31.

2. Jeff Gates, *The Ownership Solution: Toward a Shared Capitalism for the 21st Century* (Reading, Mass.: Addison-Wesley, 1998), p. 219.

3. Bill Quinn, *How Wal-Mart Is Destroying America: And What You Can Do About It* (Berkeley, Calif.: Ten Speed Press, 1998).

4. *Forbes* 1991 report on the "400 Richest," as cited by Quinn, p. xiii.

5. John Huey and Sally Solo, "America's Most Successful Merchant," *Fortune*, September 23, 1991. p. 46.

6. This report is drawn from Josh Simon, "The Mensch of Malden Mills," *Life*, May 5, 1997, p. 76; Susan Vaughn, "Firms Find Long-Term Rewards in Doing Good: A New Breed of Corporation Is Emerging Whose Leaders Place Principles Before Profits," *Los Angeles Times*, November 3, 1997, pp. D2–13; "How Malden Mills Rose Once Again from the Ashes," *New Hampshire Business Review*, October 24, 1997 19, no. 23, p. 3.

7. It is important not to confuse form and substance. Wal-Mart has an employee stock purchase plan that encourages employee ownership participation. It is not, however, linked to employee participation in the exercise of ownership rights, which were firmly in Sam Walton's control until the time of his death.

8. John Locke, *The Second Treatise of Government*, Chapter 5, paragraph 34, in David Wooten, *Political Writings of John Locke* (New York: Penguin, 1993) p. 277.

9. Locke, Chapter 5, paragraph 25, p. 273.

10. Locke, Chapter 5, paragraphs 27, 25, pp. 273–274.

11. Locke, Chapter 5, paragraph 32, p. 276.

12. Locke, Chapter 5, paragraph 25, p. 273.

13. Richard Ashcraft, "Locke's Political Philosophy," in Vere Chappell (ed.), *The Cambridge Companion to Locke* (Cambridge: Cambridge University Press, 1994), pp. 248–249.

14. Michael Hopkins and Jeffrey L. Seglin, "Americans at Work," *Inc.*, May 1997, p. 77.

15. Dee W. Hock, "The Chaordic Organization: Out of Control and into Order," *World Business Academy Perspectives* 9, no. 1, 1995., pp. 5–18.

16. Hock, p. 14.

17. For further elaboration see David C. Korten, *When Corporations Rule the World* (West Hartford, Conn.: Kumarian Press and San Francisco: Berrett-Koehler, 1995), pp. 216–220.

18. "European Economic Development Ideas Take Root in Oregon," *Transatlantic Perspectives*, no. 24, Autumn 1991, pp. 6–9.

19. "European Economic Development Ideas," pp. 6–9.

20. Based on an interview with David Bryun, the organizer of the association. For information on the Forest Stewardship Council visit www.fscus.org.

21. David C. Korten, "Community Organization and Rural Development: A Learning Process Approach," *Public Administration Review,* September/October 1980, pp. 485–486.

22. Appropriate Technology International, 1828 L Street N.W., Suite 1000, Washington, D.C. 20036; phone: (202) 293-4600; fax: (202) 293-4598; e-mail: liveableworld@ati.org.

23. The frontier versus spaceship metaphor comes from Kenneth Boulding's classic essay "The Economics of the Coming Spaceship Earth," which is discussed at greater length in David C. Korten, *When Corporations Rule the World* (West Hartford, Conn.: Kumarian Press and San Francisco: Berrett-Koehler, 1995), pp. 25–27. The original essay is reprinted in David C. Korten and Rudi Klauss (eds.), *People-Centered Development: Contributions Toward Theory and Planning Frameworks* (West Hartford, Conn.: Kumarian Press, 1984), pp. 63–73.

Chapter 10. The Rights of Living Persons

1. Thurman W. Arnold, *Folklore of Capitalism* (New Haven, Conn.: Yale University Press, 1937), p. 185, as quoted in Scott R. Bowman, *The Modern Corporation and American Thought: Law, Power, and Ideology* (Univerity Park: Pennsylvania State University Press), p. 182.

2. Richard Grossman and Frank T. Adams, *Taking Care of Business: Citizenship and the Charter of Incorporation* (Cambridge, Mass.: Charter, Inc., 1993), p. 22.

3. Grossman and Adams, p. 20.

4. Santa Clara County v. Southern Pacific Railroad Company, *118 U.S. 394* (1886). Available at www.tourolaw.edu/patch/santa.

5. Legal historians believe the assertion was based on testimony presented to the Court four years earlier by Roscoe Conkling, a former U.S. senator and a member of the congressional committee that drafted the Fourteenth Amendment. Conkling had testified that those who drafted this amendment, which states that all persons are entitled to equal protection under the law, had intended that the word *persons* include corporations—an assertion that has since been thoroughly discredited by legal scholars. Bowman, 1996, p. 323, footnote 89.

6. Robert A. G. Monks, *The Emperor's Nightingale: Restoring the Integrity of the Corporation in the Age of Shareholder Activism* (Reading, Mass.: Addison-Wesley, 1998), p. 173.

7. These data are from surveys conducted during 1996 and 1997 by CNN, *USA Today,* and the Gallup Poll, except for the data on the expectations of an

Elvis sighting, which come from an Opinion Dynamics, Inc., poll conducted for Fox News. Available at www.publicampaign.org/pubop.htmu.

8. The data on state-level campaigns are from the Web site of Public Campaign, www.publicampaign.org, which tracks and supports such initiatives on an ongoing basis.

9. For details of this assault on democracy, citizen sovereignty, and life, see Maude Barlow and Tony Clarke, *MAI: The Multilateral Agreement on Investment and the Threat to American Freedom* (New York: Stoddart Publishing, 1998). Until February 1997 the MAI negotiations had received no press coverage and were unknown to the public, suggesting that negotiators knew full well that the agreement's provisions would not stand up to democratic public scrutiny and that they intended to get it signed and slipped through the world's parliamentary bodies before the public realized that their governments had just signed away their right to regulate global capital. In that month a leaked copy of the document was posted to the Web, making the secret negotiating documents available to anyone with a computer and a modem. Using the Internet as an organizing tool, citizen groups all over the world mobilized and created a sufficient political backlash against the prospective agreement by early 1998 to place its conclusion in doubt. An article in *Foreign Policy* concludes that because of the Internet, "It will be increasingly difficult to conduct international negotiations in private, much less in secret, or to impose globalization as an elite-driven project." Stephen J. Kobrin, "The MAI and the Clash of Globalizations," *Foreign Policy*, Fall 1998, p. 108. Links to various Web sites dealing with the MAI may be found at www.foreignpolicy.com.

10. Bob Herbert, "Banana Bully," *The New York Times*, May 13, 1996, p. A15; and Brook Larmer, "Brawl Over Bananas," *Newsweek*, April 28, 1997, pp. 43–44.

11. Michael Specter, "Europe Bucking Trend in U.S., Blocks Genetically Altered Food," *The New York Times*, July 20, 1998, pp. A1 and A8, reports on the depth of citizen concern in Europe about the safety of genetically altered foods.

12. "Rougher Sailing Across the Atlantic," *Business Week*, July 27, 1998, p. 29.

13. Bernard A. Lietaer, *The Future of Money: Beyond Greed and Scarcity* (forthcoming).

14. For an authoritative and highly readable treatment of the issues and options see Michael Rowbotham, *The Grip of Death: A Study of Modern Money, Debt Slavery and Destructive Economics* (Charlbury, Oxfordshire: Jon Carpenter Publishing, 1998).

15. Lietaer.

16. Jeff Shavelson, *A Third Way: A Sourcebook: Innovations in Community-Owned Enterprise, 1990*, available from The National Center for Economic Alternatives, 2000 P Street N.W., Suite 330, Washington, D.C. 20009; phone: (202) 986-1373; fax: (202) 986-7938, provides background and contact information on a representative sampling of such enterprises.

17. Jeff Gates, *The Ownership Solution* (Reading, Mass.: Addison-Wesley, 1998), pp. 217–218.

18. Sir James Goldsmith, *The Trap* (New York: Carroll & Graf, 1993).

19. Klaus Schwab and Claude Smadja, "Start Taking the Backlash Against Globalization Seriously," *International Herald Tribune,* February 1, 1996, p. 8.

20. Barry James, "Executives' Warning on Raw Capitalism," *International Herald Tribune,* October 5, 1996.

21. James.

22. A complete report on the proceedings is published as Sadruddin Aga Khan (ed.), *Policing the Global Economy: Why, How, and for Whom?* (London: Cameron May, 1998).

23. "Needed: A New Financial Architecture," *Business Week,* October 12, 1998, p. 162.

24. The New Party, 227 West 40th Street, Suite 1303, New York 10018; phone: (800) 200-1294; e-mail: newparty@igc.org; Web: www.newparty.org.

25. Monks, pp. 170–181.

26. Michael Lerner, "Social Responsibility Amendment," *Tikkun* 12, no. 4, July/August 1997, p. 33. For further information contact the Foundation for Ethics and Meaning, 4620A West Kennedy Boulevard, Tampa, Fla., 33609; phone: (888) 538-7227; fax: (813) 251-0492; e-mail: roberts@meaning.org; Web: www.meaning.org. See also Michael Lerner, *The Politics of Meaning: Restoring Hope and Possibility in Age of Cynicism* (Reading, Mass.: Addison-Wesley, 1996).

27. For more information contact the Alliance for Democracy, P.O. Box 683, Lincoln, Mass. 01773; phone: (617) 259-9395; fax: (617) 259-0404, e-mail: peoplesall@aol.com.

28. For information contact Jeff Barber, NGO Taskforce on Business & Industry, c/o Integrative Strategies Forum, 1612 K Street, NW, Suite 600, Washington, D.C. 20006; phone: (202) 872-5339; fax: (202) 331-8166; e-mail: jbarber@igc.apc.org.

29. Program on Corporations, Law & Democracy, P.O. Box 246, South Yarmouth, Mass. 02664-0246; phone: (508) 398-1145; fax: (508) 398-1552; e-mail: people@poclad.org.

30. The Social Ventures Network, P.O. Box 29221, San Francisco 94129-0221; phone: (415) 561-6501, fax: (415) 561-6435; e-mail: svn@well.com; Web www.svn.org; Business for Social Responsibility, 609 Mission Street, 2nd Floor, San Francisco 94105-3506; phone: (415) 537-0888; fax: (415) 537-0889; Web: www.bsr.org; the World Business Academy, P.O. Box 191210, San Francisco 94119-1210; phone: (415) 393-8251; fax: (415) 393-8369; e-mail: wba@well.com.

Chapter 11. Culture Shift

1. Willis Harman, *Global Mind Change: The Promise of the Last Years of the Twentieth Century* (San Francisco: Berrett-Koehler, 1988), p. xvii.

2. Fritjof Capra, *The Web of Life: A New Scientific Understanding of Living Systems* (New York: Anchor Books, 1996), p. 4.

3. Elisabet Sahtouris reflections on UNCED in "The Evolution of Governance," *In Context,* no. 36, Fall 1993.

4. *YES! A Journal of Positive Futures* is dedicated to giving voice to the new storytellers. Published by The Positive Futures Network, P.O. Box 10818, Bain-

bridge Island, Wash. 98110; phone: (206) 842-0216; fax: (206) 842-5208; e-mail: yes@futurenet.org; Web: www.futurenet.org.

5. This discussion of Ray's research is based on Paul H. Ray, *The Integral Culture Survey: A Study of Values Subcultures and the Use of Alternative Health Care in America, A Report to Fetzer Institute and the Institute of Noetic Sciences*, October, 1995; Paul Ray, "The Great Divide: Prospects for an Integral Culture," *YES! A Journal of Positive Futures*, Fall 1996, pp. 55–58; and Paul H. Ray, "The Rise of Integral Culture," *Noetic Sciences Review*, Spring 1996, pp. 4–15. The study involved 1,036 respondents from a representative national panel of persons who have agreed to answer mail surveys, plus 245 respondents from a national sample of Cultural Creatives.

6. Ray, 1995, p. 48.

7. Ray, 1995, p. 68.

8. "Yearning for Balance: Views of Americans on Consumption, Materialism, and the Environment," July 1995, prepared by The Harwood Group for the Merck Family Fund, 6930 Carroll Avenue, Suite 500, Takoma Park, Md. 20912, p. 1. This was a nationwide random sample survey of 800 adults ages 18 years and older conducted by telephone from February 20 to March 1, 1995.

9. "Yearning for Balance," p. 18.

10. As reported by Duane Elgin and Coleen LeDrew, "Global Paradigm Report: Tracking the Shift Under Way," *YES! A Journal of Positive Futures*, Winter 1997, p. 19; and Duane Elgin with Collen LeDrew, *Global Consciousness Change: Indicators of an Emerging Paradigm* (San Anselmo, Calif.: Millennium Project, 1997). For further information visit: www.awakeningearth.org.

11. Ronald Inglehart, *Modernization and Postmodernization: Cultural, Economic, and Political Change in 43 Societies* (Princeton, N.J.: Princeton University Press, 1997). The methodology involved face-to-face interviews with national samples in each country. For a summary report see Duane Elgin and Coleen LeDrew, "Global Paradigm Report: Tracking the Shift Underway," *YES! A Journal of Positive Futures*, Winter 1997, p. 21; and Duane Elgin with Collen LeDrew, *Global Consciousness Change: Indicators of an Emerging Paradigm* (San Anselmo, Calif.: Millennium Project, 1997).

12. "Top 10 Trends for 1997 as Predicted by the Trends Research Institute in Rhinebeck, N.Y." *Detroit News*, December 29, 1996, p. A10.

13. Information provided in personal communication from Vicki Robin, June 19, 1998.

14. "Yearning for Balance," p. 18.

15. The Spring/Summer 1996 issue of *YES! A Journal of Positive Futures* features the voluntary simplicity movement and provides a guide to resources to those who want to be involved.

16. Joe Dominguez and Vicki Robin, *Your Money or Your Life: Transforming Your Relationships with Money and Achieving Financial Independence* (New York: Viking, 1992), p. 54. Joe died of cancer on January 11, 1997. Vicki and her new Road Map Foundation colleagues continue actively with their work in helping people achieve financial independence through voluntary simplicity.

17. As quoted by Joe Dominguez and Vicki Robin in the introduction to Jacqueline Blix and David Heitmiller, *Getting a Life: Real Lives Transformed by Your Money or Your Life* (New York: Viking, 1997), p. xii.
18. Blix and Heitmiller.

Chapter 12. The New Storytellers

1. Hazel Henderson, *Building a Win-Win World* (San Francisco: Berrett-Koehler, 1996), p. 162.
2. As quoted in *Sustainable Seattle, Indicators of Sustainable Community* (Seattle: Sustainable Seattle, 1998), p. 6.
3. Timothy Egan, "'Or Else' Gives Seattle Voters the Last Laugh," *The New York Times,* December 7, 1997, pp. 1, 36.
4. Tracy Rysavy, "Mothers for Eco-Justice," *YES! A Journal of Positive Futures,* Summer 1998, pp. 25–26.
5. Gavan McCormack, "Village vs. State," *The Ecologist* 27, no. 6, November/December 1997, pp. 225–228.
6. "Profile of Vandana Shiva," *PCDForum Paradigm Warrior Profile* no. 3, June 1, 1996. http://iisd.ca/pcdf.
7. "Profile of Vandana Shiva," 1996.
8. Barry Bearak, "Man of Vision or of Violence?" *The New York Times,* November 20, 1997, pp. B1, B4.
9. David Bonbright et al., *Leading Public Entrepreneurs* (Arlington, Va.: Ashoka Innovators for the Public, 1997).
10. The following stories of women environmental heroes are from Mary Joy Breton, *Women Pioneers for the Environment* (Boston: Northeastern University Press, 1998).
11. Rachel Carson, *Silent Spring* (Boston: Houghton Mifflin, 1962). Theo Colborn, Dianne Dumanoski, and John Peterson Myers, *Our Stolen Future* (New York: Penguin Books, 1996).
12. Based on NPR *All Things Considered* transcript no. 98042005-212 downloaded from Lexis-Nexis, and National Foundation for Women Business Owners press releases available on www.nfwbo.org.
13. Donella H. Meadows, "Responsible Wealth," *YES! A Journal of Positive Futures,* Spring 1998, pp. 54–55; and "Responsible Taxes," *YES! A Journal of Positive Futures,* Summer 1998, pp. 9–10. For more information contact Responsible Wealth, c/o United for a Fair Economy, 37 Temple Place, 5th Floor, Boston 02111; phone: (617) 423-2148; fax: (617) 423-0191; e-mail: rw@stw.org.
14. *YES! A Journal of Positive Futures,* Summer 1998, p. 8. For more information contact Business Leaders for Sensible Priorities, 130 William Street, 7th Floor, New York 10038, or phone: (212) 964-3534 Ext. 28.
15. Based on Frances F. Korten, "Fast Track—Dead End," *YES! A Journal of Positive Futures,* Spring 1998, pp. 56–57.
16. For more information contact Program Director, International Forum on Globalization, Foundation for Deep Ecology, P.O. Box 12218, San Francisco 94112-0218; phone: (415) 771-3394, Ext. 309; fax: (415) 771-1121.
17. "Profile of Sara Larrain R.," *PCDForum Paradigm Warrior Profile* no. 2, June 1, 1996. Based on an interview by David C. Korten; http:/iisd.ca/pcdf. For

more information contact RENACE, Ecocentro, Seminario 774, Nuñoa, Casilla 16784 Coreo 9, Santiago, Chile; phone: (56-2) 223-4483; fax: (56-2) 223-4522; e-mail: iep@ax.apc.org.

18. "Creating a National Consensus: Interview with Nicanor 'Nicky' Perlas by David C. Korten," *PCDForum Paradigm Warrior Profile* no. 4, May 20, 1997; http://iisd.ca/pcdf. For more information contact the Center for Alternative Development Initiatives (CADI), 110 Scout Rallos, Quezon City, Philippines; phone: (63-2) 928-3986; fax: (63-2) 928-7608; e-mail: CADI@phil.gn.apc.org.

19. Maude Barlow, "Globalization and the Dismantling of Canadian Democracy, Values, and Society," *PCDForum* article no. 17, June 1, 1996; http://iisd.ca/pcdf. For more information contact Council of Canadians, 904-251 Laurier Avenue W., Ottawa, Ontario K1P 5J6, Canada; phone: (613) 233-2773; fax: (613) 233-6776; e-mail: coc@web.apc.org.

Chapter 13. Life Choices

1. Matthew Fox, *The Reinvention of Work: A New Vision of Livelihood for Our Time* (San Francisco: HarperCollins, 1994), pp. 1–2.

2. Kahlil Gibran, *The Prophet* (New York: Alfred A. Knopf, 1962), p. 40

3. John Robbins, *Reclaiming Our Health: Exploding the Medical Myth and Embracing the Source of True Healing* (Tiburon, Calif.: H. J. Kramer, 1996), pp. 2–3.

4. Michael Lerner, *Choices in Healing: Integrating the Best of Conventional and Complementary Approaches to Cancer* (Cambridge, Mass.: MIT Press, 1994), p. 35.

5. Robbins, 1996, p. 260.

6. Jane E. Brody, "Alternative Care: Buyer Beware," *International Herald Tribune,* May 4, 1998, p. 9.

7. Annemarie Colbin, *Food and Healing* (New York: Ballantine Books, 1996).

8. Based on an e-mail version of "The Global Citizen," a syndicated column produced by Donella H. Meadows, September 18, 1997, and published by participating U.S. newspapers. Meadows's columns are regularly posted on the PCDForum Web site: http://iisd.ca/pcdf.

9. From an analysis of federal data by the Tufts University Center on Hunger, Poverty and Nutrition Policy as reported by *WHY,* Fall/Winter 1997, p. 30.

10. John Steinhart and Carol Steinhart, "Energy Use in the United States Food System," *Science* 184, 1974, pp. 307–316, as reported by Kenneth A. Dahlberg, in "World Food Problems: Making the Transition from Agriculture to Regenerative Food Systems," in Dennis Pirages (ed.), *Building Sustainable Societies: A Blueprint for a Post-Industrial World* (Armonk, N.Y.: M. E. Sharpe, 1996), pp. 257–274.

11. Robert McC. Netting, *Smallholders, Householders: Farm Families and the Ecology of Intensive, Sustainable Agriculture* (Stanford, Calif.: Stanford University Press, 1993), p. 124.

12. Vandana Shiva, *The Violence of the Green Revolution* (Penang, Malaysia: Third World Network, 1991), pp. 80–81; and Mae-Wan Ho, "On the Nature of Sustainable Economic Systems," *World Futures* (forthcoming).

13. Netting, 1993, p. 322.

14. Robbins, 1996, p. 338.
15. Statistics compiled by the Oregon Department of Land Conservation and Development and obtained from the University of Oregon Web site: http://darkwing.uoregon.edu/.
16. As reported by Alan Thein Durning, *This Place on Earth: Home and the Practice of Permanence* (Seattle: Sasquatch Books, 1996), pp. 114–116.
17. This story is compiled from Jay Walljasper, "Portland's Green Peace: At Play in the Fields of Urban Planning," *The Nation*, October 13, 1997, pp. 11–15; Charles E. Beggs, "Land Use Watchdog Group in Oregon Now Has 2,500 'Friends,'" Associated Press, May 16, 1994; Angela Wilson, "The Browning of the Green Movement: The Urban League Becomes an Environmental Powerhouse," *Portland Skanner* XXI, no. 31, May 22, 1996, p. 1.
18. Erik Ingram and George Snyder, "Five Antisprawl Measures Pass in Sonoma County," *San Francisco Chronicle*, November 7, 1996, p. A19.
19. Hap Cawood, "Growth Still Possible Without the Sprawl," *Dayton Daily News*, June 12, 1997, p. 18A.
20. The reasons are spelled out in Chapters 2 and 3.
21. Redefining Progress, One Kearny Street, 4th Floor, San Francisco 94108; phone: (415) 781-1191; fax: (415) 781-1198, e-mail: info@rprogress.org, publishes a number of reports on these efforts and maintains a searchable data base with Internet links to each project that may be accessed at www.rprogress.org. The *Community Indicators Handbook* is available from Redefining Progress to help interested communities get started with their own indicators projects. See also Kate Besleme and Megan Mullin, "Community Indicators and Healthy Communities," *National Civic Review* 86, no. 1, Spring 1997, pp. 43–52.
22. This discussion of Sustainable Seattle is based on its 1998 report, *Sustainable Seattle, Indicators of Sustainable Community* (Seattle: Sustainable Seattle, 1998), which is available from Sustainable Seattle, 514 Minor Avenue North, Seattle 98109-5516; phone: (206) 622-3522; fax: (206) 622-311; e-mail: sustsea@halcyon.com; Web: www.sustainable.org.

Chapter 14. Engaging the Future

1. As quoted by John Holt, *What Do I Do Monday?* (New York: Dell, 1970), p. 302.
2. Margaret J. Wheatley and Myron Kellner-Rogers, *A Simpler Way* (San Francisco: Berrett-Koehler, 1996), p. 50.
3. A curriculum for such a course, as designed and taught by Professor James Q. Wilson at the Anderson Graduate School of Management at the University of California at Los Angeles (UCLA), is presented in *The Good Society* 8, no. 1, Winter 1998, pp. 51–56, published by the Committee on the Political Economy of the Good Society, Department of Government and Politics, University of Maryland, College Park, Md. 20742.
4. International Society for Ecological Economics (ISEE), P.O. Box 1589, Solomons, Md. 20688; phone: (410) 326-7354; fax: (410) 326-7354; Web: http://kabir.umb.edu/ISEE. Note that although the ISEE is engaged in rigorous economic research toward building an alternative economics discipline, membership is open to all who are concerned with creating an earth-

and community-friendly economic system. Its journal is for the technical specialist, but its newsletter is wholly intelligible to those without specialized training in economics. The Web site is also a resource for those looking for academic programs in ecological economics.

5. Joe Dominguez and Vicki Robin, *Your Money or Your Life: Transforming Your Relationship with Money and Achieving Financial Independence* (New York: Viking, 1992), is the all-time best-selling practical guide to the practice of voluntary simplicity. Duane Elgin, *Voluntary Simplicity: Toward a Way of Life That Is Outwardly Simple, Inwardly Rich* (New York: William Morrow, 1993), is the classic work on the philosophy of voluntary simplicity. The Simple Living Network offers a comprehensive guide to relevant resources on voluntary simplicity through its Web site, www.slnet.com. If you are interested in forming a voluntary simplicity support group, take a look at the program offered by The Global Action Plan for the Earth (GAP), P.O. Box 428, Woodstock, N.Y. 12498; phone: (914) 679-4830; fax: (914) 679-4834; e-mail: info@globalactionplan.org; Web: www.globalctionplan.org. Note that the GAP Web site gives contact information for GAP programs in other countries. For further information on these and other resources see *YES! A Journal of Positive Futures*, spring/summer 1996, on "Getting Free: Moving Beyond the Consumer Culture."

6. For information on the Thanksgiving Conspiracy, contact Gerard Bentryn, owner and manager of the Bainbridge Winery, at gbentryn@seanet.com.

7. Those I find especially useful include *The Ecologist*, c/o Cissbury House, Furze View, Five Oaks Road, Slinfold, W. Sussex RH13 7RH, U.K., phone/fax (441-258) 473-476, e-mail ecologist@gn.apc.org; *Mother Jones*, P.O. Box 469024, Escondido, Calif. 92046-9838, phone(800) 438-6656, Web www.motherjones.com; *The Progressive Populist*, P.O. Box 487, Storm Lake, Iowa 50588, (1-800) 732-4992, www.eden.com/~reporter, and *The Nation*, P.O. Box 37072, Boone, Iowa 50037, phone (800) 333-8536, Web www.The Nation.com. A number of the publications that specifically cater to the business community, such as *Business Week* and *The Wall Street Journal* are filled with useful reports on economic and corporate issues neglected by publications aimed at more general readers—once you get beyond the ideological bias of the editorial content. For an excellent selection of books dealing with issues given scant attention by the corporate press, request a catalog from Apex Press, Council on International and Public Affairs, 777 United Nations Plaza, Suite 3C, New York 10017; phone/fax: (914) 271-6500.

8. *Co-op America's National Green Pages* lists a number of leading community banks. Co-op America, 1612 K Street N.W., Suite 600, Washington, D.C. 20006; phone: (800) 584-7336; fax: (202) 331-8166; Web: www.coopamerica.org.

9. Tracy Gary and Melissa Kohner, *Inspired Philanthropy: Creating a Giving Plan—A Workbook* (Berkeley, Calif.: Chardon Press, 1998), provides guidance in taking a thoughtful and organized approach to giving, no matter what amount is within your means.

10. In the United States, Working Assets Long Distance (800) 788-0898 and Affinity (800) 964-3863 offer such plans. For example, under the Affinity

long-distance program you can enjoy competitive long-distance rates and at the same time support the Positive Futures Network and *YES! A Journal of Positive Futures*. For details, call *YES!* at (800) 937-4451.

11. *The Community Indicators Handbook: Measuring Progress Toward Healthy and Sustainable Communities* offers detailed guidance. Copies are available from Redefining Progress, One Kearny Street, 4th Floor, San Francisco 94108; phone: (415) 781-1191; fax: (415) 781-1198; Web: www.rprogress.org.

12. You may find useful inspiration for such a project from *Co-op America's National Green Pages: A Directory of Products and Services for People and the Planet,* available from Co-op America. See note 8 for contact information.

13. For more information on community currencies and how to create them see the Spring 1997 issue of *YES! A Journal of Positive Futures,* featuring the theme "Money, Print Your Own!" See also Thomas H. Greco Jr., *New Money for Healthy Communities,* available for $19 from Thomas H. Greco Jr., P.O. Box 42663, Tucson, Ariz. 85733; and Edgar Cahn and Jonathan Rowe, *Time Dollars* (Emmaus, Pa.: Rodale Press, 1992).

14. Anthony Downs, *New Visions for Metropolitan America* (Washington, D.C.: Brookings Institution, 1994) examines the issues and experience relating to urban planning and growth boundaries.

15. Michael H. Shuman, *Going Local: Creating Self-Reliant Communities in a Global Age* (New York: Free Press, 1998), lays out the nature and importance of community self-reliance strategies and provide a useful sixty-eight-page resource directory as an appendix. Further information is available from The Sustainable Communities Program, Institute for Policy Studies, 733 15th Street N.W., Suite 1020, Washington, D.C.; phone: (202) 234-9382; fax: (202) 387-7915; e-mail: shuman@igc.org; Web: www.ipc-dc.org. Another useful source of ideas and experience is The International Council for Local Environmental Initiatives (ICLEI), which has offices in each major region of the world. For more information contact the World Secretariat, City Hall East Tower, 8th Floor, Toronto, Ontario M5H 2N2, Canada; phone: (416) 392-1462; fax: (416) 392-1478; e-mail: iclei@icelie.org; Web: www.cilei.org.

16. Accounts by Daniel Kemmis of his experience as mayor of Missoula, Montana, as reported in *The Good City and the Good Life* (Boston: Houghton Mifflin, 1995) and *Community and the Politics of Place* (Norman: University of Oklahoma Press, 1990), are great sources of inspiration on the importance and opportunities of local politics.

17. The New Party, 227 West 40 Street, Suite 1303, New York 10018; phone: (800) 200-1294; Web:www.newparty.org.

18. A variety of highly useful resources support political agendas that advance us toward a post-corporate world, including Public Campaign, 1320 19th Street, N.W., Suite M-1, Washington, D.C. 20036, phone (202) 293-0222, fax (202) 293-0202, Web www.publicampaign.org, which focuses on campaign finance reform; Common Cause, 1250 Connecticut Avenue, N.W., Washington, D.C. 20036, Web www.commoncause.org, which deals with a broad agenda of democratic reform issues; and Public Citizen, 1600 20th Street N.W., Washington, D.C. 20009, phone (800) 289-3787, Web www.citizen.org, which is especially strong on campaign reform, consumer eco-

nomics, safety, and trade issues. The Center for Responsive Politics, 1320 19th Street N.W., Suite 620, Washington, D.C. 20036, Web www.crp.org, reports current data on the funding sources of national political candidates. The Progressive Challenge at www.netprogress.org is a joint project of over a hundred citizen groups organized in conjunction with the Progressive Caucus of the U.S. Congress working for a common, multi-issue progressive agenda entitled the Fairness Agenda for America. Further information on the Progressive Challenge is available from the Institute for Policy Studies, 733 15th Street N.W., Suite 1020, Washington, D.C. 20005; phone: (202) 234-9382; fax: (202) 387-7915; Web: www.ips-dc.org.

19. The Alliance for Democracy, P.O. Box 683, Lincoln, Mass. 01773, phone (617) 259-9395, fax (617) 259-0404, e-mail peoplesall@aol.com; and the Politics of Meaning movement, The Foundation for Ethics and Meaning, 5445 Mariner St., Suite 314, Tampa, FL 33609, phone (888) 538-7227, fax (813) 251-0492, e-mail: roberts@meaning.org, Web: www.meaning.org, are examples in the United States. The Sierra Club, 85 Second Street, 2nd Floor, San Francisco 94105-3441; phone: (415) 977-5500; fax: (415) 977-5799; Web: www.sierraclub.org is an example of a well-established organization with a more environmentally oriented agenda that has a strong grassroots base.

20. The Public Citizen Global Trade Watch, 215 Pennsylvania Avenue S.E., Washington, D.C. 20003; phone: (202) 546-4996; Web: www.tradewatch.org, is a good place to start to find groups working on international-institutions issues.

21. Michael Shuman, *Toward a Global Village: International Community Development Initiatives* (London: Pluto Press, 1994) documents a number of such initiatives and offers useful guidance for those interested in sponsoring others.

Epilogue: Planetary Consciousness

1. Thomas Berry, *Dream of the Earth* (San Francisco: Sierra Club Books, 1988), p. 24.

2. Duane Elgin, *Collective Consciousness and Cultural Healing, A Report to the Fetzer Institute* (San Anselmo, Calif.: Millennium Project, October 1997), pp. 2–3.

Index

Abzug, B., 233
Accountability, 15, 42–43, 79, 186, 200, 204
Accountancy industry, 43
Acquisitions, 42–43
Activism. *See* Civic participation; *specific issues*
Advertising, 33
Agriculture, 95–96, 149, 228–230, 247. *See also* Environmental crisis
life-affirming, 249–253
Albania, 53
"All Things Considered," 233
Alliance for Democracy, 205
Almighty Latin King/Queen Nation, Inc., 229
Anand Milk Producers' Union, 180
Antitrust legislation, 199–200. *See also* Monopolization
APEC, 191
Apoptosis, 115
Appropriate Technology International (ATI), 180
Aristotle, 139–141, 145, 158
Ashoka Fellows Program, 230
Asian environmental crisis, 72
Asian financial crisis, 54, 55, 72, 119. *See also* Thailand
Association for Progressive Communications (APC), 273
Aurobindo, S., 214

Babolna, 249–250

Bacteria, 121, 125, 159
Banking, community, 268
restoring the concept of, 197–198
Banking system, unitary, 197–198
Banks. *See also* Loans
prohibiting from financial speculators, 195–196
Barber, J., 205
Bari, J., 232
Barlow, M., 241
Bavelas, A., 174
Beckhardt, R., 174
Bellerive Foundation, 202
Benguet Mining Company, 77
Bennis, W., 174
Bentryn, G., 263
Bentryn, J., 263
Benyus, J., 106, 122
Berry, T., 11–12, 88, 91, 94, 97, 277
Bill of Rights, 184–185
Billionaires, 80, 81, 200
Biocommunities, 110–112, 160
Blix, J., 221
Block, P., 174
Bohr, N., 113
Borders, 160
economic, 59, 62, 198, 237
national, 39, 48, 50, 60, 193, 198
paying attention to one's, 161
Bossel, H., 126
Boulding, K., 3
Boundaries, life as depending on, 123–124
Brazil, 55, 72

Breton, M. J., 231
Broad, R., 77
Brokaw, T., 166
Bruno, K., 78
Buddhism, 146–147
Bullionism, 29
Burns, E. M., 26–27
Bush administration, 204
Business Leaders for Sensible Priori-
     ties, 235–236
Businesses, small/human-scale/stake-
     holder-owned, 15, 178–181,
     267–268
  economy made up of, 157, 158
  female owners of, 234
  human, innovative, 173–176
  job satisfaction in, 174

CAMA, 178
Cameron, M., 32
Canada, 240–241
Cancer, 15, 115–117, 246, 262
  as metaphor, 116, 120, 151,
     262–263
Capital, 77
  depletion of, 76–77
  human/natural, 76, 77, 117, 169
Capital accumulation, 51–59
Capital gains tax, short-term, 196
Capital investment, 169
Capitalism, 138, 142, 152–153. See
     also specific aspects of capital-
     ism
  as a cancer, 15, 16, 40, 116, 262–263
  central planners, 61
  deceptions of, 36, 39, 40
  democracy and, 37, 205
  freedom without responsibility in,
     137
  against the market, 38–40
  meanings of, 39
  nature of, 36–38, 40, 44
  triumph of
     creation of global economic
        machine, 63
     of the few over the many, 39
  types of

finance, 51–59, 73–74
  global, 2, 40, 52, 62, 82, 112, 133,
     163, 167, 181, 262, 280
  stakeholder vs. shareholder, 172
  values of, 153
  vs. healthy markets, 40, 41
Capitalist economy, 39, 133
  dominated by a few speculators, 40
Capitalists, responsibility for conse-
     quences of actions, 154
Capra, F., 114
Carson, R., 232–233
Cavanagh, J., 77
Cells, 93, 108, 115–116
Central planning, from self-organiza-
     tion to, 59–63
Centre des Jeunes Dirigeants d'Entre-
     prise, 201–202
CEOs, 60–61, 75–76, 81, 187, 265
Change, ways to achieve, 3–4
Character, 140
Chile, 82
Chilean Ecological Action Network
     (RENACE), 238
China, 72–73
Chipko, 232
Choices, 132–133. See also Decision
     making
  mindful, 138–139
Citizen groups, 193–194, 240–241,
     263–266, 272–273. See also
     specific groups
  taking on corporate power, 7,
     203–207
Citizen Movement for Democracy,
     230
Citizen's Agenda for Canada, 240–241
Civic participation, 140, 263–266,
     271–272. See also Interven-
     tion; specific issues
Civic responsibility, 225
Civil society, 139, 140
Civilization, history and evolution of,
     95–99
Clarke, T., 203
Clinton, President William, 7, 72, 166,
     236

Clinton administration, 55
Co-op America, 243, 267
Coca-Cola, 187
Cogswell, G., 226
Cohen, B., 235
Colbin, A., 248, 251
Colborn, T., 232
Collectivization, extreme, 120
Colonialism, 30
Colonization of popular culture, 30–34
Communication, interregional electronic, 130–132
Communism, 117. *See also* Marxism
problems with, 152
Community currency, supporting and creating, 196–197, 270
Community economic self-reliance, 271
Community economy, creating a sustainable, 270
Community heroes, 226–230
Community values, 166
Community(ies), 117, 170, 225, 269. *See also* Cybercommunities
biological, 110–112, 160
ethical-political, 139
health and, 257
life as depending on inclusive, place-based, 122
Comparative advantage, theory of, 48–50
Competition, 22–24, 41, 43, 152. *See also* Wal-Mart
aggressive and unrestrained, 123
small firms *vs.* megacorporations, 40–43
Computer simulations, self-organizing, 112–113
Confucius, 139
Connecting, 264
Conscious living, 222
Consciousness, 10–14, 26, 117
ideal of civic, 139–141
planetary, 277–281
Constitution, 184–186, 204

Consumer rights and protection, 44, 158–159
Consumerism, 6, 32
Cooperation, 41
life as rewarding, 122–123
Copernicus, N., 24, 97, 116, 280
Corporate central planners, 61
Corporate excesses, 7
Corporate income tax, 47, 199
Corporate misdeeds. *See also specific topics*
strategies to stop, 187–200
Corporate personhood, doctrine of, 185–186, 190–191
Corporate power, 32, 40–41
citizen groups taking on, 7, 203–207
consolidation of unaccountable, 42–43, 186, 200
increasing, 30–31
Corporate shareholders, 184, 204
Corporate welfare and subsidies, 15, 46–48, 194–195
Corporation(s), 186–187. *See also* International corporations; Megacorporations; *specific issues and corporations*
as agent, 75–79
efforts to control, 15, 183
as engines of wealth extraction, 48
increasing prestige of, 30–31
influence on values, 32
limited liability for-profit public, eliminating, 15
organized around self-managing business units or cost centers, 176
personification of, 75, 183, 185–186
political participation, 15
as property of shareholders, 184, 185, 186
rights, freedoms, and protections of, 15, 183–186, 190–191, 205
uncontrollability of, 186–187
Cultural Creatives (CCs), 214–217
Cultural diversity, 125, 133
Cultural fields, 31–32

Cultural groupings, 214–216
Culture, integral, 215, 216, 223
Culture shift, 211–214
    new culture in the making,
        214–217
Currencies
    creation of national, 197
    local/community, 196–197, 270
Cybercommunities, 131. *See also*
        Internet

Daly, H., 76
Darwin, C., 123
Dawkins, R., 115, 123
Dead universe story, 9–11, 13, 24–28
Debt, 35, 49. *See also* Loans
Decision makers, putting costs on the,
        156–157, 164
Decision making, 164. *See also*
        Choices
Democracy, 163, 184, 205, 275. *See
    also* Self-rule
    capitalism and, 37, 205
    economic, 198–200, 265
    representative, 144
    restoring political, 188–190
Democratic rights, 193
Deregulation, 60, 142
Descartes, R., 24–25
Development. *See also* Progress
    waves of extractive, 68–69
Devi, A., 231–232
Dietary practice, 247–249
Disclosure, full, 158–159
Diversity, 124–125, 133, 160–161, 230
DNA, 89, 90, 93, 109, 115
Dobbin, M., 79
Dole Fruit Company, 80
Dominguez, J., 220–222
Dream of the Earth (Berry), 11–12
Drug companies, 45–46
Duggins, Reverend Gordon, 229–230
Dumanoski, D., 232
Durning, A., 68

Earth, history of the, 88–95
Economic equity *vs.* incentives, 143

Economic growth, 169
    and increasing poverty, 73–75, 79
    measures of, 255–259
    relentless pursuit of, 6
    social and environmental decline
        due to, 70–73
Economic inequality, 6, 7, 79, 158
Economic institutions. *See also spe-
        cific institutions*
    restructuring, 8–9
Economic measures, 75, 156, 255–259
Economic relationships, 127
    decisions regarding, 132–133
Economic theory, 39
Economic well-being, global decline
        in, 71–72
Economics. *See also specific topics*
    philosophy of, 27
Ecosystem, as model of economic sys-
        tem, 120
Egalitarianism, 143. *See also* Equity
Elgin, D., 33, 215, 223
Elite consensus, cracks in the,
        200–203
Elite privilege, 200, 221–222
Elites, 80–81, 133, 221–222
    rule by, 98
    of Third World, 82
Emilia-Romagna, 178
Employee stock ownership plans
        (ESOPs), 199. *See also* Owner-
        ship, forms of, local/stake-
        holder
Energy, 108, 111, 112, 129, 130. *See
    also* Physics
Energy self-reliance, renewable, 128
Environment, 160, 227, 257. *See also*
        Natural capital
    harm done to, 70–73, 76–79,
        82–83, 129, 187, 194, 228, 258
Environmental balance, regional, 129
Environmental crisis, 75
    root causes of, 66–69
Environmental movement, 239
    women in, 231–234
Environmental use fees, 194
Equity *vs.* inequity, 79, 143, 158

Estes, R., 48, 194
Ethical approach to business, 166
Ethical culture, maintaining an, 162
Ethical Impact Report, 204–205
Ethics, 27–28, 187
   philosophy of, 26–27
Eukaryotes, 93
Evolution, 66–67, 69–73, 114
   of civilization, 95–99
   of life, 88–95
Exploitation, 66. *See also* Environ-
   ment, harm done to

Falkenbury, D., 226
Farming. *See* Agriculture
Fast track legislation, 7, 236–237
Federal Reserve, 196
Fermentation, 90–92, 123
Fernandez, A., 229
Feuerstein, A., 165–167
Fields, 31–32
Finance capital, 51–59, 73–74. *See also*
   Money
Finance excesses, 51–52
Financial bubbles, 53–56, 73–74, 81,
   198
Financial institutions. *See also specific*
   institutions
   influence on corporations, 60–61
Financial pyramids, 53, 57
Financial speculation, 15, 40, 51, 53,
   57, 81, 195–196, 202
Fiscal and regulatory policy, 15, 60,
   129, 142
Fisheries, 82
Food. *See* Agriculture; Dietary prac-
   tice
Food liable laws, 45
Foreign policy. *See also specific issues*
   municipal, 273–274
Forest Stewardship Council, 180
Free market, 138
Free speech, 190
Freedom, 143
   government protection of, 140, 161
   paradox of, 144–146
   promise of universal, 3

responsibility and, 138, 144, 150

Gabel, P., 204
Galileo Galilei, 24
Gates, B., 81, 158, 164
Gates, J., 199
Gender. *See* Women
General Agreement on Tariffs and
   Trade (GATT), 191, 236, 239
General Motors, 187
Genetic diversity, 125, 133
Gesber, J., 214
Giuliani, Mayor, 47
Global Action Plan (GAP), 147–148
Global corporate rule, 185
Global financial markets, unregu-
   lated, 202
Global institutions, 272–273. *See also*
   International corporations
Global networks, 272
Globalization, 201–202
   forces of economic, 2, 60–61,
     240–241
GLOBE International, 202
Goldman Prize, 229–230
Goldschmidt, N., 254
Goldsmith, J., 200
Goodman, E., 221
Goodman, P., 261
Government
   caretaking *vs.* authoritarian ten-
     dencies, 143
   role of, 41, 153, 161–162
Government-corporate collusion,
   movements to end the, 205
Government policies, 58, 265–266.
   See also specific issues and poli-
   cies
Government regulation and interven-
   tion, 15, 60, 129, 142, 157,
   191–194
   in economics, 58, 161
   requirement for coercive, 140
Government subsidies. *See* Corporate
   welfare and subsidies
Gravitz, Alisa, 243–244
Great Depression of 1930s, 51

Greed, 6, 65–66, 115, 140, 151–153, 200. *See also* Competition; Exploitation; Self-restraint
Greer, J., 78
Gross domestic product (GDP), 69–71, 73, 74, 75, 256
Grossman, R., 205
Growth, unrestrained, 22, 270. *See also* Cancer

Hanh, Thich Nhat, 138, 146–147
Hansen, G. B., 265
Harman, W., 1, 97, 99, 211
Harwood Group, 217–219
Havel, V., 119
Hawken, P., 47, 65, 162
Health, 257. *See also* Dietary practice
Health costs, 48
Health of the Planet survey, 218
Heartlanders, 214–216
Hedge funds, 195–196
Hedonism, 24–28, 32
Heitmiller, D., 221
Herbert, B., 77
Hermannsdorf farm, 250–251
Heroes, ordinary, 226–230
Hewlett, B., 174
Hierarchies, organizational, 174–176, 178
Ho, M-W., 8, 9, 14, 103, 104, 105, 109
Hobbes, T., 26–29, 31–32, 116, 141, 142, 145
Hock, D., 176
Holarchy, 114
Holistic health, 149–150, 152, 245–247
Holistic movements, 238–242
Holon, 114
Hominids, 94–95
Housing, affordable, 270
Human capital, depletion of, 76
Human development, 12
Human potential, latent, 106–110
Human scale, on a large scale, 176–182
Humane institutions, 165–167

Ideals, 98
Ideologies, extreme, 120
Image (Boulding), 3
Images, 3–4
Immune system, 115
Income inequity, 79, 158
Index of sustainable economic welfare, 75
India's National Dairy Development Board, 180
Indicators projects, 269
Individualism, extreme, 120, 152
Individuality, 124–125
Information
    access to, 158–159, 268
    sharing *vs.* monopolizing of, 44–46
Inglehart, R., 219, 223
Institute for Global Communications (IGC), 273
Institute of Noetic Sciences, 248
Institutional capital, 77
Institutional change, ways to achieve, 3–4
Institutions, humane, 165–167
Intelligence, 12, 14
International accounts, balanced rooted *vs.* global capital, 48–51
International borders, 193
International corporations and finance, 33, 116, 203. *See also* Trade
    regulation, 15, 191–194
International Forum on Globalization (IFG), 237
International investment flows, 48–49, 202
International Monetary Fund (IMF), 55, 57, 193, 272, 273
Internet, 177–178, 279. *See also* Cybercommunities
Intervention. *See also specific issues*
    at multiple levels, 266–267
    community level, 269–271
    international level, 272–274
    national level, 271–272
    personal and family level, 267–269

Intrapreneuring, 174
Investment capital, 54
Investments, 195–196. *See also* Capitalism, types of, finance; Stock market
   capital, 169
   productive *vs.* extractive, 51–59
   socially responsible, 148–149, 265, 268–269

Japan, 55, 56, 171, 227–228
Jennings, P., 166
Job satisfaction in small businesses, 174
Jobs, life-affirming, 268
Jobs, S., 174
Justice, 153

Kalaw, J., 239
Kenya's Green Belt Movement, 232
Keynes, J. M., 119
"King Tone," 229
Kinsley, M. J., 270
Kito village, 227–228
Knight, P., 78
Koestler, A., 114
Korea, 55
Korten, D. C., 4–5
   When Corporations Rule the World, 1, 2, 6, 8, 14–16, 18
Kotze, E., 230
Kravck, M., 230

Langton, C., 145
Larrain, S., 238
Latin Kings, 229
Law enforcement, 153, 161
Leach, W., 32
Learning, shared, 124–125
Leavitt, H., 174
LeDrew, C., 215
Lerner, M., 204
Liability, 45. *See also* Accountability
   lack of corporate, 15, 186
Liberalism
   challenge to monarchy, 141–144
   economic, 138, 142

   appeal to frustrated capitalist classes, 142
   freedom and, 145
   meanings of, 142–144
Liberals, economic *vs.* political, 143–144
Libertarianism, 61
Lietaer, B., 35, 196, 197
Life, 35–36. *See also* Organism
   evolution, 88–95
   lessons of ancient wisdom of, 121–125
   meaning and purpose of, 10, 26, 141
   nurturing, 262–263
   potentials of, 12–14
   securing the right to live, 168–170
   simplifying one's, 267
   vs. money, as measure of evaluation, 156
Life-affirming jobs, 268
Life-centered nations, 238–242
Life choices, 243–244
Likert, R., 174
Linux, 175
Living, essential elements of good, 243–244
Living capital, 117
Living consciously, 222
Living places, 253–255
Living systems, 8–9, 14
Living world, 22–23
Loans, 34, 35, 49, 51, 52, 55, 195–197
   financial assets as collateral, 198
   foreign, 49, 57
Localism, positive, 236–237
Locke, J., 25, 168–169, 181
Long-Term Capital Management, 195–196
Love, 146
Lovelock, J., 89
Lukas Klinik, 246
Lumber industry, 179–180

Maathi, W., 232
Maharajah of Jodhpur, 231–232
Malaysian forests, 82–83

Malden Mills, 164–167

Management. *See also* CEOs
  authoritarian *vs.* participatory, 174,
    176
  obligation to set aside personal val-
    ues, 187

Management styles, sex differences in,
    234

Manila, 80

Manufacturing, 178

Margulis, L., 37, 88, 89, 90, 93, 100,
    103, 106

Market. *See also* Mindful markets
  feedback from, 156
  free, 138. *See also* Capitalism
  healthy, 152, 154–155, 181
  invisible hand of the, 152–154
  self-organizing, 40, 59–60. *See also*
    Smith, A.

Market economy, 43, 133

Market efficiency, 161

Market relationships, 181

Market theory, 38–40, 44, 46, 48, 158

Market value, 57, 58

Markets, nature of, 62, 151–152. *See
    also specific aspects of markets*

Marxism, 120

Material advantage, ruthless pursuit
    of, 140

Materialism
  culture of, 213–214
  rise of, 28–31

Materialistic hedonism, 24–28

Materialistic values, 33, 214, 215,
    217–218. *See also* Modernism

Materials use, closed-cycle, 129

McCall, T., 254–255

McCormack, G., 228

McCrory, C., 232

McGregor, D., 174

McKinsey, 72, 73

Meadows, D., 249–250

Megacorporations, 40–43
  breaking down into stakeholder-
    owned firms, 198, 265

Mercantilism, 29

Merck Family Fund, 217–218

Mergers, 42–43

Mexican collapse, 55

Microsoft Corporation, 40–41, 175

Midas curse, 65–66, 72, 73, 78, 83

Milk producers, 180

Mindful markets, 270
  ten rules for, 154–162
  vs. capitalist economy, 155–156

Mindfulness, 138–139, 146, 150, 164
  in the marketplace, 146–150

Modernism, 222–223
  in trouble, 217–220

Modernists, 214, 215, 217, 221

Monarchy, liberalism's challenge to,
    141–144

Money. *See also* Capitalism, types of,
    finance; Finance
  demurrage charge on, 197
  illusions about, 23
  importance of, 98
  as means *vs.* ends, 3, 41
  as medium of exchange, restora-
    tion of, 195–198
  nature of, 23–24, 34–35
  rise of, 28–31
  triumph over life, 17

Money world, 23

Money-world indicators, 75

Monks, R., 186, 204

Monopolization, 40–41, 45–46, 157.
    See also Antitrust legislation;
    Wal-Mart
  capitalism and, 43
  vs. sharing, 44–46

Monsanto, 187

Moore, T., 254

Moral responsibility, 27–28. *See also*
    Ethics, philosophy of
  vs. profitability, 187

Morehouse, W., 205

Mothers of East L.A. (MELASI),
    226–227

Motorola, 46

Multilateral Agreement Investment
    (MAI), 191–192, 274

Mutuality, 114

Myers, J. P., 232–233

National goals and institutions, holistic movements aimed at changing, 238–242
Natural capital, depletion of, 76, 77. *See also* Environmental crisis
Natural Step, 66, 147–148
Natural wealth, 169
Neighborhood settlements, 127–128
Neoliberals, 142
Nervous system, central, 109
Nestle, 187
Netting, R., 252
Networking, creative power of, 175
Networks, 178–179
New Party, 203–204, 271
Newton, I., 25, 113
NGO Global Firm, 212
NGO Taskforce on Business and Industry, 205
NGOs, Philippine, 238–240
Nike, 61, 77–78
Nixon, President Richard, 24
Nongovernment organization. *See* NGOs
North, R., 4
North American Free Trade Agreement (NAFTA), 55, 191, 236

Odyssey, 21–22, 274, 275
Oil companies, 77
Organism
    nature of the, 107–110, 117
    shifting metaphor from machine to, 104–106
Organization for Economic Cooperation and Development (OECD) countries, 73–74
Organizations, chaordic, 176–178
Owen, H., 174
Ownership, 41, 157
    combining management and, 167
    forms of
        absentee, 164, 199, 207
        family, 167
        local/stakeholder, 157, 164, 170–173, 177, 181, 198–200, 207, 267–268

self, 176
    rights, responsibilities, and, 171–172
    separation from production, 51
Ownership control, 178
Ownership rights, 45, 60, 133, 163–164

Packard, D., 174
Paradigms of science, 103–104
Participation in decision making, 157, 173
Patel, A., 230
Patents, 45. *See also* Property rights, intellectual
Perlas, N., 239
Peters, T., 174
Philippine Agenda 21, 240
Philippine Council on Sustainable Development (PCSD), 239, 240
Philippine nongovernmental organizations (NGOs), 238–240
Philippines, 80, 238–240
Photosynthesis, 90–93
Physics, 9, 11, 24, 105–106, 108, 113–114
Pinchot, E., 174
Pinchot, G., 174
Political activism. *See* Civic participation
Political campaign contributions, 81, 189
Political campaign reform, 15, 189–190
Political corruption, 189
Political philosophy
    of Aristotle, 140–141
    of Hobbes, 141, 142, 145
Political rights, connected to property *vs.* persons, 184
Political society/community, 139
Politics
    influence of money on, 15, 189
    seeds of a new citizen-led, 203–208
Politics of Meaning, 204
Ponzi scheme, 53

Population and resources, 253–257
Portland, Oregon, 254–255
Positive Futures Network (PFN), 7–8, 264
Post-capitalist civilization, 2–3
Post-corporate world, 2–3, 138
  guidelines for developing, 15, 182
  system design for a, 126–133
  task of creating, 133
Power, reclaiming, 7
Power shift, 59, 60
Press, corporate-controlled, 7
Price. *See also* Financial bubbles
  full costs *vs.* public subsidies and, 46–48
  market, 157
Program on Corporations, Law, and Democracy (POCLAD), 205
Progress, 5–6
  as evolution in reverse, 66–67, 69–73
  measuring, 255–259
Prokaryotes, 93
Property, political rights connected to persons *vs.*, 184
Property rights, 168, 169, 170, 181, 183
  intellectual, 159
  vs. rights of property, 184–186
Property tax, 47
Public facilities fee, 195
Pyramid scheme, 53

Quinn, B., 164, 165

R. J. Reynolds corporation, 187
Rational materialism, 27, 28, 30, 31
Ray, P., 214, 218, 223
Reagan administration, 204
Regional centers, 128
Regulation. *See* Government regulation
Religious beliefs, 12, 25, 96, 146–147
RENACE, 238
Resource allocation, 46, 158
Resources, international, 273

Responsibility, 27–28, 148, 151, 155, 167, 174, 207, 275
  civic, 144, 225
  corporate, 187
  freedom and, 137, 155, 157
  moral, 27–28, 153, 187
  ownership, 171–172
  shared, 154
  wealth and, 235–236, 275
Responsible Wealth, 235–236
Ricardo, D., 48–50
Right Livelihoods Award, 229–230
Rights, 143, 183
  corporate *vs.* human, 183
  government protection of, 161
  human, 168, 183, 184, 185, 191
  to live, 168–170
  of the living, restoring the, 186–188
Rio de Janeiro, 239, 278
Riskin, C., 72
Robbins, J., 245–246, 252–253
Robèrt, K-H., 66–67, 148
Robin, V., 220–223
Rocky Mountain Institute (RMI), 270
Roman Empire, 97
Rosales, L., 230
Russian crisis, 55

Sagan, D., 26, 88, 90, 93, 100, 103, 106, 114
Sahtouris, E., 8–9, 14, 88, 92, 110, 123, 212
Santa Clara County v. Southern Pacific Railroad, 185
Santa Fe Institute, 106, 112–113
Savings, personal
  investment and, 51
Scarcity, in the guise of plenty, 34–36
Schwab, K., 201
Schweisfurth, K. L., 250
Science, 9, 11, 14, 96–98, 104, 112–113. *See also* Physics
  Newtonian, 24–25
Scientific-industrial era, 26
"Securities: The New Wealth Machine," 56–58
Securitization, 56–57

Self-assertion, 114
Self-awareness, 108, 138, 145, 280
Self-interest, 153
Self-managed teams, 174, 176
Self-organization, 107, 116, 124–125, 133
  human-scale, 126–127
  life as favoring, 121
  vs. central planning, 59–63
Self-organizing computer simulations, 112–113
Self-organizing systems, 145
  creative power of, 176
Self-owned and directed firms, 176
Self-reliance, 128, 160–161
Self-restraint, 144–146, 152, 161, 162
Self-rule, 141
Selfishness, 115, 140, 153. *See also* Greed
Senge, P., 174
Shared learning, 124–125
Sharing, 121–122, 130
  of knowledge and technology, 159
Shiva, V., 228, 252
Silent Spring (Carson), 232–233
Smadja, C., 201
"Smart Growth" law, 255
Smith, A., 27, 38, 39, 40, 60
  on monopoly, 44, 46
  on motivation and morality, 152–154
  on role of state, 153
  ten rules for mindful markets, 154–162
  The Theory of Moral Sentiments, 153, 154
  The Wealth of Nations, 38, 152–154
Smolin, L., 99, 123–124
Social capital, 77
Social Darwinists, 14
Social Responsibility Amendment, 204–205
Socialism, 120
  death of, 2–3
  from self-organization to central planning of, 59–63
Society(ies)

healthy, 154
  ideal of civil, 145
  life-centered, 8
  reclaiming power, 7
Sociobiologists, 14
Sorokin, P. A., 214
Soros, G., 39, 200–201
South Korea, 55
Space, physical, 132. *See also* Boundaries
Spain, 171
Speculation. *See* Financial speculation
Sprawl, 253–255
Stakeholder buyouts, 198, 265
Stakeholder-owned enterprises, 15, 198–200, 267–268
"Star Trek," 120
State. *See* Government
Stock market, 53–55, 75
Supply and demand. *See* Scarcity
Sustainable Seattle, 257–258
Swimme, B., 88, 91, 94, 97

Tarnas, R., 28
"Tax shift" proposals, 157
Taxation, 30, 47, 129, 199
  corporate income, 47, 199
  of short-term capital gains, 196
Technology, 133, 201
  development of, 96–99
Television, influence of, 33–34
Thailand, 82
  encounter with global finance capitalism, 54, 56–57
"Thanksgiving conspiracy," 267–268
Thatcher, M., 120
Third World, elites of the, 82
Timber industry, 179–180
Towns, 128
Trade, 97–98
  balanced *vs.* unbalanced, 160, 161
  free *vs.* restricted, 48–50, 142, 191–194
Trade agreements, 7, 191–194, 236
Trade dependence, 160
Trade secrets. *See* Information
Transportation, 266, 269, 270

history of, 98–99
Trends Research Institute, 219–220
Trust, in civilized society, 154

Uiguen, J. I., 230
United Nations Commission on Sustainable Development, 205
United Nations Conference on Environment and Development (UNCED), 211–212, 239, 241, 278
Universal Declaration of Human Rights of the United Nations, 168
Universe
history of, 87–89, 99–100, 103–104
nature of, 9–13, 24–26

Value, scarcity and, 34
Values, 70, 98, 219. See also Ideals
community, 166
societal, 207, 214–216
Vermont Family Forests, 179
Vietnam, 119–120
Village patterns, 127–128
Visa International, 176–178
Voluntary simplicity, 147–148, 222–223

Waite, M. R., 185
Wal-Mart, 42, 164–167, 173, 187
Waldrop, M., 112–113
Wall Street bankers, 55

Walton, S., 164
Wealth, 34–36. See also Economic inequality; Elites
promise of universal, 3
responsibility and, 235–236, 275
Weill, S., 81
Werner, D., 80
Wheatley, M., 174
Whirlpool, 47
Whole-part relationships, 113–114
Wholeness and coherence, 145–146, 245–247
Wild spaces, 132
Women
active in forest protection, 231–232, 233
as business owners, 233, 234
place of, 231–234
Women Pioneers for the Environment (Breton), 231–232
Women's Environment and Development Organization (WEDO), 233
Workers. See Natural capital
World Bank, 193, 272–273
World Conference of the Society for International Development, 8
World Trade Organization (WTO), 192–193, 272, 273
Worldwatch Institute, 67

YES!, 7–8, 17, 215, 264

About the Author

DR. DAVID C. KORTEN has over thirty-five years of experience in pre-eminent business, academic, and international development institutions as well as in contemporary citizen action organizations. He is a co-founder and president of The People-Centered Development Forum.

Korten earned his M.B.A. and Ph.D. degrees at the Stanford University Graduate School of Business. Trained in economics, organization theory, and business strategy, his early career was devoted to setting up business schools in low income countries—starting with Ethiopia—in the hope that creating a new class of professional business entrepreneurs would be the key to ending poverty. He completed his military service during the Vietnam War as a captain in the U.S. Air Force, serving in Air Force headquarters command and the Office of the Secretary of Defense.

Korten then served for five and a half years as a faculty member of the Harvard University Graduate School of Business and taught in Harvard's middle management and M.B.A. programs. He also served as Harvard's advisor to the Nicaragua-based Central American Management Institute. He subsequently joined the staff of the Harvard Institute for International Development, where he headed a Ford Foundation-funded project to strengthen the organization and management of national family planning programs.

In the late 1970s, Korten left U.S. academia and moved to Southeast Asia, where he lived for nearly fifteen years, serving first as a Ford Foundation project specialist, and later as Asia regional advisor on development management to the U.S. Agency for International Development (USAID). His work there won him international recognition for his contributions to pioneering the development of powerful strategies for transforming public bureaucracies into responsive support systems dedicated to strengthening community control and management of land, water, and forestry resources.

Disillusioned by the evident inability of USAID and other large official aid donors to apply the approaches that had been proven effective by the nongovernmental Ford Foundation., Korten broke with the official aid system. His last five years in Asia were devoted to working with leaders of Asian nongovernmental organizations on identifying the root causes of development failure in the region and building the capacity of civil society organizations to function as strategic catalysts of national- and global-level change.

Korten came to realize that the crisis of deepening poverty, growing inequality, environmental devastation, and social disintegration he was observing in Asia was also being experienced in nearly every country in the world—including the United States and other "developed" countries. Furthermore, he came to the conclusion that the United States was actively promoting—both at home and abroad—the very policies that were deepening the resulting global crisis. For the world to survive, the United States must change. He returned to the United States in 1992 to help advance that change.

Dr. Korten's publications are required reading in university courses around the world. He has authored or edited numerous books, including *When Corporations Rule the World* published by Kumarian Press and Berrett-Koehler Publishers and *Getting to the 21st Century: Voluntary Action and the Global Agenda; Community Management; People Centered Development* (edited with Rudi Klauss); *Bureaucracy and the Poor: Closing the Gap* (edited with Felipe B. Alfonso), all published by Kumarian Press. He contributes regularly to edited books and professional journals, and to a wide variety of periodical publications. He is also a popular international speaker and a regular guest on talk radio and television.

What People are saying about YES!

YES! is the best source I know for inspiration, information, connections, and stories for those of us who believe there is an alternative to a world torn apart by greed and violence—that for every "no" there is a "Yes".

David C. Korten

YES! is a joy to read -- it does a beautiful job of telling the new story of what people are doing to create hope in a difficult world. It carries an unspoken spirituality where actions are valued and a longed for tomorrow seems a little closer than we realized.

Peter Block, author
Stewardship

YES! is.... the bible of the sustainability movement.

The Seattle Weekly

YES! is published by the Positive Futures Network, an independent, non-profit organization based on Bainbridge Island, Washington in the United States. The organization was founded in 1996 by David Korten, YES! Editor Sarah van Gelder, and other visionaries concerned about the social, ecological, economic, and spiritual crises of our times. The Network's purpose is to illuminate and encourage the deep shifts in culture and institutions that lead to a more just, sustainable, and compassionate future.

THE POSITIVE FUTURES NETWORK
P. O. Box 10818, Bainbridge Island, WA, 98110 USA

www.futurenet.org

Selected Titles from Berrett-Koehler Publishers

Global Mind Change: The Promise of the 21st Century (2nd Edition) Willis Harman, Ph.D.

Building a Win-Win World: Life Beyond Global Economic Warfare Hazel Henderson

The Age of Participation: New Governance for the Workplace and the World Patricia McLagan and Christo Nel

Economic Insanity: How Growth-Driven Capitalism Is Devouring the American Dream Roger Terry

Putting Democracy to Work: A Practical Guide for Starting and Managing Worker-Owned Businesses Frank T. Adams and Gary B. Hansen

A Higher Standard of Leadership: Lessons from the Life of Gandhi Keshavan Nair

Stewardship: Choosing Service Over Self-Interest Peter Block

The New Management: Bringing Democracy and Markets Inside Organizations William E. Halal

Tyranny of the Bottom Line: Why Corporations Make Good People Do Bad Things Ralph Estes

The Courageous Follower: Standing Up To and For Our Leaders Ira Chaleff

EcoManagement: The Elmwood Guide to Ecological Auditing and Sustainable Business Ernest Callenbach, Fritjof Capra, Lenore Goldman, Rüdiger Lutz, and Sandra Marburg

Corporate Social Investing: The Breakthrough Strategy for Giving and Getting Corporate Contributions Curt Weeden

Leadership and the New Science Margaret J. Wheatley

Berrett-Koehler Publishers, Inc.
San Francisco

Send orders to:
Berrett-Koehler Publishers, Inc.
PO Box 565
Williston, VT 05495

Or call toll-free:
(800) 929-2929 7 AM–12 midnight (U.S. only)

Or fax: (802) 864-7625

Internet: www.bkpub.com

Selected Titles from Kumarian Press

Globalization

When Corporations Rule the World David C. Korten

Creating Alternative Futures: The End of Economics Hazel Henderson

Unequal Freedoms: The Global Market as an Ethical System
John McMurtry

Getting to the 21st Century: Voluntary Action and the Global Agenda
David C. Korten

Other Books from Kumarian Press

Promises Not Kept: The Betrayal of Social Change in the Third World
(Fourth Edition) John Isbister

Achieving Broad-Based Sustainable Development: Governance, Environment, and Growth with Equity James H. Weaver, Michael T. Rock, and Kenneth Kusterer

The New World of Microenterprise Finance: Building Healthy Financial Institutions for the Poor Maria Otero and Elisabeth Rhyne, editors

Nongovernments: NGOs and the Political Development of the Third World
Julie Fisher

Knowledge Shared: Participatory Evaluation in Development Cooperation
Edward T. Jackson and Yusuf Kassam, editors

Aiding Violence: The Development Enterprise In Rwanda Peter Uvin

Mediating Sustainability: Growing Policy from the Grassroots
Jutta Blauert and Simon Zadek, editors

Policy, Politics and Gender: Women Gaining Ground Kathleen Staudt

Governance, Administration and Development: Making the State Work
Mark Turner and David Hulme

Multi-Track Diplomacy: A Systems Approach to Peace
Louise Diamond and Ambassador John McDonald

Kumarian Press
14 Oakwood Avenue
West Hartford, CT 06119

Order toll-free: (800) 289-2664

Call for complete catalog anytime!

Inquiries: (860) 233-5895
Fax: (860) 233-6072
Web: www.kpbooks.com
Email: kpbooks@aol.com

yes! yes!

Subscribe to

yes!

Your link to the global community of people, organizations, and ideas that are helping to create a just, sustainable, and compassionate future that works for all.

1-800-937-4451

www.futurenet.org

Subscribe Now!

ONE FULL YEAR FOR $19

You are invited to become a new subscriber to *YES!* magazine. You'll receive four quarterly issues at the introductory price of $19, a $5 savings off the cover price. Price guaranteed through December 31, 2001.

Please send a subscription to:

Name (please print clearly)

Address

City/State/Zip

☐ Payment enclosed ☐ Bill me later
(U.S. Only)

Canadian orders add $5. All other foreign orders add $7 (send pre-paid in U.S. funds).

KOR1

Get Informed. Get Yes!

|||||

BUSINESS REPLY MAIL
FIRST-CLASS MAIL PERMIT NO. 1521 SEATTLE, WA

POSTAGE WILL BE PAID BY ADDRESSEE

POSITIVE FUTURES NETWORK
P O BOX 10818
BAINBRIDGE ISLAND WA 98110-9940